A Foucauldian Interpretation of Modern Law

A Foucauldian Interpretation of Modern Law

From Sovereignty to Normalisation and Beyond

Jacopo Martire

EDINBURGH
University Press

Edinburgh University Press is one of the leading university presses
in the UK. We publish academic books and journals in our selected
subject areas across the humanities and social sciences, combining
cutting-edge scholarship with high editorial and production values to
produce academic works of lasting importance. For more information
visit our website: edinburghuniversitypress.com

© Jacopo Martire, 2017

Edinburgh University Press Ltd
The Tun – Holyrood Road
12 (2f) Jackson's Entry
Edinburgh EH8 8PJ

Typeset in 11/13 Goudy Old Style by
Servis Filmsetting Ltd, Stockport, Cheshire

A CIP record for this book is available from the British Library

ISBN 978 1 4744 1192 9 (hardback)
ISBN 978 1 4744 4572 6 (pbk.)
ISBN 978 1 4744 1193 6 (webready PDF)
ISBN 978 1 4744 1194 3 (epub)

The right of Jacopo Martire to be identified as author of this work
has been asserted in accordance with the Copyright, Designs and
Patents Act 1988 and the Copyright and Related Rights Regulations
2003 (SI No. 2498).

Contents

Acknowledgements vii

1 An Outline for a Foucauldian Interpretation of Modern Law 1
    Introduction 1
    Foucault and the law: an indigestible meal? 4
    Foucauldian responses 11
    An alternative approach: back to Foucault's 'toolbox' 21
    A framework of analysis 30

2 A Genealogy of Modern Law I: The Political Truth of the Individual 37
    Introduction 37
    From medieval theology to secularisation 38
    The new foundations of politics 46
    The dilemma of democracy 56
    The features of a new politics 69

3 A Genealogy of Modern Law II: The Political Truth of Society 72
    Introduction 72
    Three revolutionary declensions of a paradigm shift 73
    The long English Revolution: government as an institution 77
    The American Revolution: government as a process 84
    The French Revolution: government as a programme 91
    The normalising constitutional horizon of modernity 101

4 The Normalising Complex and the Challenges of Virtualisation 104
    Introduction 104
    The illocutionary effect of modern law: the creation of the universal subject 106

Law and other apparatuses: the normalising complex	113
Liquid modernity and the biopolitics of control: a tale of virtualisation	119
The collapse of the normalising complex?	126
The normative and functional crisis of modern law	134
Conclusions	**141**
The current status of legal theory	141
The blockage of the liberal camp	142
The blockage of the critical camp	151
An opening towards new avenues	160
Notes	**163**
Bibliography	**215**
Index	**239**

Acknowledgements

This book has been a while in the making, accompanying me, in one form or another, since my LLM, through my Ph.D., and in my academic career as a lecturer. On and off I have spent almost ten years preoccupied with this project and with the questions it addresses. Unsurprisingly, during this period, which has been as much an existential as an intellectual journey, I have met many people from whom, discussing my ideas and hypothesis, I have learned a great deal, and because of this I have incurred many debts which are difficult to define in words.

First and foremost, I am deeply grateful to my supervisor, Professor Mary Vogel. We first met when I was an LLM student at King's College London, where she was the Law and Social Theory module leader. Throughout my Master's and Ph.D. years she has been an inspiring mentor whose unwavering support, acumen and intellectual rigour have helped me in countless ways. Mary showed tireless patience and dedication, encouraging me to expand and refine my intuitions and to critically reflect upon my own work. Her guidance has enabled me to grow as a person and as a scholar. Similarly, I am deeply indebted to my other supervisor, Professor Roger Brownsword. He introduced me to new areas of research which have proven fundamental for the development of my argument, and has provided me with an invaluable wealth of knowledge and expertise which has greatly enriched my mind and fostered my scholarly growth. His wisdom and generosity are an example that I hope to carry on as an academic and as a man.

I am also thankful to my two Ph.D. examiners, Professor Patrick Hanafin and Professor Gerry Johnstone. Their comments and observations have enabled me to view my work in a fresh light and have helped me to sharpen the ideas presented herein. Their contributions and criticisms have crucially shaped the structure of my argument and made possible its transition from a Ph.D. thesis to a scholarly monograph. I could not have completed my thesis without the stimulus provided by a lively and intellectually challenging environment at King's College London's School of Law. I would therefore wish to thank Professor Raymond Plant, Professor Susan Marx, Professor Maleiha Malik, Professor Alan Norrie and Professor Penny Green for sharing some of their academic brilliance with me during this time, as well as offering me illuminating insights into several fundamental topics. I would also like to acknowledge the financial support from the AHRC and the *Modern Law Review*, without which it would have been impossible for me to have produced my Ph.D.

At the University of Stirling I have found an excellent environment in which to develop and expand my research. All my colleagues have been wonderful in helping me in the first steps of my career, and I have learned from them more than I can consciously perceive. In particular, I have enjoyed and benefited from several friendly conversations with Dr Rowan Cruft, Professor Gavin Little and Dr Oles Andriychuk, all of whom I thank. I had the opportunity to discuss parts of my work as seminar papers at several academic institutions such as the University of Stirling, the University of Glasgow, the University of Malmö, the New School for Social Research, the University of Stellenbosch, the University of Ljubljana, and the Università degli Studi Federico II. I am grateful to both the organisers of and the participants in each event for the lively exchanges and the thoughtful conversations.

Much of this book was rewritten and revised during academic leave granted to me by the School of Law at the University of Stirling. I spent this period as Visiting Fellow at two prestigious institutions: the École des Hautes Études en Sciences Sociales in Paris and the New School for Social Research in New York City. In both cases I have found a vibrant academic atmosphere which has undoubtedly improved the quality of my work. I would hence like to thank Professor Paolo Napoli and Professor Nancy Fraser, respectively, as without their support and sponsorship I would have not had this superb opportunity. In New York, especially, I found an intellectually stimulating community that has motivated me immeasurably. Professor Andreas Kalyvas, Professor Andrew Arato, Professor Michel Rosenfeld, and Professor Bernard E. Harcourt have all made valuable contributions which challenged and improved my ideas in new unexpected ways. Professor Peter Goodrich has been exceptionally generous towards me. Not only did he offer precious advice during several conversations, but he also invited me to the symposium 'West of Everything', held at the Cardozo School of Law, where I had a chance to present part of the final draft of my manuscript and received invaluable feedback from the attendees – all of whom I thank. I am greatly honoured to have known Professor Goodrich as an intellectual, as a person, and as a surprisingly good chef. In New York, I was also very lucky to rely on the good-humoured company of my friend Dr Diego Acosta. While working on his own projects, he had the endurance to listen and probe many of my elucubrations, and to read the final draft of my typescript, making several useful suggestions on how to make more accessible the delivery of my argument. I also owe a debt of gratitude to Dr Ben Golder – whose works on Foucault and the law I admire greatly – who acted as my peer reviewer, providing me with insightful comments and generous encouragements.

Of course, all errors and shortcomings in the present work remain my own. They would have been many more and much graver without the positive influence of those benevolent enough to help me throughout this project.

I do not think that it would have been possible for me to finish this work without the support of my friends. They have eased me through the hard times and made memorable the happy ones. They all deserve a mention here, but I would like to thank three in particular: Andrea, Paolo, and Sara. They, more than anyone else, withstood my periods of desperation and shouldered my occasional lamentations. Nevertheless, and for reasons that escape my understanding or any rational explanation, they have faithfully stood by me. Certainly, at times, they must have thought of our friendship as an undeserved and unrelenting affliction, but my days have been brighter because of them and my worries lighter. I hope that in the future I will be able to repay them for their patience and their smiles.

Finally, I want to thank my family for their help – without which I would have never been able to follow the academic path I have chosen – and especially my grandmother Nella. Her courage, strength, and kindness do not cease to fill me with awe and inspiration. If I have ever achieved anything in my life it is because of her. And it is to her that I dedicate this book, even though she has not passed on to me any of her qualities.

1
An Outline for a Foucauldian Interpretation of Modern Law

Introduction

As of today, probably few academic pronouncements have been more neglected than Jean Baudrillard's now (in)famous remark, 'Forget Foucault!'.[1] Michel Foucault's theories, ideas, and concepts, more than thirty years after his death, remain at the centre of intellectual debates in fields as diverse as philosophy, history, political science, sociology, media studies, gender studies, criminology, and postcolonial studies.[2] Although Foucault can rightly be seen as one of the most influential thinkers of our times, his ideas have hardly been received without also generating controversy. His vision of law in the modern era, in particular, has drawn severe criticism from many circles. Established scholars as diverse as Jürgen Habermas and Nicos Poulantzas have expressed strong reservations about aspects of Foucault's approach to the legal phenomenon, accusing him of downplaying and distorting the role of law in modern society.[3] He has been criticised for portraying law as a mere spectacle for the manipulative ploys of a fathomless power, and, as a consequence, for being unable to recognise the development of legal rights as tools designed to contain the pervasive influence of power, and as instruments to promote individual and collective freedom, and self-determination. These attacks are far from unwarranted. Foucault's argument appears almost counterfactual: how is it possible to claim that, in the modern 'age of rights',[4] the individual, formally protected by a sphere of legal autonomy, is, in fact, subject to the omnipresent gaze of power?

Such a reading of Foucault's work in relation to law, however, is ultimately quite misleading as it takes Foucault's passing remarks on the regression of law in our times[5] at face value without considering the broader context of his genealogical enterprise. Those sharing the conclusion that Foucault disregarded the liberating potential that modern law could offer to the individual implicitly assume that, according to the French philosopher, in modern societies, the individual is not freer than before, or at least, she is only apparently free, while in fact secretly manipulated by the cunning of power. It is easy, though, to demonstrate that Foucault did not address the relationship between autonomy and power in the crude terms of a zero-sum game (more autonomy, less power, and vice versa), but, more subtly, as a matter of *different* regimes of freedom. In this regard, he suggested that power and freedom are almost coextensive. Power does not subjugate the individual; rather, it activates certain patterns of behaviour and thinking that follow power's own impersonal discourse and that need a certain space of freedom to flourish and be effective.

The question of law within a Foucauldian framework, therefore, should not be posed in terms of a stark alternative ('Does modern law effectively grants us an individual sphere of autonomy or not?'), but, instead, should be understood as an inquiry concerning the ambiguous landscape of freedom that law contributes to generating against the background of contemporary dynamics of power. It has recently been suggested that the entirety of Foucault's oeuvre can be understood as an exercise in problematisation understood as an inquiry into the conditions of possibility of the present.[6] Seen in this light, Foucault's work becomes suddenly relevant for the legal field as it offers a series of theoretical tools that could open up new, previously foreclosed, avenues of research. The present work is an attempt in following this path. Its scope is that of provoking a problematisation of law that would unearth the unseen postulates and implicit assumptions that delineate the limits and establish the conditions of truth of our current legal horizon. Its goal is that of demonstrating that the very concept of law that we moderns silently accept and incessantly utilise is not a transhistorical reality, but rather an evolving eminently historical formation, operating according to distinctive discursive rules.

Such an endeavour promises to be doubly fruitful. First, it would resolve a longstanding conundrum which has faced many Foucauldian scholars and critics alike, showing not just the possibility of situating law within the broader Foucauldian project, but how Foucauldian conceptions of power, freedom, truth, and subjectivity are key to illuminating the progressive establishment of the modern legal discourse and to elucidating its internal workings. Second, and most importantly, it would break new ground for legal theory more generally, as the ultimate purpose of any problematisation is precisely that of making visible a problem that we could not see in the first place. Anticipating the results of my interpretation, I would posit that law and modern (biopolitical) regimes of power are not to be seen as incompatible or heterogeneous. Rather, they both evolved isomorphically as normalising technologies of government of the living, and exist in a relationship of co-production: law creates the universal subject of rights, who is reflected in the normal subject of biopolitical regimes, and vice versa. While this relationship established a largely functional complex for a long time, this complex is nowadays progressively collapsing in the face of the shift towards what Zygmunt Bauman calls 'liquid modernity' and the consequent displacing of normalising dynamics that it brings along. This mismatch between what remains a fundamentally normalising legal discourse and an increasingly non-normalisable subjectivity is, I suggest, at the root of the normative and functional crisis of modern law. Through my analysis, I will make this problem visible, while exposing contemporary legal theory's inability to properly theorise it because of its failure to question law as a historical construct. If my argument will prove convincing, I will have revealed how modern law should not be treated as a given universal and how contemporary legal theory should search for the solutions to some – or possibly many – of the normative and functional predicaments of our age by breaking away from the increasingly fragile mould of a discourse conceived in other times and built to answer different problems from the ones that challenge us now, and those that loom ahead in the coming future.

To achieve this ambitious result, I propose to perform the most typical Foucauldian methodological manoeuvre: a genealogical analysis. Foucault's genealogical method, mentioned in his writings as early as 1967,[7] drew explicitly from Friedrich Nietzsche's works. Broadly speaking, it can be described as a kind of approach that 'examines the constraints, the "regimes of truth" that underlie the historically variable divisions between the true and the false in knowledge and culture'.[8] In a different way from his archaeological method[9] – which focused on the 'system of conceptual possibilities that determines the boundaries of thought in a given domain and period'[10] – genealogy investigated more specifically the interplay of power in the shift from one system of thinking to another.[11]

Genealogy thus addresses the progressive formation of the complex and contingent nexus formed by power, knowledge, and truth, which constitute the seemingly absolute horizon of our social reality. It attempts to contextualise the order of the present so as to show not only that the most fundamental assumptions structuring our living environment are, in fact, the product of incidental historical junctures but, most crucially, how these have actually emerged. In its demystifying task, genealogy does not represent a form of judgement of the present, but rather the most radical form of its critique that is propaedeutic to judgement.[12] It is a form of inquiry that, desedimentising the concretations of history, allows us to see beyond a present which 'is always conditioned by its own inertia',[13] and to imagine previously unthinkable alternatives.

I will explain more precisely the contours of my genealogical project and how it partially departs from the Foucauldian canon in the following pages. First, however, in order to provide a more solid background to my subsequent analysis, I will focus on some relevant aspects of Foucault's theory and on the controversial role that law plays within it.

Foucault and the law: an indigestible meal?

Foucault famously claimed that modern forms of power are biopolitical as they place the lives of individuals at the centre of explicit political machinations.[14] The idea of biopolitics was brought to the forefront of academic debate by Michel Foucault, who first mentioned the term in 1974.[15] He later developed the concept in *The Will to Knowledge*[16] and in his courses at the Collège de France.[17] The statement that best seems to encapsulate his fluid ideas on the matter is this, taken from *The Will to Knowledge*:

> One would have to speak of [biopolitics] to designate what brought life and its mechanisms into the realm of explicit calculations and made knowledge/power an agent of transformation of human life . . . For millennia, man remained what he was for Aristotle: a living animal with the additional capacity for a political existence; modern man is an animal whose politics places his existence as a living being into question.[18]

Foucault provided a historical account of the rise of biopolitics. According to his view, it evolved from a framework that focused on the body of the single individual to one that took into its calculations the life of populations as a whole.

Foucault famously argued that modernity is marked by an abandonment of the juridico-political model of sovereignty. Increasingly supplementing it,[19] between the end of the sixteenth and the whole of the eighteenth century, a vast array of techniques conceived to dominate the body of the individual emerged, aiming at enhancing the body's 'productive force'.[20] In *Discipline and Punish*,[21] his most systematic study of this topic, Foucault delineated the general characteristics of 'disciplinary societies'. He argued that societies came to be informed by an 'anatomo-politics', that is a 'micro-physics' of self-regulated power. Through a complex and multi-layered system of surveillance, hierarchy, inspections, reports upon the object of the body – suddenly understood as a powerful tool of production itself – 'disciplinary techniques' were conceived and implemented. This disciplinary power was born within various heterogeneous institutions – the prison, the asylum, the factory, the army, etc. – as a dispersed set of norms and practices that fostered efficiency and effectiveness. It coupled perfectly with the rising capitalistic mode of production.[22] As Foucault puts it:

> The historical moment of the disciplines was the moment when an art of the human body was born, which was directed not only at the growth of its skills, nor at the intensification of its subjection, but at the formation of a relation that in the mechanism itself makes it more obedient as it becomes more useful, and conversely.[23]

From the second half of the eighteenth century onwards, Foucault saw another technology of power that does not exclude or substitute for discipline but that, installing itself on the substrate formed by it, operates at a 'different level' using 'different instruments'.[24]

The object of this emerging technique is not the single body of the individual any more but, more abstractly, the life of men itself. As Foucault says, it is a 'new body, a multiple body, a body with so many heads, that, while they might not be infinite in number, [they] cannot necessarily be counted'.[25] This body has the name of 'population'. The problems arising along with this new object of power are of a statistical nature: probabilities, series, and aleatory circumstances are the kind of events affecting it. The mechanisms characterising this new technique of power make use of the biological body similarly to disciplinary techniques, but they follow a completely different path. They do not deal any more with the taming of the body of the single individual but take into account the global entirety of a species: hence they do not discipline but regulate. To this kind of technology of power Foucault gave the name 'governmentality'.[26]

With the individuation of the field of governmentality, Foucault attempted to study all of those activities that could 'concern the relation between self and self, private interpersonal relations involving some form of control or guidance, relations within social institutions and communities and, finally, relations concerned with the exercise of political sovereignty'.[27] His thesis was that at a certain point in history, the state ceased to be derived from the divine order of the universe and started to be conceived as an object with its own autonomous rationality of government and concerned mainly with the correct management of the productive life of its population.[28] This new conceptualisation marked a profound shift in the art of government as it moved from the administration of a territory with its population to the administration of

> men in their relations, their links, their imbrication with those other things which are wealth, resources, means of subsistence, the territory ... men in their relation to that other kind of things, customs, habits, ways of acting and thinking ... lastly, men in their relation to that other kind of things, accidents and misfortunes such as famine, epidemics, death, etc.[29]

The dynamics of power, in other words, moved from the scheme of sovereignty or the limited focus of disciplines in order to surround the individual and the population as a whole within a triangle formed by sovereignty–discipline–government that aimed at an efficient and rational management of the national community.[30] The modern state, consequently, has to be seen as the product of this new network of practices and, according to Foucault, the history of modern Western society is, all things considered, that of the 'governmentalisation of the state'.[31] Foucault further argued that the emergence of this new rationality of government derived genealogically from the Christian 'pastoral power'.[32] Foucault also suggested that this form of power was organised around certain basic tenets that were starkly at odds with the typical dynamics of sovereign power as it focused on protecting and fostering the individual instead of asking for their sacrifice.[33]

Pastoral power influenced governmentality in two distinct ways. In the first place, it entered into a direct dialogical relationship with the individual, enveloping her within its rational discourse and pushing her to internalise ideological, behavioural, practical standards of conduct. Secondly, it treated the subject both as a single individual and as a constituent part of a flock, thus giving rise to a discourse of power that would at once 'totalise' and 'individualise'.[34] As a consequence. Foucault claimed that 'we should [not] consider "the modern state" as an entity which was developed above individuals, ignoring what they are and even their very existence, but on the contrary, as a very sophisticated structure, in which individuals can be integrated, under one condition: that this individuality would be shaped in a new form and submitted to a set of very specific patterns'.[35] Foucault, in short, understood the state as a by-product of disciplines, governmentality, and a pastoral vision of power. He seemed to downplay to the largest extent the function that law exercised in the emergence of the state and in informing its structure.[36]

Discipline and governmentality, notwithstanding their differences, were seen by Foucault as parts of common dynamics of power that, focusing on the biological, aimed at managing the subject both as a single individual and as a member of the social body.[37] Together they surrounded the subject, forcing her to internalise standards of practice, behaviours, and ideology, and giving rise to a dynamics of power where abiding by rational standards and rules of conduct was of paramount importance.[38] Within this context Foucault stressed that power, in modern society, and through discipline/governmentality, abandons what he called a Hobbesian model of sovereignty and moves towards a model of 'normalisation'.[39] In this model, power is not obsessed any more with prohibition or repression; rather, it tries to enforce upon society the ideal of the normal. The concept of 'normal' comes to represent a fundamental key to manage society as it provides power with a guideline for its regulatory operations. It does not only offer a matrix by which to interpret society, but also a scale by which to judge and differentiate each individual from the next. As Foucault observed, 'the power of normalisation imposes homogeneity; but it individualises by making it possible to measure gaps, to determine levels, to fix specialties and to render the differences useful by fitting them one to another'.[40] The emergence of a normalising dynamics of power during the late eighteenth and the nineteenth century has to be seen as the completion of a unitary surrounding manoeuvre around the body, the final stage of a siege that puts in check man understood as a biological machine: 'We are, then, in a power that has taken control of both the bodies and life or that has, if you like, taken control of life in general – with the body as one pole and the population as the other.'[41]

Foucault, following Canguilhem,[42] derived the concept 'normal' from that of the 'norm' understood in a socio-scientific sense as a rule that functions as 'a minimal threshold, as an average to be respected or as an optimum towards which one must move'.[43] Within this context Foucault stressed that power, in modern society, largely ceases to be articulated along the scheme of sovereign commands, and is instead structured along the logic of the norm.[44] The norm, according to Foucault, is a concept that is not limited exclusively to the moral, ethical or legal realm, but defines a whole mode of thinking that is distinctively modern. François Ewald, following Foucault, suggests that the concept of the norm, at the beginning of the nineteenth century, ceased to be plainly equated with the legal or moral rule and came to be linked with the idea of normality. In the modern sense the norm designates both 'a particular variety of rules and a way of producing them and, perhaps most significantly of all, a principle of valorization . . . Its essential reference is . . . to the average; the norm now refers to the play of oppositions between the normal and the abnormal or pathological.'[45]

The norm, understood in this way, becomes something akin to an epistemological and ordaining idea of the world. The norm, in other words, functions both as a scheme that allows us to efficiently categorise reality and also as a parameter by which to regulate it. To this extent, the norm fulfils two functions. In the first place it works as a method of communication as it allows the comparison of different entities on the basis of a common standard. At the same time, it transforms reality with its illocutionary force: the norm divides reality into discrete comparable entities that can be articulated through the norm itself. As Ewald puts it:

> the norm implies a rule of judgement, as well as a means of producing that rule. It is a *principle of communication*, a highly specific means of resolving the problem of intersubjectivity. The norm is equalising; it makes each individual *comparable* to all others; it provides the standard of measurement. Essentially, we are all alike and, if not altogether interchangeable, at least similar, never different enough from one another to imagine ourselves as entirely apart from the rest. If the establishment of norms implies classification, this is primarily because the norm creates classes of equivalency.[46]

The Foucauldian tools of biopolitics, discipline and governmentality, fascinating though they might be, have not always been welcomed, especially by those thinkers working in the liberal legal tradition. Liberal scholars have generally rejected Foucault's arguments as a distorted historical interpretation, offering, instead, a more straightforward vision of the relationship between power, law, and freedom in our society. It is clear that these scholars do not claim that our era is characterised by an unbridled state of individual liberty (that would be almost a contradiction in terms); nevertheless, they argue that in modern societies the individual is protected from the ploys of power to an unprecedented extent. This result has been achieved, above all, thanks to the development of a complex and sophisticated system of rights ensuring an autonomous sphere of action for the individual both at a formal and a substantive level.[47]

Such attacks are not entirely misdirected. The province of law seems to represent for adherents to Foucauldian theory a somewhat indigestible meal (an expression Foucault used with regard to the notion of the state).[48] Foucault himself produced, as is well-known, very sparse and sometimes contradictory comments on the subject, and has never offered a comprehensive analysis of law within the context of his theory, sometimes, even, seemingly resorting to the generally accepted idea of legal rights as a vehicle for expressions of resistance and subversion against practices of subjection promoted by the incessant workings of a faceless power.[49]

If one had to choose a standard-bearer for the liberal dissatisfaction – a dissatisfaction that verges on irritation – towards the generality of Foucault's theories, and in particular his ideas about power and modernity, that would be Jürgen Habermas. Habermas mounts a full-scale critique of the Foucauldian approach to law. Taking into consideration *Discipline and Punish*, Habermas claims that Foucault's understanding of the changes in penal practice around the close of the eighteenth century as the inception of a disciplinary turn in the dynamics of power is 'false in its generality'.[50] According to Habermas, Foucault can only put forward his thesis by moving from the premises of a 'theory of power for which the normative structures of the development of law remain elusive'.[51] As a result, Foucault disregards the normative impact that philosophies like utilitarianism and the Kantian theory of morality and law – which he sees connected with the emergence of discipline – have had on modernity. He simply 'does not go into the fact that these in turn serve the revolutionary establishment of a constitutionalised state power, which is to say, a political order transferred ideologically from the sovereignty of the prince to the sovereignty of the people'.[52] In Habermas's opinion, Foucault – precisely because of his normative hollow theory of power – neglects 'the development of normative structures in connection with the modern formation of power'.[53] Within this perspective, the modern discourse of law is heavily underestimated with regard to its internal rational content:

> whereas the sovereign power of classical formations of power is constituted in concepts of right and law, this normative language game is supposed to be inapplicable to the disciplinary power of the modern age; the latter is suited only to empirical, at least nonjuridical, concepts having to do with the factual steering and organisation of the behavioural modes and the motives of a population rendered increasingly manipulable by science.[54]

Overall, in Habermas's interpretation, it is the entire object represented by modern law that is overlooked in Foucault's grim account of the modern penal system. Foucault is bound to disregard it, otherwise

> he would have to submit the unmistakable gains in liberality and legal security, and the expansion of civil-rights guarantees even in this area, to an exact interpretation in terms of the theory of power. However his presentation is utterly distorted by the fact that he also filters out the history of penal practices itself as aspects of legal regulation. In prisons, indeed, just as in clinics, schools, and military installations, there do

exist those 'special power relationships' that have by no means remained undisturbed by an energetically advancing enactment of legal rights.[55]

Habermas, in other words, accuses Foucault of ignoring the normative dimension of law to subscribe to a grim vision of the modern legal phenomenon. Law is understood as a mere spectacle for the manipulating play of a fathomless power, and Foucault is consequently unable to recognise the development of legal rights as limits to the influence of power and as instruments for individual and collective self-determination.

The claim that Foucault, in his account of modern forms of power, did not pay enough attention to or grossly misinterpreted the role of law in our times has been endorsed by more sympathetic readers of the French philosopher than Habermas. Alan Hunt and Gary Wickham are among those who have stated more clearly the case proposing the so-called 'expulsion thesis' in their book *Foucault and Law*.[56] Their argument, although developed in a broader and more nuanced fashion, reaches in practice the same conclusions as Habermas's: Foucault, in his version of modernity, downplayed excessively the force of law within the dynamics of society. Relying too much on discipline and governmentality, he effectively expelled law from the locus of power. According to this thesis, Foucault saw law as a hollowed-out discourse colonised by external sets of knowledge and devoid of any effective autonomous directive role.[57]

Hunt and Wickham's description of Foucault's thoughts on law (which they claim cannot form a Foucauldian theory of law because of their sparse and cursory nature)[58] rests heavily on the idea that Foucault himself proposed a very grim account of law. They suggest that Foucault saw law as inextricably linked with sovereign expressions of authority, as the vehicle of a kind of power that manifested itself negatively as a form of a prohibition. Law was the pure command of the sovereign that told its subjects what not to do and which activities and behaviours they should avoid so as not to suffer the punishment of his violent wrath. In this sense law and power always worked as a limit not to be surpassed, its exemplar being criminal law accompanied by its sanctions.[59] In the wake of modernity, power changed its shape and embraced a new dynamic. The emergence of disciplinary societies marked a mutation in the relationship between power and the individual which abandoned a purely negative dimension. As already mentioned, according to Foucault, modern forms of power embraced a positive stance towards the subject and began to shape and mould her. In this context, the simply repressive function of law faded into the background as power became more and more diffuse in the way it worked, creating the subject from the inside – acting on her routines and conducts, entrapping her into a panoptical gaze – instead of punishing her from the outside. As a consequence, Hunt and Wickham conclude, Foucault relegates law to a minor role in today's society.[60] The legal field is colonised by the norms of human sciences and has lost its normative pre-eminence in the face of a more penetrative form of normalising power. Hence the expulsion thesis: within the dynamics of modern power, law has little or no place.[61] [62]

Foucauldian responses

Foucauldian scholars, on the other hand, have frequently addressed the issue of law in modern society. They have done so mainly from an applied perspective, by 'deploying Foucault's various methodologies or concepts in the service of a range of different critical approaches to law (and in a range of different legal contexts)'.[63] Nikolas Rose and Mariana Valverde, in particular, offer a range of methodological suggestions for how to explore law from a biopolitical perspective and can be considered exemplars of this approach.[64] They urge us to study law in concatenation with specific disciplinary and governmental practices and strategies in order to unearth its biopolitical usages. Namely, they intimate that we should focus on law as a phenomenon that produces practices of subjectivation through 'a series of productive antagonisms and alliances between different conceptions of the objects, subjects and mechanisms of government'[65] and a heterogeneous patchwork of different authorities which intermix inextricably legal and extra-legal authorities and mentalities.[66] Such an approach implies that, in practice, law falls far from the ideal of freedom, following instead biopolitical lines of subjection.[67]

While Rose and Valverde's propositions are indeed stimulating, the premise of their reasoning is troublesome. By arguing that '[l]aw, as a unified phenomenon governed by certain general principles is a fiction'[68], and claiming that conducts are governed facially through law 'but by ways of thinking, regulating and enforcing that are very different from those usually associated with legality', [69] they repeat some of the most trite tropes of the expulsion thesis, leaving their approach open to two serious lines of criticism. In the first place, the work of the legal scholar is hereby made redundant or, at best, parasitic, in the study of the legal field. If law is little more than a veneer, then the legal scholarship can offer no proper insights into the workings of law and can only be subservient to the task of the sociologist or the historian. Secondly, denying substance to the legal discourse proper seems to be in plain contradiction with its development and importance in modern society, an implausible and unacceptable conclusion.

Much of Foucauldian legal scholarship, therefore, while offering useful and provocative insights, appears to miss the point of the liberal challenge to a Foucauldian reading of power and, as a consequence, of freedom. Liberals, to their credit, do not dismiss out of hand the idea that modern societies can be oppressive notwithstanding the presence of a developed legal system and individual rights. On the contrary, they often recognise the wrongs of our times. They suggest, however, that law is the primary instrument to right those wrongs. No doubt, certain laws and rules can be an integral part of the process of legitimising oppressive and freedom-quashing discourses when strategically situated within a broader biopolitical landscape; nevertheless, the idea that fundamental legal rights protect the individual against the abuses of power still retains its theoretical validity.

Hence, much of the current Foucauldian legal scholarship does a praiseworthy job in criticising law in its practical application and contextuality, but does not fundamentally question the liberal ideal of freedom that (reformed) law can still theoretically offer. The Foucauldian argument that power and freedom are coextensive therefore appears to be weakened when we are confronted with the legal field. The theoretical *enjeu* here is particularly high: if law can, at least in principle, serve the purposes of enabling individual freedom, then Foucault's vision of modern forms of power loses a good deal of its appeal as it seems to follow the lines of an internal analysis of the liberal project, unearthing in novel ways its inconsistencies, but seemingly incapable of a truly radical critique of its overarching discursive dimension.

The conundrum that Foucauldian legal scholars have to address is therefore the following: how can one describe law without falling back within the schemes of commands and socio-scientific norms? Recognising a certain catch in Hunt and Wickham's argument: how is it possible to avoid the trap of the expulsion thesis? Several authors who have taken seriously Foucault's thoughts on law have tried to resolve this dilemma. They have certainly offered valuable improvements towards a new understanding of modern law, but, I would argue, they are eventually unable to provide an account of law that clearly escapes the command/norm gravitational field.

François Ewald is, of course, one of these authors. His work is fundamental to grasping clearly Foucault's understanding of law as a discourse that, in modernity, was dramatically reframed by the rise of normalising scientific regimes. Ewald reads Foucault as providing a distinction in law between a juridico-political dimension and a legal dimension,[70] and suggests that the turn towards the norm implicates, in general, the emergence within the legal field of a new rationality that he calls 'normative' (in the sense that it is built on the concept of the norm as explained above) in the place of the one that Foucault termed 'juridical'. This shift caused the ingraining of rational-scientific, socially generated norms within the legal discourse and the abandonment of the arbitrary impositions of a sovereign will. Modern law and society are thus both 'normative' because they both follow the same paradigm of the norm.[71] This is a very promising insight, but the way in which Ewald develops it is problematic. This can be seen in his ponderous study on 'insurance societies', where his legal ideas are more thoroughly expounded. In *État Providence*,[72] Ewald attempts to describe the juridical experience[73] of historical legal systems and the rule of judgement[74] that underscores coeval modes of legal thinking. More precisely, he analyses what he sees as the rise of 'insurance societies' in the nineteenth century.

His argument – crudely summarised – is that the complexity of modern society requires that the subject of law is not any more the single individual but society as whole – as a multitude with all its intricacies and interconnections.[75] He claims that the consequent socialisation of risk that is inherent in this kind of society imposes a new legal rationality that eschews the concepts of personal fault and individual responsibility,[76] in order to adopt the concepts of error and balance.[77,78] The juridical experience that emerges from this transformation is that of a Social Law (an order where collective claims are paramount) which is opposed to the old system of Civil Law (roughly, a legal system based on individual absolute rights), characterised by a rule of judgement that establishes the norm as its paradigm, pushing into the background law understood as a static set of universalising standards.[79] In this context, the norm appears as a shifting and modulating operator of socialisation that is capable of ensuring the correct balance of the community, generating an efficient distribution of resources among different interest groups.[80] Applying this new rule of judgement – this new law of the law – the judge does not any more subsume the concrete case under a legal categorisation; rather, she resorts to a norm that will rearrange societal conflicts on a case-by-case basis so as to reach an optimal equilibrium among parties.[81] The frame of reference moves from an absolute justice to a relativised social justice where what is due to each party is not determined on the basis of some abstract scheme, but is calculated to ensure the most desirable result concretely achievable in a given society at a given time.[82]

While I generally agree (as it will become apparent later in the present work) with the broad characterisation that Ewald proposes of the medieval and modern legal period (which he – idiosyncratically – dubs classical natural law and modern natural law) as two historical stages which, respectively, had as their frames of reference a metaphysical heavenly plan and an idealised vision of secular society, and I concur with much that he has to say with regard to the contemporary period (namely, the idea that we are progressively abandoning any idealisation of society and shifting our concern to the concrete possibilities of managerial articulation of the social body), I believe that his approach suffers from one serious flaw. Namely, Ewald does not develop a specific account of how law itself changed during its evolutionary process. He fails to offer a description of how the very structure of law was transformed by changing regimes of power and how it achieved a distinct specificity, in the face of the normalising complex. This is quite surprising, as in his analysis he urges us to focus on the changing structure of the 'law of law'[83] – that is to say, the structural logic informing the legal discourse. However, when he claims that the modern 'law of law' increasingly moved towards the norm, he does not offer a satisfying explanation of the syntactical effects that this change had on the legal language. Ewald apparently fails to appreciate that the normalising dynamic common to disciplinary, and later to governmental, mechanisms did not establish itself as 'the law of law', but, quite differently, forced law to adapt its structure so as to include normalising forms of rationality. On the contrary, it is necessary to avoid to uncritically identifying socio-scientific norms as the new structural logic of law and to be aware that modern law developed its own specific logic which, in turn, does have an impact on related regimes of power. Certainly the 'law of law' did change in reaction to the rising truth claims of normalising regimes but, at the same time, did not collapse within their dimension as it produced a peculiar distinctive syntax. Overlooking this would imply that law is only a reflection of a game of power that takes place somewhere else.

Ewald's reasoning, in sum, falls into the expulsion thesis trap. To say that there are certain rules of judgement, external to the legal discourse proper, that determine the meaning of legal statements (*énoncés*) is to say that the legal discourse itself has no proper identity and must be complemented by an external discourse.[84] What appears, in other words, is that the legal discourse has no autonomous or independent logic of its own whose dynamics are always heterodirected. Law is thus depicted once again as a veneer behind which power exercises its ploys, a hardly acceptable conclusion.[85]

Victor Tadros has tried to avoid such pitfalls, trying to demonstrate the relative autonomy of the legal field and its impact on society when confronted with disciplinary and governmental regimes. Moving from Ewald's interpretation, he recognises that Foucault's position on law was complex and nuanced and that the juridical is by no means to be equated to the legal. He suggests:

> We must consider three different phenomena if we are to understand the sophistication of Foucault's argument about law; firstly there is the law itself (which may take a number of different forms), secondly there is the network of power relations (which, at different times, may be either juridical or disciplinary, for example) and finally there is the code by which power presents itself (which for Foucault is consistently juridical).[86]

Building on this understanding, Tadros further claims that, in the passage from the Middle Ages to the modern age, the advancing of disciplines (that he sees as a restructuring of the network of power relations) involved a mutation in the forms of law, which abandoned a purely juridical expression and became the central mechanism of what Deleuze and Guattari call an 'assemblage of capture'.[87] Tadros writes:

> [Modern] law succeeded not by exerting violence but by unifying through the alliance of power relations that were already in place. By the beginning of the Classical Age the codification of power relations was sufficiently established to have converted the prior mechanisms of power into a legal mechanism. The law, then, co-ordinated the pre-existing relationships of power and reduced the potential for conflict between the structures that they formed.[88]

A few pages later, he specifies his claim using one of Foucault's most fundamental ideas, namely, that modern power has a distinctive creative effect vis-à-vis the individual:

> The primary aim of law was no longer to prescribe general rules which defined a level of transgression, it was to intervene into the relationships between particular groups of people according to information carefully collected and analysed in the form of the economy ... The modern regulatory aspect of law, then, ought not to be understood merely as 'power-conferring' but should be seen as intervening in the social construction and government of the modern subject.[89]

Differentiating between discipline and governmentality, Tadros concludes that this construction was made possible by a system of law that worked as a relay, as a connective tissue between these two normalising regimes, transferring the subject among various normalising mechanisms.[90]

This is certainly a valuable contribution, and provides a useful touchstone with which to explore the potentialities of an approach that would take Foucault's thoughts about law seriously. Most importantly, this position, albeit implicitly, approaches law as a historical discourse within broader biopolitical dynamics. Closer scrutiny, however, reveals a weakness in Tadros's proposal.

One should notice that Tadros – emphasising the normalising nature of modern networks of power relations – configures the sovereign dimension of power mainly as a rhetorical function.[91] This has a quite problematic effect: if the sovereign dimension of power is broadly rhetorical, should one not conclude that the *only* source of power resides in the truth of normalisation? How is it possible, then, to avoid the conclusion that law is just an empty space occupied *manu scientiae* by the swarming machinations of disciplines and governmentality? To this end, it is not sufficient to declare that modern law moved from a 'commanding' to a 'co-ordinative' and 'connective' mode, as this amounts to begging the question: the issue, in fact, is not 'what is the effect of modern law?' but, more fundamentally, 'what is the change internal to law itself in the face of emerging biopolitical (normalising) forms of power?'. Avoiding this issue creates the illusion of a law that is always heterodetermined in its formulations, a by-product of normalising scientific regimes that always lie beyond the reach of law. If, as Tadros argues, power networks are in place before law's codification, what is then law's proper dimension?[92] Does not this reading depict law once more, in a somewhat crude fashion, as a deceiving smokescreen skilfully deployed by the cunning of power? Are we not falling again into the expulsion thesis trap?

Such problems have not passed unnoticed. Golder and Fitzpatrick, in their book *Foucault's Law*, offer an excellent overview of Foucauldian interpretations of law and raise similar concerns to those rehearsed above. One of their main goals is to reject the 'expulsion thesis'. As it happens, they make short work of the crudest version of the thesis, the one which depicts law as a completely overlooked topic in Foucault's work. Through a close reading of Foucault's texts,[93] they easily demonstrate that Foucault addressed the question of law repeatedly both in his publications and in his lectures, and never actually claimed that law is obliterated from the horizon of modernity, insisting, on the contrary, that law is an integral part of our social life. Against the more insidious version of the 'expulsion thesis' – the one claiming that Foucault considered law as a discourse that has little influence on the distinctively modern and pervasive systems of power embodied by discipline and governmentality – Golder and Fitzpatrick muster two concurring arguments. First, they suggest that law, far from playing a subservient role to biopolitical forms of power,[94] is linked to them by a complex and mutually enforcing relationship. More precisely, they argue that law legitimises the disciplinary/governmental regimes of human sciences by providing a final epistemological horizon to their practices, and implementing their orders upon recalcitrant subjects.[95] At the same time, law bases its legitimation on the truth produced by human sciences and implemented by normalising regimes.[96] Second, law is not described by Golder and Fitzpatrick just in positive relational terms with regard to normality. Building on Foucault's idea of co-dependency between power and resistance, Golder and Fitzpatrick argue that law's determinacy – its commandeering aspect – is 'only one side of the equation of the law',[97] the other being law's necessary flexibility towards the undetermined and yet-to-be-known.[98] Law thus exhibits a responsiveness to new interrogations by unruly subjects that opens up possibilities of subversion against normalising practices and institutions.[99]

Such a reading looks like a promising perspective on Foucauldian theorisations of law. The suggestion that law and discipline/governmentality work in concatenation, mutually enforcing their authority and legitimacy, is powerful, fertile, and thought-provoking. In effect, the idea that disciplinary and governmental apparatuses established with law a positive – that is, a productive – relationship seems to fit squarely within Foucault's theoretical framework, and points towards a nuanced and sophisticated understanding of the modern legal phenomenon. Notwithstanding their insightfulness, however, Golder and Fitzpatrick's propositions against the more insidious version of the 'expulsion thesis' present some troubling limitations.

At the outset, it is not entirely clear how law would be capable of legitimising normalising practices. The authors are quite vague on how exactly law exercises its supporting epistemological role by framing discipline/governmentality: what would be law's legitimating force – which is supposed to be overarching – in the face of normality's truth claims? On this point the Foucauldian textual grounds that Golder and Fitzpatrick select from *Discipline and Punish* to corroborate their thesis[100] are worryingly shaky, since to say that the involvement of the judicial system with normalising discourses gave 'legal justification' to the latter is a rather underdetermined claim as it begs the crucial question: how is this legalisation complementing the scientific truth of discipline and governmentality beyond merely adding a supplement of coercive force to their implementation? Golder and Fitzpatrick's suggestion that law vouches for the appropriateness of normalising claims by limiting their most extreme applications does not solve this dilemma.[101] The kind of legitimation that a legal system operating only at the peripheries would offer would be a flimsy one indeed, looking like little more than a deceitful smokescreen which, behind the veneer of a modicum of legal constraint, in fact lets normalising practices run loose. Curbing only the most dominating aspects of disciplinary/governmental regimes, law seemingly operates as a decoy that appears to limit normalising practices but, in fact, generally rubber-stamps their truth claims.

Further, their claim that law operates in modernity by restraining the excesses of law implies two consequences. First, if law generally operates at the margins, it follows that the overwhelming majority of disciplinary and governmental practices go unchallenged. Discipline/governmentality therefore represent a province which law only seldom dares to explore, and one must conclude that, in modernity, biopolitical forms of power have indeed hollowed out or colonised the territory previously overseen by law, greatly reducing the reach of the legal field. Second, even if we accept this submission – if we accept that the law operates mainly at the margins and turn a blind eye to the innumerable instances of the fine and penetrating intervention of law in social practices – Golder and Fitzpatrick's argument implies that that there is only an external relationship between law, on the one hand, and discipline/governmentality on the other; the two systems operate with distinct and different rationalities and purposes. This picture describes law and discipline/governmentality as absolutely heterogeneous. Law's discourse, while still present in our societies and attached to disciplinary and governmental regimes, is ultimately external to them and to their underlying dynamics. Law therefore represents a system which is fundamentally alien to the modern biopolitical horizon of power, a relic of a sovereign past which still casts a shadow upon us. What we end up with is not exactly a replica of the subtler version of the 'expulsion thesis', but something akin to what we could call a 'heterogeneity thesis'.

The problem with such an interpretation is that it does not dispel the embarrassment that legal scholars must endure when facing the liberal challenge to Foucauldian theories of law. How is it possible to claim that the legal discourse has a marginal function in the structuring of power in modernity? How to square this fundamental heterogeneity with the role that law has played in the establishment of modernity itself? Anybody can see that law regulates our social body extensively and minutely, that rights and obligations are central to the workings of power, that the very fabric of modernity has been weaved thanks to the language of law. In this perspective, Golder and Fitzpatrick's suggestion that law provides the individual with a transformative space of resistance against the swarming of discipline/governmentality is too reductive. Law in modern societies does not just operate at the margin, serving either as an ultimate horizon of legitimation or as a final opportunity for subversion. Law is central to power in a much deeper way than Golder and Fitzpatrick's Foucauldian interpretation caters for.

While Golder and Fitzpatrick's propositions are open to criticism,[102] it must be recognised that their reading closely follows Foucault's own reflections about the relationship between the legal discourse, on the one hand, and biopolitical forms of power, which he saw as intertwined with the ideology of liberalism, on the other. Foucault's argument, foreshadowed in the 'Society Must Be Defended' and the 'Security, Territory, Population' courses at the Collège de France in 1975–6 and 1977–8 respectively, was spelled out more properly in the subsequent course 'The Birth of Biopolitics' in 1978–9.

As we have seen, Foucault argues that around the sixteenth and seventeenth centuries we have the dawning of a new governmental rationality that represents a distinctively modern technology of power. Between 1580 and 1650 we have the emergence – through works such as *Della Ragion di Stato* by Giovanni Botero (1589) – of a new vision of government which is not focused any more on territorial expansion, on an economy of subtraction, and on an increase in the sovereign's glory,[103] but is instead devoted to the multiplication of the forces of the population, which is pursued through a form of pastoral care involving each and every individual. It is in this phase of his research that Foucault made some of his most controversial observations about law, seemingly defining it in negative terms[104] and proclaiming the juridical model of sovereignty (and law) as fundamentally incompatible with the core tenets of liberalism.[105] Such incompatibility is rooted in the essentially divergent rationalities that, according to Foucault, animate the legal and the normalising discourse.

In his 'Birth of Biopolitics' course at the Collège de France, Foucault traced the rise of liberalism and neo-liberalism as the dominant ideologies at the root of contemporary governmental forms. In his analysis, he suggested that with the advent of modern economy in the eighteenth century, the subject of government is no longer the *Homo Juridicus*, the holder of rights typical of juridico-political thought, but the *Homo Economicus*, an absolute agent of human interest guided by the invisible hand of the market. These two subjects are fundamentally different, with a completely unlike relation to political power.[106] In one case the presence of a sovereign is necessary, in the other it is superfluous or damaging. According to Foucault, in the juridico-political discourse,

> the subject of right is, by definition, a subject who accepts negativity, who agrees to a self-renunciation and splits himself, as it were, to be, on one level, the possessor of a number of natural and immediate rights and, on another level, someone who agrees to the principle of relinquishing them and who is thereby constituted as a different subject.[107]

The individual, in order to protect her interest, enters into the social contract and, as a consequence, becomes the subservient subject of rights, obedient to the supreme will of the sovereign. The *Homo Economicus*, by contrast, is a subject who can never relinquish her interest. She cannot do that for two concurrent reasons. First, personal interests are seen as overriding the bindingness of any social contract – if the contract no longer is functional to the subject's interests, it no longer has force.[108] Second, interests are only personal and cannot be pursued collectively. The common interest is therefore seen not as an interest pertaining to the generality of the population, but is more like the aggregate result of single interests. Hence, it is impossible for 'the sovereign to have a point of view on the economic mechanism which totalizes every element and enables them to be combined artificially or voluntarily'.[109] The two regulatory systems that emerge from these different visions of the subject and her relationship with her interest are fundamentally divergent. The system linked with the *Homo Juridicus* is one where there is a ruling sovereign who represents the absolute will of all, and which imposes limitations on its subjects. The system which centres on the *Homo Economicus*, on the other hand, rejects to the largest extent possible any form of government on the basis that society is capable of finding its own equilibrium. There is therefore, according to Foucault, a fundamental incompatibility between 'the non-totalizable multiplicity of economic subjects of interest and the totalizing unity of the juridical sovereign'.[110]

The discourse of law is therefore 'alien'[111] to that of dawning normalising regimes. There is an absolute break in the rationalities of power whereby law appears as a theoretical (and yet very encumbering) residue of the sovereign past and discipline/governmentality are intertwined with the liberal ideology. People such as Hobbes, Rousseau, Montesquieu, Locke, and their political theories, are therefore characterised by a non-modern matrix that makes them allegedly superfluous for the understanding of the dynamics of power in our societies.[112] Moving from these considerations, it is no surprise that Foucault dedicated little time to law in his analytics of power.

The time has come to recognise that this 'heterogeneity thesis' was a mistake on the part of Foucault. I am convinced, on the contrary, that the legal discourse has been fundamental in shaping the diagram of power in modernity. I believe that that we should attempt an analysis of law that, using Foucault's 'toolbox', will allow us to go beyond Foucault's own limits and provide us with an original approach to the legal field.

An alternative approach: back to Foucault's 'toolbox'

In the light of the above considerations, we can sum up the problem of current Foucauldian approaches to law thus: in one way or another, they always depict law as a phantasmatic presence, either a proxy that has no a force of its own, and is dominated (or almost completely informed, or systemically functional and subservient) to discipline and governmentality, or as a residual discourse that is, at its core, radically non-modern and only very limitedly participates in the constitution of the environment of power in our societies. Critics of Foucault (like Habermas) have, therefore, an easy time in attacking this juncture; to argue that law in modernity plays such a marginal role leads to a gross oversimplification that largely disregards the power that is intrinsic to law as a self-standing normative discourse – a vague and rightly unacceptable conclusion.

In order to avoid a characterisation of the legal field that would fall prey to the expulsion thesis we do not need to abandon Foucault altogether. Quite the opposite – we need to be even more Foucauldian in our endeavours. With this goal in mind, I will now dig deeper into Foucault's theoretical 'toolbox'. First, I will briefly expound Foucault's understanding of the complex intertwining of power, truth, knowledge, subjectivity, and freedom. Second, I will scrutinise more closely some of his writings that are more specifically concerned with the evolution of juridical forms, namely his Rio[113] and Louvain lectures.[114]

Power is a problematic that did emerge immediately in Foucault's work, but came to prominence roughly around the time of the publication of *Discipline and Punish* and was further explored in *The Will to Knowledge* and other subsequent texts.[115] It must be clarified that Foucault never offered a clear-cut theory of power but preferred, instead, to proceed by means of an 'analytics' of power, that would lead towards 'a definition of the specific domain formed by the relations of power, and towards a determination of the instruments that will make possible its analysis'.[116] Hence, while in his works Foucault tried to be as nominalistic as possible with regard to the actual configurations that power acquired during history and eschewed all-encompassing definitions, he nevertheless provided some stipulations concerning how to study power.[117] According to Foucault, power is not a tool that can be owned and used, but rather a dynamic, 'the name that one attributes to a complex strategic situation in a particular society'.[118] It implies a set of practices – routinised and reiterated processes understood as 'programs of conduct which have both prescriptive effects regarding what is to be done . . . and codifying effects regarding what is to be known'[119] – that work as a logical ensemble and are not guided by the will of individual subjects.[120] Power is therefore not seen by Foucault as an object or a quality that one has or has not; rather, it is seen as an omnipresent field that 'is produced from one moment to the next, at every point, or rather in every relation from one point to another', and it is everywhere 'not because it embraces everything but because it comes from everywhere'.[121]

The omnipresent quality of power logically implies that power relationships are 'not in a position of exteriority with respect with other types of relationships . . . but are immanent [in them]'.[122] In particular, power establishes a strong correlative relationship with knowledge, where the two are so inextricably intertwined as to form a sort of *unicum*, which Foucault described with the neologism *power-knowledge*. According to him, the production of knowledge always takes place within formations (institutional, social, interpersonal, etc.) that are already invested by power and, on the other hand, there is no power relation which does not itself produce knowledge as a discourse that ordains, explains, legitimises, and propagates the operations of power.[123] This connection is not at all an impermeable self-feeding mechanism where power and knowledge mutually support each other *ad infinitum*, but an unstable link where the two poles enable and limit each other in a relationship which is as productive as it is perpetually problematic and subject to continuous reframing.[124]

The conviction that power and knowledge are co-dependent led Foucault (in the footsteps of Nietzsche) to reject the idea of truth (inherited by the Enlightenment) as the correct description of an objective reality,[125] and embrace a vision of truth as a regime of formation of true and false claims, focusing more on the conditions that allow one to make a statement than on the quality of the validity of the assertions themselves.[126] As he put it:

> by truth I do not mean 'the ensemble of truths which are to be discovered and accepted', but rather 'the ensemble of rules according to which

the true and the false are separated and specific effects of power attached to the true' . . . 'Truth' is to be understood as a system of ordered procedures for the production, regulation, distribution, circulation and operation of statements. 'Truth' is linked in a circular relation with systems of power which produce and sustain it, and to effects of power which it induces and which extend it. A 'regime' of truth.[127]

We can therefore see that power, knowledge and truth constitute a sort of triangle where each element both supports and draws support from the other two. Most importantly, we can see that this structure is not negative or repressive, but rather, is chiefly aimed at the positive production of social effects. Building on this approach, Foucault offered a peculiar and intriguing understanding of subjectivity which eschewed the primacy of the subject as something already given and firmly places it as the primary product of the ensemble formed by power–knowledge–truth. The place that the individual occupies in the play of power is crucial, as she ceases to be opposed to its working but becomes integral to its mechanisms:

> The individual is not to be conceived of as a sort of elementary nucleus, a primitive atom, a multiple and inert material on which power comes to fasten or against which it happens to strike, and in doing so subdues or crushes individuals. In fact, it is already one of the prime effects of power that certain bodies, certain gestures, certain discourses, certain desires, come to be identified and constituted as individuals. The individual, that is, is not vis-à-vis of power; it is, I believe, one of its prime effects.[128]

Contrary to some simplistic interpretations, Foucault does not present a 'power-determined' vision of the subject.[129] Rather, he sees the individual as intrinsically enmeshed with the discourses of power/knowledge.[130] In this sense, 'Foucault's interest is in showing the extent to which subjects are the effects of discourses or [sic] power by bracketing the relative autonomy of the subject'.[131] Foucault further argues that power, within the horizon of modernity, is not seen in opposition to freedom but as coextensive to it. Power, constituting the individual, also takes the individual as its main vector and the means of its propagation. Internalised by the subject, power does not subjugate the individual completely; rather, it activates certain patterns of behaviour and thinking that will implement power's own discourse and that need a certain space of freedom to flourish and to be effective:

> Power is exercised only over free subjects, and only insofar as they are free . . . [F]reedom may well appear as the condition for the exercise of

power (at the same time its precondition, since freedom must exist for power to be exerted, and also its permanent support, since without the possibility of recalcitrance, power would be equivalent to a physical determination).[132]

Following Foucault's penchant for neologism, we could invent the neologism 'subjactivation' to indicate precisely this effect of power on the individual, an effect which implies a positive working of power, not repressive but creative, and which transforms her into an agent who is both the passive recipient of norms of conduct and their active (and therefore potentially subversive) operator. In modernity, thus, power operates upon individual subjectivity in order to create and mould the person into a well-integrated member of society. Hence, the idea of personal conduct comes to prominence as the most important factor in pursuing positive change, charging the subject with a specific responsibility to act in relation to herself and society. The individual is not the passive recipient of heteronomous principles of conduct, but emerges as an autonomous agent that, following her own egoistic interest, also contributes to the greater good.[133] In this sense, the single person is not only free to choose her own path, but she is also 'obliged to be free', invited to actively shape her life in accordance with the standards of optimisation that are generally accepted.[134]

Foucauldian studies – and in particular governmental ones[135] – have thus shown how the freedom we enjoy as individuals in modern society is built into an inextricable web of rationalities, policies, and practices that inexorably influence an individual's mind set, choices, and world view. These studies suggest that such a freedom is not an unqualified one; rather, it represents a spectrum of strategic possibilities that are acceptable – even favoured and fostered – within a given historically and contextually specific dynamic of power. As Peter Miller and Nikolas Rose contend:

> The practices of modern freedom have been constructed out of an arduous, haphazard and contingent concatenation of problematisations, strategies of government and techniques of regulation. This is not to say that our freedom is a sham. It is to say that the agonistic relation between liberty and government is an intrinsic part of what we have come to know as freedom.[136]

The upshot of this complex picture is that the individual is turned into a subject by the deployment of a series of discourses that inscribe the person into a triangle formed by power, knowledge and truth which designates the environment of the subject's freedom, both enabling her actions and limiting her possibilities in a fluctuating, continuously changing equilibrium. The ensemble of the mechanisms that make possible processes of subjectivation is called, in Foucauldian terminology, a *dispositif*, normally translated into English as *apparatus*.[137] The meaning of the term 'apparatus' is never explicitly described by Foucault, who came closest to a definition in an interview in 1977 in which he said that a *dispositif* is the strategic network formed by a

> heterogeneous set consisting of discourses, institutions, architectural forms, regulatory decisions, laws, administrative measures, scientific statements, philosophical, moral, and philanthropic propositions – in short, the said as much as the unsaid ... The apparatus is ... always inscribed into a play of power, but it is also always linked to certain limits of knowledge that arise from it and, to an equal degree, condition it. The apparatus is precisely this: a set of strategies of the relations of forces supporting, and supported by, certain types of knowledge.[138]

The meaning of apparatus has been further expounded by other thinkers in the Foucauldian tradition, most importantly Gilles Deleuze and Giorgio Agamben. Deleuze, offering his idiosyncratic take on Foucault's term, argues that an apparatus is a machine both of visibility (a mechanism which makes an object apparent in our world as a problematic) and of enunciation (a mechanism which imposes rules of knowledge and truth upon a certain discourse) which works along lines of power and subjectivity (that is, it imposes specific meanings and connections while being open to human manipulation).[139] Agamben, on his part, building on both Foucault and Deleuze, has intimated that an apparatus is 'anything that has in some way the capacity to capture, orient, determine, intercept, model, control, or secure the gestures, behaviours, opinions, or discourses of living beings',[140] hence stressing that the main effect of any apparatus is to produce a process of subjectivation which will mould living beings into social subjects.[141] It must not be overlooked, however, that processes of subjectivation are not absolute. Building on the Foucauldian principle of co-extensiveness between power and resistance, Sandro Chignola acutely observes that no apparatus can perform a complete overdetermination of the subject, as no apparatus can ever fully foreclose lines of flight that allow for opposition and subversion.[142] An apparatus, then, can be described as, on the one hand, one of the machines that embody and operationalise the co-dependent relation between a given historical epistemic order and a given historical network of power and, on the other, the performative place of a subjectivity that perpetually (yet only partially and imperfectly) escapes the overdeterminations of power.

But what is the role that law plays, if any, within this dynamic? The lectures that Foucault gave in Rio de Janeiro in 1973[143] and in Louvain in 1981,[144] both chiefly concerned with the problem of how specific historical forms of subjectivity are created through regimes of knowledge imbued with power,[145] point towards what seems to me a fruitful line of inquiry. In *Truth and Juridical Forms* Foucault's goal is to study 'juridical forms and their evolution in the field of penal law as the generative locus for a given number of forms of truth'.[146] It is not my intention here to analyse in depth his studies on the Germanic test, the late medieval inquiry, or the modern examination; rather, I would like to point out Foucault's broader argument that closely links specific truth-producing mechanisms with broader social dynamics, demonstrating that there is a relationship between the judicial production of truth and more general schemata of power-knowledge which inform societies at large.[147] By looking at judicial procedures Foucault attempted to gain access to 'models of truth which still circulate in our society, are still imposed on it, and operate not only in the political domain and in the domain of everyday behaviour, but even in the realm of science'.[148]

In *Wrong-Doing, Truth-Telling*, Foucault's goal is similar, but his focus homes in on how the individual is subjectivated through her participation in certain judicial procedures, namely that of avowal. Having qualified avowal as a very special kind of declaration associated with a certain 'cost of enunciation',[149] Foucault suggests that the avowal is a 'verbal act through which the subject affirms who he is, binds himself to this truth, places himself in a relationship of dependence with regard to another, and modifies at the same time his relationship to himself'.[150] An analysis of the history of the avowal, therefore, is part and parcel of a general critical history of those processes of veridiction through which the individual becomes a subject and finds herself tied to certain forms of truth instigated by specific regimes of power/knowledge.[151]

What emerges from the Rio and Louvain lectures is Foucault's idea that the legal field is a privileged one with which to explore the relationship between forms of veridiction and subjectivation, dynamics of power, and regimes of knowledge.[152] Unfortunately, Foucault did not pursue this avenue to its fullest extent. As already mentioned, he was persuaded that the discourse of law and that of normalising regimes (which embraced the ideology of liberalism) were fundamentally incompatible, and that there was an absolute heterogeneity between the subject of right and the liberal subject of interest.[153] Hence, he took into consideration juridical forms only as those reflected broader schemes of veridiction in a given historical era, but never investigated properly how law was related to the emergence of the subject of interest in the political realm.

I believe that we need to address precisely this space. My working hypothesis is thus the following: law should be studied as a *sui generis* apparatus which, working along the lines of jurisdiction/veridiction, inscribes subjectivity within a triangle formed by power, knowledge, and truth. More precisely, and against Foucault's heterogeneity thesis, I intimate that law is that particular apparatus which, in modernity, establishes the political truth of the subject by making visible her interests. It is within this context that I will proceed towards a genealogy of modern law. When conceived as a proper apparatus, law is by no means an exception to the Foucauldian genealogical rule. Once we realise that the discourse of law can be understood as a distinctive channel of subjectivation – according to Agamben's and Deleuze's meaning of apparatus – we are bound to attempt an analysis of such an apparatus that would disentangle the strands of its peculiar discursive formation while trying, as much as it is possible, to treat it as a discrete entity. An approach that would take seriously Foucault's teaching – to the extent of contradicting Foucault himself – should face this problem squarely. One should use his 'conceptual toolbox' to scrutinise the shifting meaning of law, its changing structure and configuration, in order to glimpse its specificity in relation to different societies and systems of power.

By means of a genealogical analysis, I aim to link the problematisation of modern law with its eventalisation. Achieving a 'breach of self-evidence, of those self-evidences on which our knowledges, aquiescences, and practices rest',[154] I will be able to approach modern law from a fresh angle and to question it as an original problematic object. The kind of analysis I propose is currently lacking not only in legal theory as generally understood, but, more surprisingly, in Foucauldian approaches to law as well. This void – which is puzzling in legal theory and quite frankly striking in Foucauldian studies – has brought about two dire consequences: first, the legal discourse is seen as an inert object which is never analysed on its own and it is therefore necessarily relegated to a sort of ancillary role with respect to other power nexuses; second, the word 'law' is always used in an unqualified way as a historical invariant that does not need to be properly investigated, and whose internal continuities and discontinuities are therefore forgotten and neglected.[155]

To be sure, localised and field-specific legal genealogies have been attempted.[156] What I am suggesting here, however, is something much broader and deeper. What I want to scrutinise in the present work is the transformation of what we could call the internal logic that informs modern law – what one could call its fundamental syntax[157] or the *properly legal* 'law of law'.[158][159] In this regard, I would like to distinguish my views from other commentators' and suggest that the general epistemological structure linked with normalisation did not lead socio-scientific norms to bluntly colonise the legal field or made law a relic of the past; rather, it transformed the very structure of the legal discourse from within. Law, I would thus argue, in developing through the centuries into what we could now identify as the modern form of law, progressively adopted the underlying logic of contemporary biopolitical regimes – which for Foucault had a normalising nature. My claim is that law, under the pressure of normalisation, ceased to be only and exclusively a mere *sign* of power to become the general *discourse* of power in modern societies. To put it differently, I believe that, progressing towards the modern age, law gradually ceased to be an order that was – by and large – the mere signification of sovereign commands (the social form in which a heteronomous sovereign entity manifested itself) and instead became a self-standing discourse structured upon the paradigm of the norm (understood in a Foucauldian sense) which delineated the general environment of power. Law, according to my thesis, was not slowly 'hollowed out' by the swarming of norms belonging to various external socio-scientific discourses but, by adopting the paradigm of the norm as its internal structuring principle, underwent a mutation that fundamentally changed its own discursive nature and, as a consequence, its role as an apparatus within the broader context of power.[160]

Before I proceed further, some caveats are in order. It must have not gone unnoticed (for the informed Foucauldian reader at least) that I plan to address law as an apparatus in a quite peculiar fashion. The term 'apparatus' normally refers to a varied array of ideas, practices, institutions, etc., and is therefore marked by a distinctive heterogeneity in its constitutive elements. Hence, law as a (more or less self-contained) discursive formation should be excluded from this definition, as law should be examined only in its social applications together with the practices and institutions that actualise its existence in society. My investigation would therefore resemble more an archaeology than a genealogy, and allegedly should not make use of the notion of apparatus as a conceptual tool. I would reject such a reading. In the first place, genealogies cannot take place if not in conjunction with archaeologies, and the two operations cannot be neatly separated.[161] In the second place, it is important to point out that while the orthodox conception of apparatus is that of a heterogeneity, the core of this idea – its problematising function, so to say – is that of a machine capable of producing subjectivity. In this sense, law indeed represents a specific sort of subjectivising machine because it is one of the few apparatuses – maybe the only one – that by its discursive force alone is capable of creating subjectivity. Sure enough, any discursive formation imports a subjectivising effect, but modern law is uniquely effective and transformative in this respect. As is widely recognised and as I will make clear through my subsequent analysis, modern law performs this function by linking together at a political level truth, knowledge, and power in a distinctively potent way. Through its injunctions, therefore, law literally structures our social environment and creates subjectivities (the citizen, the criminal, the minor, etc.) to a historically unparalleled degree. To that extent, focusing on the syntax of modern law is a genuinely genealogical enterprise as it traces the development of an overarching diagram of truth, knowledge, and power in our society and problematically frames its dynamics with regard to the subject. This is not to deny that we can thus serenely eschew the study of law in practice; as a matter of fact, the study of the concrete deployments of the legal discourse is of the utmost importance. I believe, though, that it is also very important – indeed, necessary and fundamental in terms of its logical priority – to address as well the discourse of law as a *sui generis* apparatus so as to open up the intellectual 'black box'[162] represented by its syntax and critically examine its inner workings.

Further, the reader (again, especially one versed in Foucault's works) might be disoriented by my subsequent rather conceptual and analytical reading of the emergence of modern law, and by the relative absence of the intertwining of intellectual ideas and a rich social history which characterises much of Foucault's work and that of those – like Rabinow, Rose, Hacking, etc. – whom he inspired. I readily admit the charges, but I would plead clemency on two grounds. First, my conceptual interpretation is to be read against the background of Foucault's more general description of the historical evolution of forms of power. As such, my study should be read as an addendum to that project, building upon the general lines of the social history it describes (even if I sometimes depart from the Foucauldian canon). Second, my project, while ambitious in its scope and goal, cannot hope to account for a detailed genealogy of the modern legal discourse. An enterprise of this sort appears titanic in its breadth and would probably require several volumes to complete. More modestly, the present work only represents an outline of such a genealogy as it attempts to indicate the broad paths of development undertaken by modern law. Keeping with the inquiring spirit of a genealogy, my study aims at making visible a certain problem. It does not pretend to offer a complete picture of our complex reality; rather, it aims at shedding light on previously overlooked fissures and lines of flight in it so that we can work on them. Future work will be needed for this purpose. Here I only dedicate myself to the most urgent task of indicating the existence of such a field and to delineating its general contours.

A framework of analysis

One of Foucault's most important methodological rules is that the analysis of any phenomenon should avoid ontological questions and should focus instead on more historical ones. Foucault famously tried to circumvent anthropological universals in order to treat them as historical constructs and unearth the hidden meanings of their actual articulation through time. A genealogical scrutiny of modern law is bound to follow this rule. Consequently, I will not address the conceptual conundrum of what law is in and of itself but will explore the discursive effects that modern law has produced on our society. In order to answer this question, it must be recognised that it is almost impossible to initiate a discussion of modern law without bringing in the notion of the modern state that frames it.

Foucault claimed that the state is the effect rather than the cause of a whole range of power relations,[163] and that it represents for them a sort of 'quilting point' towards which various apparatuses have gravitated and by which they have been absorbed or sanctioned.[164] The rise of the state is, at least at the level of social institutions, the single most important phenomenon of modern times, a phenomenon that is inextricably linked with the development of modern law. The aetiological relationship between these two elements, however, does not concern me here. What interests me is to evoke the notion of the state so as to provide a sound basis from which to address the discourse of modern law. What I want to do, in other words, is to provide a notion of the state that will help us to see how law was developed in relation to the problem of social order and worked instrumentally to provide its solution. Looking at the fundamental features associated with the state, we will be able to see, as in reverse, the fields of operations where law played a constitutive role. As a preliminary step towards a genealogical account, I will therefore have to clarify what is generally understood by the modern state.

The term 'state' finds its roots in fourteenth-century political thought.[165] At that time, the term (and its Latin equivalent *status*), however, did not have the meaning we currently attach to it. It referred to the particular personal standing of rulers themselves so that, within the political language of the day, state meant 'the state of the king', a condition of stateliness. Only subsequently, and namely with the works by Guicciardini and Machiavelli (fifteenth to sixteenth centuries), did the idea of the state come to be detached from that of the people actually governing a given community in order to define the community of the governed as such or the commonwealth. The modern theoretical usage of the term 'state' was developed by Bodin and Hobbes. These authors in effect rejected the idea of the state as a direct emanation either of the governors or of the governed, and attached to the state a 'doubly impersonal character'.[166] In doing so, they emphasised the autonomous quality of the state as an organisation whose supreme territorial authority is independent both 'from that of the rulers or magistrates entrusted with the exercise of is power for the time being' and 'from that of the whole society or community over which its powers are exercised'.[167] As such, the state can be broadly defined as a particular historical form and manifestation of political power.[168] More precisely, it is 'an apparatus of power whose existence remains independent of those who may happen to have control of it at any given time'.[169]

The state has been defined as the master noun[170] of modern political language. As such, and beyond the very general definition provided above, it is associated with multifaceted, and often overlapping, meanings.[171] The idea of the state could thus give us divergent answers with regard to the nature of the modern state.[172] By way of an example, to illustrate this point, the answer to the question 'what is the state?' would produce very different answers depending on the standpoint taken: genetic ('What were the conditions that led to the emergence of the state?');[173] functionalist ('What is it that the state does?');[174] or political ('What groups or dynamics does it help or undermine?').[175] For the purpose of the present work, I will focus on its more formal characteristics and sketch out its basic institutional outline.

The state, in effect, can be seen as a modality of the institutionalisation of political power.[176] That being the case, the idea of the state, which implies the existence of a supreme public power continuous in time over a given territory,[177] comprises three distinct, yet interlocked, aspects: the depersonalisation of power relations; the formalisation of the exercise of power; and the integration of power relations into a comprehensive order.[178]

The first feature – depersonalisation – reflects the fact that, in modern states, political power does not depend on an individual's identity but, instead, is objectified in the administrative and bureaucratic structure of the state. In a different way from interpretations derived from the feudal and absolutist model, the organisation of the modern state detaches political power from personal statuses in two senses. Firstly, public officials do not act on the basis of their personal authority; rather, their authority derives almost entirely from the neutral powers of the state itself. Secondly, power relations are depersonalised in the sense that individuals are, in principle, treated in an objective way by the state; in other words, political power addresses the individuals as abstract citizens regardless of their personal identity. The second feature – formalisation – refers to the fact that state power is normally exercised following standardised rules of conduct. State power, thus conceived, does not operate on the basis of arbitrary personal decisions but is always directed and limited by formal dispositions. Finally, the third feature – integration – involves the interconnectedness of the private and public spheres and therefore a link between the individual and her own state. The state and the individual do not exist as two extraneous bodies, but are related by some kind of political integration forming a mutually dependent whole.[179]

It is largely recognised that the first two features have been achieved historically mainly by means of legal rules,[180] famously leading Weber to identify the modern state with a 'legal-rational' ideal-type of domination.[181] The state could thus be defined as the societal organisation that holds the monopoly of violence by means of a supreme and binding legislative authority over a given territory.[182] Linking this well-known idea with Foucault's suggestions concerning the role of the state in power networks, an interesting intersection emerges: what was the role that law exercised in elaborating, rationalising and centralising a heterogeneous set of power relations under the banner of the state?

To answer this question – which must be central to any genealogical analysis of modern law that would avoid the expulsion thesis – we need to examine law as an apparatus and turn to the third feature of the institutionalisation of power (integration) to build a framework of analysis. The integrative feature of the state is, as David Held has suggested, the central matter of modern political theory, and can be condensed as follows: 'How should the "sovereign state" be related to the "sovereign people" who were in principle the source of its power?'[183] This (integrally modern) question is properly associated with the democratic basis of the modern state and poses at the centre of the political discourse the issue of how to model a societal order that would operate in line with the subjective interests of its members. It will not be necessary here to provide an extensive definition of what democracy is;[184] suffice it to say that, at its core, lies the idea that the only legitimate government is the one that is upheld by the voluntary consent of the people.[185] The outcome of a consensual process, the very essence of democracy, should consist of a symmetry and congruence between citizens and government on the one hand, and between the outputs of government (decision, policies, and similar) and its constituency (i.e. the citizens) on the other,[186] thus allowing (ideally) a reflection of subjective interests in the actions of government and in the structure of state and society.

It is clear that law is central to the working of democracy, and one needs only to invoke the idea of the rule of law to demonstrate the close relationship between legal rules and democratic practices. Crucially, the democratic regime based on law necessarily implies a process of subjectivation that makes visible the individual as a member of the state while animating the state (in the literal sense of giving the institutionalised society an *animus*, a soul) through the will of the individual. Even more importantly, such a process of subjectivation has the important effect of 'redoubling' the subject, which is made visible both as a single individual and as a member of society, two entities whose volition and interests (as theorists of social contract have pointed out) can sometimes be in conflict. In this context, law appears as the apparatus of subjectivation that can resolve the great modern question concerning the relationship between a sovereign people and a sovereign state: how to know the truth about the interests of the individual and use it to rule the constituted society? The emergence of the apparatus represented by modern law, therefore (not dissimilarly from what Foucault said about the state), is not really the cause of a certain mode of government, but rather its most fundamental effect.

For analytical purposes, I propose that modern law can be differentiated from earlier legal systems with reference to the presence of four key operators: generality, abstraction, equality, and freedom. Modern laws, in other words, are construed as general and abstract rules which ensure equality and freedom before the law. The fundamental role these four operators play in structuring modern law has been elucidated by F. A. Hayek in *The Constitution of Liberty* – his vision was shared, to a large extent, by Weber, Neumann, Kelsen, and Hart, among others.[187] Hayek defined freedom as 'that condition of men in which coercion of some by others is reduced as much as is possible in society'.[188] He took it as the central struggle that has guided the social evolution of mankind. In addition, he argued that '[t]he great aim of the struggle for liberty has been equality before the law'.[189] He then described laws as general and abstract commands, rules that apply to everyone irrespective of their peculiar conditions: 'Law in its ideal form might be described as a "once-and-for-all" command that is directed to unknown people and that is abstracted from all particular circumstances of time and place and refers only to such conditions as may occur anywhere and at any time.'[190] Hayek's suggestion is that only laws articulated and formulated in this way can effectively guarantee equality of individuals before the law and thus protect freedom from arbitrary coercion: 'when we obey laws, in the sense of general abstract rules laid down irrespective of their application to us, we are not subject to another man's will and are therefore free.'[191] According to this reading, generality, abstraction, equality, and freedom delimit the most fundamental generative principle of what we have called above the syntax of modern law.[192] Bearing in mind this scheme, I will proceed with the view of delineating the historical emergence of these concepts, and their structural and functional relationship within the context of coeval dynamics of normalising power.

In the remainder of the present work, my Foucauldian interpretation of modern law will develop as follows. The aim of Chapters 2 and 3 is to offer a genealogical analysis of law as an apparatus by addressing its subjectivating function from a double perspective: law as the apparatus to extract and enforce the truth of the interests of the individual, and law as the apparatus to extract and enforce the truth of the interests of society.[193] My genealogical analysis would focus on two distinct, but related objects. In Chapter 2, I will explore the emergence of law as an apparatus that makes visible the political truth of the individual by analysing the works of some key philosophers ranging from Aquinas to Hegel. More precisely, I will demonstrate that, in the shift from a metaphysical to a post-metaphysical way of thinking, the foundation of political power was identified in the secular interests of the single person, and that the syntax of law was reconceived to transform the legal discourse into a machine capable of making those interests manifest through the paradigm of the norm. In Chapter 3, I will turn to the development of law as an apparatus that makes visible the political truth of society by scrutinising the English, American, and French Revolutions as the main events that have established the constitutional horizon of modernity. Namely, I will show how each revolution, in its own distinct way, established innovative constitutional mechanisms which ensured a structural correspondence between the institutional exercise of political power and a political truth reflecting the interests of society. Those mechanisms, I will prove, were founded on a new conception of law that was normalising in scope and function, framing both government action and human will within absolute operational limits marked by the paradigm of the norm.

Through my genealogy, I will show how modern law works as an apparatus along the two lines of normalisation that Foucault termed 'normation' and 'normalisation in a strict sense'. Normation, Foucault argued, entails the primacy of the norm over the conduct: the norm is set in advance and people have to abide to it.[194] Normalisation in the strict sense, on the other hand, 'consists in establishing an interplay between . . . different distributions of normality and in acting to bring the most unfavourable in line with the more favourable'.[195] Modern law presents clearly this Janus-faced nature: on the one hand it imposes rules of formation on power, knowledge, truth, and subjectivity, thus delimiting their field of existence; on the other hand, those very same rules allow power, knowledge, truth, and subjectivity to become visible and to mould the social environment. With my genealogical analysis, I will unearth the development of this syntax while exploring some politico-historical questions. How did these operators emerge in the course of the historical development of the state? How did their meaning change through the centuries? How did this shifting meaning transform the discourse of law from an order delimited by sovereign commands to one generated by the logic of the norm?

These questions will prove propaedeutic to my endeavour in Chapter 4, which is to delineate in greater detail how modern law operates as a *sui generis* apparatus establishing the general environment of biopolitical forms of power, and how it works in concatenation with other disciplinary/governmental apparatuses. In doing so, I will tackle head on the challenge posed by the expulsion thesis by claiming that modern law and apparatuses of normalisation form a coherent self-feeding assemblage which, through a dynamic of co-production, inscribes the subject within an isomorphic space where the paradigm of the norm dominates both the legal and the socio-scientific dimension. Given this picture, I will investigate the workings of the normalising complex in our contemporary times, which Zygmunt Bauman has famously described as 'liquid modernity'. My suggestion is that the social fluidity characteristic of liquid modernity is reflective of a profound biopolitical shift, which is conducive to an understanding of the individual as a 'virtual entity'.[196] This dynamic, I contend, fundamentally challenges the paradigm of the norm and is therefore bringing us to the absolute limit of the normalising complex, ushering in a seemingly unsurpassable normative and functional crisis for the legal discourse connected with it.

Finally, my interpretation of modern law will bring me to question, in the Conclusions, what I see as a theoretical blockage in legal thinking in both the (broadly speaking) liberal and the critical camps. In short, I argue that both defenders and critics of liberalism – the political system coextensive with the modern legal discourse – because of a lack of genealogical perspective on the legal discourse fail to appreciate the extent of the inherently and inescapable normalising effects that modern law imposes on the subject, and thus are unable to offer viable solutions to the normative and functional crisis that modern law is suffering (and will suffer even more in the years to come) in the face of an increasingly liquid, non-normalisable, social body. Against this state of affairs, I plead for a Foucauldian approach to law that, far from expelling law from the locus of power, can indicate new and unforeseen avenues that we need to explore if we wish to tackle the challenges looming ahead.

2

A Genealogy of Modern Law I: The Political Truth of the Individual

Introduction

As intimated in the first chapter, by scrutinising the formation of the syntax of the modern legal discourse, I will attempt a genealogical analysis of law as an apparatus whose function is that of knowing the truth and the interests of the subject as an individual and as a member of society. The present chapter will be devoted to the first limb of the analysis. To this end, I will now turn to the formation, within the history of political theory, of ideas of political legitimation, examining how the source of political legitimation abandoned metaphysical foundations and was gradually conceived in a secular way focusing on individual interests seen through the prism of the paradigm of the norm and the dynamics of normalisation. Law slowly ceased to be conceived as a set of commands issued by a supreme sovereign, to become chiefly a body of worldly norms generated by individuals themselves. Thus, political theory progressively shifted towards the logic of normality, focusing on law, understood as an order of norms, as a mechanism of legitimation.

Such a shift occurred, in very general terms, in three successive historical phases. In the early phase (thirteenth to sixteenth centuries), the widely held idea that political legitimation rested on metaphysical foundations – an idea connected with the logic of sovereignty as described by Foucault – came to be contested, opening the way to a secular thinking that progressively turned to the paradigm of the norm as its ordering principle. In the second phase (sixteenth to eighteenth centuries), political legitimation was conceived as being dependent on certain norms that are recognisable in human nature and that reflect secular individual interests. Law, at his stage, was seen as instrumental in building a society that would respect those norms, but was still articulated as a set of commands issued by a virtually unrestrained sovereign. Consequently, law, in this period of political thinking, continued to be articulated through the paradigm of the sovereign command, but it was, as it were, overdetermined, in its scope, by the paradigm of the norm. Finally, in the third phase (eighteenth to nineteenth centuries), which established the horizon of the modern discourse of legitimation and law as we know it today, we can see that the paradigm of the norm penetrated the legal field, transforming it from within. Law, in other words, ceased to be understood simply as a means to implement certain given natural norms that establish society's legitimate order; rather, it was conceived as a mechanism through which society itself could elaborate these norms and structure political legitimation by making visible the individual interest of the subject. In this sense, law integrates, to the largest degree, the paradigm of the norm, abandoning almost entirely the logic of sovereignty. I will devote the present chapter to developing my argument by analysing the ideas of several thinkers who played an important part in the evolution just delineated. My analysis will not be a comprehensive philosophical survey; rather, following a Foucauldian stance, I will mainly address those authors who played an instrumental role in establishing a new way of thinking. As a consequence, certain notable thinkers such as Machiavelli and Montesquieu will be put aside because, much as they were important for the development of political thinking, they focused mainly on the craftsmanship or a taxonomy of the political form of their times, and avoided the fundamental question (for the purposes of this research) of what makes a political order legitimate or not.[1]

From medieval theology to secularisation

Generally speaking, in feudal times the fact that political power was theoretically and practically founded upon the supremacy of the sovereign over his subjects was almost unquestionably accepted. Foucault labelled this scheme of power relations with the term 'sovereignty' and explored it the greatest detail in *Discipline and Punish*.[2] At the beginning of the book, Foucault – as he previously did with *Madness and Civilisation*[3] and *The Order of Things*[4] – sets up an effective narrative device. He describes a powerful image of torture, the fearsome suffering that a certain Damiens, guilty of attempted regicide, had to endure before death. The description is not only rhetorical, but has a substantive function in delineating the logic of the system of power that was intrinsic to sovereignty. In the face of such gruesome violence, questions arise concerning the torture of Damiens. Why was the torment necessary? Why had it to be so publicly exhibited? And why was it so thoroughly construed, so minutely regulated? The answer, according to Foucault, lies in the scheme of power that he termed sovereignty.

As Anne Barron has pointed out, up until the seventeenth and eighteenth centuries there was a direct equation between power and sovereignty, because the latter 'reflected the actual mode of power's exercise: actual power relations in society took the same forms as that of the sovereign–subject relation'.[5] Foucault's study of the criminal and her body within the scheme of sovereignty is therefore to be read as part of a broader analysis of the fundamental logic of power. More precisely, it shows how power reacted to the continual attack on its order represented by the criminal act. Hence, Damien's torment is not to be interpreted just as a violent and almost sadistic knee-jerk reaction that the authorities displayed against criminals. On the contrary, it stands as a 'political ritual' and it is part of 'the ceremonies by which power is manifested'.[6] The infringement of the law was to be considered less as an offence against the victim personally and more as a wrongdoing against the sovereign – a felony committed against his authority and will.

The injury caused to the victim by the pettiest criminal, therefore, was not simply a matter that needed to be settled between two subjects. The offence ascended along the chain of authority like an electrical pulse directed towards the lord.[7] Faced with this challenge to his authority, the sovereign had to strike back in a proportion commensurate with the seriousness of the crime. He had to make use of violence in a calculated, yet public and fearsome, manner by way of an example to the population and as a restoration of the perceived order between the sovereign himself and the offending criminal:

> It brought to a solemn end a war, the outcome of which was decided in advance, between the criminal and the sovereign; it had to manifest the disproportion of power of the sovereign over those whom he had reduced to impotence. The dissymmetry, the irreversible imbalance of forces were an essential element in the public execution.[8]

The horrific ritual of the torment, whose ferocity increased in direct proportion to the harm the sovereign had suffered, reached its peak in cases of attempted regicide. It was a vivid as well as a technical example of the right of life and death which the sovereign had over his enemies and his subjects. This is the reason why the torment of Damiens is a perfect manifestation of sovereignty: the individual who made an attempt on the king's life should be annihilated, thereby demonstrating the absolute power and glory of the ruler. The force of the king had to be shown to its greatest extent, the spectacle of protracted and mutilating violence being the evidence of the total disposal that the king possessed over all his subjects.

In that context, law was mainly understood as a set of commands issued by the ruler, a model that Foucault defined in general terms as Hobbesian.[9] This paradigm had a double implication, at the theoretical level and at the political/historical level. At a theoretical level, it characterised problems of legality, legitimation, and authority in metaphysical terms strictly related to theological issues.[10] At a political/historical level, it ignited a harsh conflict between ecclesiastical and secular power that culminated in the investitures controversy,[11] and later on in the conflict between Phillip the Fair and Boniface VIII[12] and in the Golden Bull of 1356.[13] Our genealogy should start by delineating the contours of that kind of medieval political thinking that reflected the sovereign discourse of power as delineated by Foucault.

The ideas of Thomas Aquinas[14] (1225–74) provide a telling example. His theories are addressed here to show the inherent metaphysical traits of medieval philosophy, which rested on theological assumptions. It bound politics with the design of God's will, and conceived law as a language that could not create legitimacy by itself, but that to be legitimate had to reflect the lines of a heavenly plan. This kind of philosophy attempted to conjoin Greek philosophy, especially the works of Aristotle that had been rediscovered during the twelfth century, and Christian doctrine. Aquinas's theoretical system, and in particular his political and legal philosophy, were framed by Christian values but rooted in Aristotelian thought.

Aquinas, because of his veneration for Aristotle,[15] resolved differently from other Christian scholars such as Saint Augustine the tension between divine will and divine intellect in favour of the second.[16] Saint Thomas accepted the Christian concept of the universe as a place where everything follows a teleological plan and enriched it with the Aristotelian suggestion that things naturally developed according to their ideal form.[17] The universe, for Aquinas, is thus governed by a *lex aeterna* that is reflected in the *lex naturalis*, which represents the inherent tendency of worldly things to develop in accordance with their intrinsic, God-fixed nature.[18] Man participates in this *lex naturalis* through the use of reason, which is specific to his nature. The basis of natural law, therefore, does not reside simply in human beings, but is to be found in the eternal law and articulated as a projection of the divine plan onto the legal system.[19] *Lex humana* can access the divine plan pictured in the *lex aeterna* only through natural law. Human law then participates in God's plan by completing the general principles of natural law by means of deduction or specific determination.[20] Consequently, there is no appreciable difference between reality and metaphysics as the earthly nature of an object is determined in the first place by its ideal nature set by God.[21] Conversely, human laws are 'part and parcel of the whole system of divine government whereby everything both in heaven and earth is ruled'.[22]

From the point of view of political legitimation, Aquinas's ideas reflect the metaphysical tendency that dominated medieval thought at the time. Aquinas's disregard for the need to found authority on the secular interest of individuals emanates from the subordination of political problems to metaphysical theological questions[23] and reveals a sense of vertical political hierarchy that is closely linked with the dynamics of sovereignty. In this perspective, it is quite telling regarding this whole mode of thinking that it was impossible for humans to question God's plan and that popular consent was irrelevant in framing the legitimation of medieval monarchy. Aquinas firmly believed that power is something that emanates from above and exerts its unquestionable domination over subordinate subjects. As Foucault himself remarked, in Aquinas's thought – given that the sovereign must reproduce the government of God on Earth – there is a great continuum between sovereignty and government, which will be challenged only in the sixteenth century.[24]

More specifically with regard to law, we can see that, in Aquinas's thought, the concepts of generality, abstraction, equality, and freedom had a meaning that is very different from our modern understanding of these terms. As Orlando Patterson has clearly shown, the medieval conceptualisations of equality and freedom are very different from modern configurations. The person had no worth in herself. She was not considered as a singularity, but only as a static part of the wider community. This perception of the person (and of the universe more generally) was linked to Augustine's organic vision of society. Such a conception, which dominated the early Middle Ages and heavily influenced Aquinas as well, presented human society as a mirror of the divine order.[25] Consequently, persons were indeed equal in the eyes of God, but had different roles – and thus actual earthly duties and liberties – in the secular dimension, in order to fulfil the divine plan. In the same vein, freedom was not the freedom to do as one pleased as the only legitimate expression of individual freedom was to obey the divine will. In this context, the references to the generality and abstractness of law – that were indeed present in the works of Aquinas[26] – had a different sense from those of today. Generality, abstraction, equality, and freedom were thus subordinated to the idea of a predetermined metaphysical scheme that differentiated among individuals and organised them into strict hierarchies. While the most powerful secular and religious authorities would struggle over who should have the upper hand in political matters according to the divine plan, the bulk of the population was forced into a demeaning pattern of subordination and excluded from active participation in political discourse.

The heavy conflation between the legal and the religious discourse prevented law from having a distinctive subjectivating function. Law was not conceived as a discourse that, on its own, could know, and even less as one that could create, the political truth of the individual and determine the legitimacy of political power. Such a truth had already been eternally established by God, the allocation of power set in the divine dimension. Law could only reflect or attempt to resemble as much as possible an order that was superordinate to it, whose contents and functions absolutely resisted modification, and whose schemata had to be investigated through different (theological) instruments.

This dynamic – which firmly anchored political legitimacy in religious metaphysical claims and was deeply informed by the logic of sovereignty – encountered a formidable shift between the thirteenth and fourteenth centuries, an era marked by the struggle between the Church and the Kingdom of France as well as the Avignonese Captivity of the Pope.[27] This shift, on the one hand, reasserted at its strongest the sovereign theory of power, while on the other hand it marked the beginning of the latter's detachment from metaphysical claims.

As a consequence, Aquinas's theories were not left unchallenged. Their questioning reflected a timid reframing of political thinking towards the normalising paradigm. In France, in particular, the idea of hierocracy was rejected at a theoretical level most notably by Jean de Paris (1255–1306),[28] who asserted the supremacy of the temporal ruler in temporal matters while retaining the Church's supremacy in spiritual matters. In his *De potestate regia et papali* (1302), Jean de Paris argued that only in the spiritual sphere was there a central supreme authority because the ecclesiastic hierarchy was to be structured to mirror the heavenly hierarchy.[29] In earthly matters, however, the sovereignty of a single individual is needed for a different reason, in that only a single ruler could effectively govern the masses.[30] On the basis of this reasoning, Jean de Paris identifies the distinction between the two powers as residing not in their subject matters or ends as such, but in their means. Consequently, 'each power [was] limited to its own appropriate means of action; the secular power [to] natural means, the Church [to] supernatural means (the sacraments, which confer God's grace)'.[31] The Church, devoted to the spiritual upbringing of peoples, did not need to deploy coercive powers, while the same powers were to be used by temporal sovereigns to govern the unruly population.[32] The ideas of Jean de Paris are extremely interesting from our perspective for at least two reasons. First, Jean is one of the first scholars who, despite being a member of the Church, limits explicitly ecclesiastical temporal claims by invoking a principle of empirical effectiveness in governance. Secondly, he also rejected the authority of the Empire[33] by suggesting that different governments are created for different populations.[34] In this way, he was instrumental both for the process of secularisation that would prove to be fundamental for the development of modern practical thinking, and for construing an idea of temporal sovereignty dissociated from the traditional one of the Empire.[35]

This line of thinking that sought to limit papal authority to solely spiritual matters was pursued vigorously by Marsilius of Padua (1275–1342). In his *Defensor Pacis* (1324),[36] one of the most revolutionary and influential political treatises of the time, Marsilius proposed a very advanced theory of separation between religious and secular power. For him the state is a *'communitas perfecta'*, a natural congregation based on men's reason and experience. To the administration of such a community ecclesiastical power is perfectly extraneous[37] as it is aimed at a completely different goal, namely, the teaching and defence of faith.[38] The governments of secular and religious matters are therefore completely separated matters, and also law – that in Aquinas was inherently connected with the *lex aeterna* as imposed by God[39] – is clearly distinct from the divine order.[40] The latter is a command issued by God for the sake of the heavenly world to come, while the former is constituted by a set of rules that, determined by society, concern earthly conducts that have to be followed or avoided to achieve a desired earthly goal.[41] The state and law, therefore, are human constructions and find their legitimation in being posited by the human will rather than a godly one.[42] Marsilius's thought stands in stark opposition to any idea of papal political supremacy in temporal matters and, in a broader context, sets itself apart from Aquinas's theories. It has been suggested that, owing to Averroist Aristotelianism,[43] Marsilius was able to reject the interrelation between theology and philosophy that was so prominent in Thomism. If reason was disconnected from religious metaphysical claims, it thus became possible to explore the contours of political structures from a humanist point of view. This development opened the way towards a rational analysis of social relations and interests, a perspective which was subdued and discouraged in large part in favour of the strict ontologism of Christian doctrines.[44]

The renewed use of a secular rationality bore a new understanding of reality. The secularisation of political legitimation dented the theory of sovereignty that characterised the preceding era, as it implicitly included the persons forming a community in the political discourse. If the organisation of society and its laws was a human matter, then the vision that all individuals could in principle participate democratically in politics and that government was a matter of managing individual interests was no longer anathema, although certainly it was far from an accepted idea. Indeed, society was still heavily segmented and divided into orders, its organisation pyramidal, and in the hand of rulers who were, to a large extent, unrestrained in their exercise of authority. Nevertheless, the seeds of change were sown, setting in motion a slow democratic political and legal evolution. We are certainly very far from a vision of society where political legitimation is structured according to the paradigm of the norm. Nonetheless, theory's movement towards secularisation caused a reshuffling in political assumptions. The idea that the order of society should be conceived as moving from earthly interests and not metaphysical plans logically questioned the ordering value of sovereign commands in favour of the norm. Such a shift, at this stage, hardly affected the law and its structural logic. The features of generality, abstraction, equality, and freedom as understood in the modern sense were certainly not present at this stage. However, the secularisation of political thinking and the implicit attack on the logic of sovereignty, represented an initial step towards a discourse of law framed within those contours. The idea that law should be general and abstract, guaranteeing legal freedom and equality, seems to find a fundamental cornerstone in this historical movement from a metaphysical to a secularised approach to legitimation. Most importantly, this shift prepared the terrain for a different conception of law as a subjectivating apparatus directly connecting the political truth of the individual with that of power, excluding metaphysical and heavenly frames of references.

The Renaissance period[45] is closely associated with the dynamic which centred on a renewed focus on human affairs. Earthly matters were reassessed more critically, challenging established traditions and eager to explore the world of man from a humanist perspective. Both the individual and nature were seen as fresh objects of research, and the rigid metaphysical framework of the previous centuries was weakened irreparably, leading to a more empirical and objective analysis of the world.[46] In this context, we can see that the paradigm of normalisation began to emerge more and more clearly within the field of political legitimation and law.

It is important to mention at this juncture the ideas of Jean Bodin (1530–96), probably the most important interpreter of absolutism and the divine right of kings to rule. He was one of the first scholars (probably the very first, as he claimed to have coined the term 'political science'[47]) to approach legal and political problems from a genuine empirical point of view. He investigated the political origins of absolutism and its role in granting peace and order.[48] [49] For the purpose of the present analysis, Bodin is particularly interesting as his theoretical approach demonstrates how the discourse of absolutism, far from being simply an intensification of the regime of sovereignty, represented a hybrid regime incorporating some important traits of normalisation. Bodin's theory on the one hand strongly reasserts the need for a central ruler with absolute power over her subjects – the central case of the logic of sovereignty – while, on the other, conceiving its existence only instrumentally, as a solution that serves not only the heavenly plans of God but the very secular needs of society. Bodin's main concern is less the figure of the sovereign, and more the safety of the common people: the idea of securing peace for all individuals is one that, in his view, necessitates the creation of the absolute monarch. We can see that Bodin's fundamentally secular reasoning, while reinforcing the idea of an unrestrained sovereign, also focuses on the concept of the normal individual, pitting the whole population against the absolute ruler, thus reflecting the ambiguous route taken from one biopolitical regime to another. From this point of view it is no surprise that Foucault identifies him as one of the foremost thinkers of the *raison d'État* that announces a new rationality of government based on the principles of pastoral power, but it is also quite surprising that he did not explore in greater detail how Bodin's theories reflected a change in the legal discourse proper.[50]

It is undeniable, however, that, for all practical purposes, political decisions were still taken in a highly authoritarian fashion. In practice, legal systems largely fell in line with the commands of the sovereign. The source of political power did not come from the needs and desires of individuals, but rested in some metaphysical plan which treated secular interests as a confused echo of the truth about the universe. In this sense, law was not a mechanism meant to identify and make explicit the interests of the multitude of individuals composing the body politics; rather, it was to a very large extent the linguistic veneer behind which political power used to manifest itself. The legal discourse, in other words, was external to the locus of power; it did not dictate its formation and hardly imposed any limit upon it. Its role in shaping individuals into subjects was also basically absent. We will now see how, with the movement towards the secularisation of natural law which occurred in the following two centuries, the relationship between law, subjectivity, power, knowledge, and truth veered decisively towards normalisation.

The new foundations of politics

In the sixteenth and seventeenth centuries, it is possible to observe a consistent tendency towards the secularisation of rational thinking, which is particularly strong in political thought.[51] Notwithstanding this trend, politics is still caught somewhere between divine and secular discourses. As we have seen with Bodin, the state is at the same time completely secularised in its functional terms (the state has the empirical scope of organising society) and yet entangled with religious and metaphysical systems of legitimation (kings are still representatives of God on earth, society needs to follow the heavenly plan, etc.). I turn now to the political thought of the seventeenth and eighteenth centuries to explore how legal and political thinking advanced further in its adoption of a secular perspective and normalisation. In doing so, I will probe the theories of Grotius, Hobbes, and Locke. These scholars revived and modernised the idea of natural law – which was already present in Aquinas's works – by detaching it increasingly from its metaphysical foundations and reinterpreting it as a set of rules that are generated by the social interests of mankind.

The secularised version of natural law, unifying all individuals under an umbrella of shared social needs and traits, delineated a set of universal natural norms that could be applied to each person. Such a picture – upholding a normalising vision of mankind as sharing common traits and following similar behaviours – stands in stark contrast with the idea of an ontological difference between individuals which characterised the order of sovereignty. As I will argue, this had a profound impact on how the language of political legitimation evolved and how the changing ideas of generality, abstraction, equality, and freedom came to frame it and to transform law itself. The emerging conception of law reflects this complex passage from the logic of sovereignty to that of normality. On the one hand, law is still mainly conceived as following the scheme of sovereign command as the ruler orders society from above and is largely unrestrained in his authority. Law, however, is seen as instrumental in implementing the norms of human nature. Consequently, we are confronted with a vision of law that is externally framed by the paradigm of the norm – in other words, law is legitimised insofar as it implements the norms of nature – but, internally, is still structured as a set of commands. Crucially, law begins to be characterised as an apparatus that can tell us the truth about human social nature. At this stage, law is not yet that peculiar mechanism of subjective inscription that identifies the truth of human interest by imposing on her its rules and interrogating her on the basis of those rules; rather, it is a science that treats humans as somewhat unconscious objects of volition, not too differently from stones or stars. It observes the regularities of historical societies and on that basis it declares the basic structure of their political arrangement. Such an approach largely recognises the fact that the truth about human interest in situated in humankind itself, but, quite paradoxically, it deems the single individual and society at large unable to grasp it. Only the historians and the philosophers can access a truth which is locked in the depth of human experience.

The seventeenth century is a major turning point in legal and political thinking, primarily because of works published by the political theorist Hugo Grotius (1583–1645). Grotius's main contribution to political theory was to redefine the contours of natural law and to transpose it in an almost completely secular dimension, a fact unprecedented at the time.[52] I have shown that, especially in relation to Aquinas, also during the Middle Ages natural law was the basis of political legitimation, but it was strictly linked with the metaphysical schemes of the divine will and teleological doctrines of Aristotelian ascendancy. Grotius, while retaining certain aspects of scholastic thought,[53] proposed a new outlook by way of a so called '*etiamsi daremus*' hypothesis.[54]

Grotius's main idea is that man is inherently a rational and social animal and that he has an innate desire for self-preservation. This desire, however, is not an end in itself as it represents an instrumental instinct to serve the true nature of man as set forth by God: to live sociably and develop as a rational being.[55] Man, in growing and developing as a rational subject, follows the laws of his own nature. However, and this is the point at which he breaks with the past, Grotius suggests that the laws of nature would be valid even if God were not to exist (*etiamsi daremus non esse Deum*).[56] It is in the expression of this hypothesis that we can see the ideas that ensured Grotius's place in history as one of the most important actors who defined the trend towards secularisation in philosophy and political theory.[57] Even if this hypothesis is immediately discarded by Grotius himself as blasphemous,[58] it indicates the possibility for mankind to understand autonomously the most fundamental rules that govern social living. His hypothesis also recognises the intrinsic dignity and rationality of civil society even in the absence of any superior heavenly entity.

In Grotius's vision, law is not only a reflection of God's will, but also a practical instrument for achieving peace and order. Most importantly, his analysis of the nature of human beings and their inherent tendencies shows the emergence of the idea that men are equal and free subjects. All men, in fact, are equal at a fundamental level as they are similar subjects sharing the same sense of sociability and rationality, and they are not ordered according to a metaphysical hierarchy. At the same time, even if the argument does not appear clearly delineated, individuals are also understood to be ultimately free subjects. If, according to Grotius, individuals are to be true to their nature as rational beings then this cannot be achieved if they are meant to abide by a predetermined divine plan. On the contrary, their responsibility in developing their self-government implies a basic freedom to explore their rational nature without following predetermined schemes. Within this context, law is no longer simply an emanation of a higher godly order, but is something that is situated directly in a person's inner intellect and that needs to be rationally developed.[59] Law remains linked to the fundamental commands of God; nevertheless, it ceases to be a theological subject and is strongly identified as being a matter for the earthly world. It is in such light that the *etiamsi daremus* hypothesis stands as a powerful and innovative theoretical break, as it indicates a virtually free human rationality.

The most important innovative aspect of Grotius's thinking, however, lies in his analytical approach to law.[60] Here, too, he demonstrates a strong inclination for secular thinking that will have a lasting impact on his successors. Grotius accounts for the content of law in a peculiar and innovative way, as he is the first to use historical evidence as a guide to finding the substantive content of natural law.[61] Grotius proposed two methods for analysing the content of natural law. The first is based on an a priori proof. The content of natural law is discovered using exclusively human reasoning in order to identify the necessary characteristics of law. However, Grotius claimed that this method was extremely difficult and complex to use. For this reason, he shied away from a purely logical analysis of the content of natural law.[62]

Alternatively, Grotius applied a historical scientific approach based on an a posteriori proof. This method proceeded 'by supplying evidence of that which is believed by all nations, or at least by learned men from all civilised countries, to be binding on all men'.[63] [64] Grotius thus attached great importance to the actual history of societies. He shifted his attention from metaphysical speculation – that could hardly lead to substantive agreement – and, in order to find a common ground of political convergence, focused on a secular analysis of what were at the time the shared traits of actual political communities. Consequently, we can say that to investigate the content of natural laws, Grotius, in his a posteriori proof, undertook a process of abstraction and generalisation. Taking into consideration the whole of historical human experience, he abstracted from contingent occurrences in order to find a general pattern common to the whole of mankind.

In addition, Grotius moved decisively towards a 'subjectivation' of law. A right, according to Grotius, is 'a quality of or belonging to persons, and usually refers to the rightful power to have or to do something'.[65] This definition allowed Grotius to link the idea of right specifically to the person as such. In other words, with his innovative idea of right (an idea that is now part of our legal heritage), Grotius transformed the 'right' from something that an action or a state of affairs is when it is in accordance with law ('to be right') to something that a person has ('to have a right').[66] In this sense, it has been argued that Grotius is a precursor of the modern idea of subjective rights, that is, rights that pertain to a person *qua* person, even prior to any political association.[67]

With Grotius, we see a shift in the ways in which political legitimation and law are framed. He highlighted a basic natural equality among men, a certain freedom in developing their rationality and an individualistic undertone that undermined political models based on the scheme of sovereignty. The consideration that the person is a bearer of rights in her own right generated a new awareness concerning the relation between each single individual and political power. Certainly, we are still far from law as a subjectivating apparatus interlocking individual interests and political power through a game of knowledge and truth. The legitimacy of power stems from legal principles that are constructed only through an idealised theorisation and not through an actual interrogation of individuals in the legislative process. The central dilemma of modern democracy – 'How can individuals be at the same time rulers and ruled?' – cannot yet be delineated properly at this stage. The way in which law is conceived and placed in relation to legitimacy, according to Grotius, however, opens up new avenues of enquiry that will bring us genealogically to that question. Law is no longer simply a set of commands imposed from above by an unrestrained power but, instead, now stems from an ensemble of rational norms that have to be followed in order to root legitimate political power. Within this context the discovery of natural law's content, presupposing the existence of a common practice developed by following freely human rationality, relies on a process of abstraction and generalisation of human experience and does not require any actual form of democratic confrontation; individuals do not need to be consulted, their truth is something foreclosed to themselves. The modern version of the concepts of generality, abstraction, equality, and freedom start to transpire nonetheless, if not as structural elements of the syntax of law, then as important ideas in the theorisation of law and in the transformation of the language in which it is expressed.

Similarly, the reference to human nature is central in Hobbes's theories on law and the state. Hobbes (1588–1679), with his major work *Leviathan* (1651), paved the way for a new method of thinking about the state that reflected an innovative secular understanding of the nature of man and his society. Hobbes was the first to try to build a theory of political philosophy that was entirely rational, rejected metaphysical assumptions and was entirely rooted in the material nature of man. Fascinated by geometric sciences,[68] he attempted a wholly mechanistic description of human conduct.[69] Hobbes's political system is grounded in the assumption that the fundamental human instinct is that of self-preservation.[70] In a pre-political condition, however, survival is menaced by the human state of nature.[71] In nature, according to Hobbes, men are all fundamentally equal, at least in their instincts and basic capacities.[72] Men are also similar in terms of their natural rights, as all have a 'right to everything' that is driven by their boundless desire for power.[73] This condition, worsened by the scarcity of resources, leads to a hellish state of war that pits all against all.[74] In order to overcome this dangerous state of affairs, individuals are forced to co-operate and come together and delegate their rights to a supreme, absolute sovereign by means of a collective agreement.[75] The latter, in turn, sets up a system of laws that is designed to protect them and let them live peacefully together.[76]

Hobbes's vision, therefore, sees the state's role as one that is not meant to establish an ideal realm in accordance with the divine plan, but, instead derives its function prosaically from the social necessity of limiting individual rights[77] in order to protect the life of each citizen.[78] By detaching societal organisation from metaphysical claims and insisting on the primacy of self-preservation as the first cause of human actions,[79] Hobbes changed dramatically the linguistic meaning of what he called the laws of nature. These were not to be understood as direct commands emanating from God, but, on the contrary, are to be seen as the rules that, through rationality and reasoning, can ensure that self-preservation is a realisable goal.[80]

In his materialistic account of human society, Hobbes goes so far as to suggest that the concepts of good and evil are not present *per se* in nature. On the contrary, good and evil are qualities that acquire meaning only within the structure of law as posited by the sovereign: only what the sovereign decrees to be good or evil is so.[81] In this way, Hobbes clearly suggests that the sovereign is nothing less than an earthly God.[82] The consequence of this reasoning is that – logically speaking – the sovereign is never wrong, insofar as, in exercising his authority, he guarantees the protection of its subjects.[83] In Hobbes we see that the foundation of political legitimation and, more broadly, the substance of any ethical framework are not linked with the plan of God, but only with the concrete nature of mankind. The necessary and sufficient condition for political power to be legitimate is fulfilled if it can guarantee at a societal level that instinct to self-preservation which is innate in human nature.[84] Such a theoretical system could strike the modern reader for its morally neutral account of law, sovereignty and the state, and be criticised for its lack of a substantive ethical dimension.[85] Human desires are considered by Hobbes in a very mechanistic way, and the whole system of societal organisation is built upon such foundational concepts in a successive sequence of logical deductions.

In Hobbes, we can see that the theories of sovereignty based on divine rights are 'turned upside down'. A secular path has been clearly taken. The legitimation of the ruler does not derive any more from a special relationship with God, but it is constructed 'from below' taking as starting point the earthly natural interests of men and the norms of their conducts. The outcome, however, under the point of view of popular political legitimation of laws and state, is largely at odds with contemporary democratic theories as it establishes a boundless sovereign. In a way that is reminiscent of established metaphysical theories of legitimation, in Hobbes a framework that could sustain a democratic dynamic is also substantially lacking. Hobbes is capable of demonstrating the necessity of the existence of the state and of the absolute power of the sovereign on a purely rational basis, but he is ultimately incapable of (or uninterested in) providing a deeper legitimation for its politics. He thus sidesteps what we have identified as the central dilemma of modern democracy. Hobbes, while able to justify the state's authority at a certain basic functional level (that of granting protection to its citizens), largely rejects the possibility of an active political role for citizenry.[86] Not surprisingly, Hobbes's idea of the legal system is closely associated with a concept of law understood as a set of commands issued by a sovereign who is characteristically above civil law.[87] In this sense, the citizens never participate in the creation of law; rather, they are the mere passive subjects of its force.

This is evidence, in my opinion, of the fact that Hobbes's reasoning is caught between the discourses of sovereignty and normalisation. He embraces the logic of normality at the most fundamental level of political legitimation, since for him the norms of nature are fundamental in structuring the political field. Laws, however, are still imagined within the contours of a sovereign discourse as they do not significantly contribute to the elaboration of the norms according to which society should function – these are to be theorised by philosophers alone through a geometric method of reasoning. As I have argued at the beginning of the present section, law is suspended between two paradigms: externally it is overdetermined by the idea of the norm, but, internally, it is still articulated as a command. Hence Hobbes, against Foucault's canonical interpretation,[88] represents not so much the last defender of an old conception of power and sovereignty as one of the scholars who were crucial in opening up and questioning the discourse of law by introducing within it the paradigm of the norm alongside that of command.

I have sought to outline the principal elements of the theories of Grotius and Hobbes so that it is possible to present a clearer vision of the movement of secularisation that divides classical and modern political thinking, in that it seems to reflect the passage from sovereignty to normalisation. This movement entailed the creation of a chasm between the metaphysical dimension of theological nature and the practical functional level of political structures and discourses. Along with the development of strong national states and the firm establishment of absolutism as historical phenomena, political thinking abandoned the problems of legitimation between secular and religious power typical of the preceding era and explored the earthly motivations that pushed people to come together, and form societies and communities. The main problem shifted from an inquiry into how the human world could resemble and replicate the heavenly order and respect the divine hierarchy to an exploration of what human nature was *per se*, and how society could organise itself on the basis of that knowledge. In this sense, the concept of natural law became associated with the idea of regularities and standards – that is, norms – that could be recognised in human conduct (e.g. natural equality, instinct of self-preservation, etc.). The idea that mankind is defined by taking into consideration a benchmark of normality in turn allows the discourse of normality to be integrated with the discourse of sovereignty and to start changing the latter from the inside. Hobbes, in particular, realigns the theory of sovereignty according to this dynamic. For him, the sovereign is still an absolute ruler and yet he is not legitimised because he is the delegate of God. He is ontologically superior to his subjects, but only because his existence ensures that society is ruled in accordance with the norms of human conduct.

This philosophical rupture, however, still meant that political issues were analysed in a predominantly static manner as both history and the rational laws of nature influenced the structure of the state in a necessary way, as it were. This mode of thinking was largely unable to come to terms with its own understanding of society as something created by men. As a result, the political discourse was framed within formal structures that excluded the truth of the individual from shaping the organisation of her own community. In other words, if the political world came to be interpreted as a dimension circumscribed to human matters, then rigid limits were posited to the actual freedom of people to rationally and consciously construct their own world. The evolution of society was deemed to a large extent to be causally predetermined by the intrinsic features of man's own nature and instincts. Consequently, political structures were constrained from the outset in their shape and rules of functioning, and the actual individual could not actively contribute to this game of power and truth. The abandonment of such a mode of thinking will be made possible through a reframing of law's internal structure along normalising lines.

The theories of John Locke (1632–1704) well represent the limits of an idea of law that is trapped between sovereignty and normalisation. With Locke, for the first time, the laws of nature – understood as norms – have a direct impact on the laws that restrain governmental action, and thus sovereign commands. Locke, however, seems unable to go beyond this point and to conceive law in fully normalising terms. In other words, in Locke's theory, the norm establishes law's boundaries, but it is not adopted as the paradigm with which to elaborate law itself. Hence, with Locke we see in a clearer fashion Hobbes's dilemma: on the one hand, the norm structures law's limits, but, on the other, the norm has not yet become the paradigm of law itself, its ordering principle.

Locke tried to elaborate an explicitly democratic theory of law and the state. He proposed one of the most radical political theories of his times, an inversion of the relationship between the state and the individual. In Locke's view, the individual was no longer simply a subject of the state, a cog in the mechanism of its organisation. On the contrary: the state was to be conceived as an organisation entirely dedicated to the protection of the personal sphere of individual freedom and autonomy. In his *Two Treatises of Government* (1689)[89] Locke addressed the problem of political power and its legitimation.[90] He refuted the idea of an absolute sovereign in favour of a form of government which would have as its main goal the protection of the natural rights of the individual and whose legitimation would rest on the consent of the governed.[91] In order to develop his political theory, Locke takes as a starting point a human state of nature that is opposite to that of Hobbes.[92] It is not characterised by mutual violence and mistrust, but by a 'State of freedom . . . within the bounds of the Law of Nature'.[93] This state of nature, however, is not without inconveniences,[94] but with the aim of peace and self-preservation[95] individuals come together, establishing by means of agreement an independent society and subsequently a common government.[96] It was envisioned as one that would preserve the fundamental natural rights of life, liberty and estate.[97]

According to Locke, the state aims at protecting a personal sphere of independence where the individual could enjoy her natural rights – legitimate government exists only insofar as it is able to protect this sphere.[98] Locke proposes a political theory that is modern in many aspects and that explicitly challenges the traditional scheme of sovereignty. Popular sovereignty, majority rule, division of powers, constitutional government are central in his thinking as he constructs a system where individual rights would be granted to all citizens.[99] Political legitimation, in this sense, is oriented towards a scheme of normality where there is no supreme authority dominating its subjects, but a society populated by citizens and whose foundation is built upon universal norms. Nonetheless, he retained certain elements that prevented him from building a more consequential democratic political theory. Locke's political theory is certainly based on individual rights – thus boldly moving in the direction of a liberal stance; however, it was still construed around rights descending directly from God.[100] Hence, the content of natural law was to a certain extent still predetermined by a metaphysical discourse.[101] The law of nature was understood as a framework handed down by God rather than a set of rules chosen by free and equal individuals.[102]

Locke's political theory is unable to formulate a proper relation between individual interests and government, and ultimately fails to provide a working mechanism of democratic legitimation for the state.[103] In particular, the participation of individuals in politics is not really necessary for legitimation.[104] As such, the role of consent in Locke's theory appears perfunctory because consent either has an almost superfluous function in assessing the legitimacy of government (what counts is the activity of government that should coincide with natural law[105]) or amounts to a bland 'voluntary acquiescence' in the foundation of the state.[106] [107] Locke thus envisions a society where political legitimacy is present even if political participation is minimal. In this sense, it can be rightly said that '[p]olitical activity for Locke is instrumental . . . [t]he creation of a political community or government is the burden individuals have to bear to secure their ends'.[108] Locke, in other words, has in mind a somewhat atomised society where a 'thin' idea of political connection between individuals prevails. In Locke's thought, notwithstanding his vision of a representative government, political struggle and civic participation are almost absent, as citizens, in his view, play a small role in shaping the actual dynamics of politics.

With Locke we reach the limit of the discourse of natural law developed by Grotius and Hobbes. We have seen above how natural law reshaped the theory of sovereignty, detaching it from metaphysical plans and linking it with an idea of human nature constructed along the lines of 'normal' instincts, inclinations and behaviours. Within this context the sovereign is no longer unrestrained and ontologically superior to her subjects, but is instead legitimised to the extent that she guides her society in accordance with the norms of human nature. This scheme, however, is caught in a contradiction, because on the one hand the sovereign (or the government) is bound by the norms of nature but, on the other, there is no mechanism to ensure that she follows them, no method that would allow a confrontation between sovereign and subjects on the legitimacy of political decisions. Within the confines of natural law theories, no rules are suggested to overcome disagreement between rulers and ruled and any political stalemate is resolvable only by recourse to the confrontation typical of the sovereign scheme, that is, war.[109] It is clear, then, that no true democratic dynamic is possible, and it is also clear how political legitimation was caught between sovereignty and normalisation: the political structure still follows the lines set by the sovereign power, but the increasing importance of norms is nevertheless evident.

It should be remarked that norms, at this stage, still refer to a mythical human nature, to a more or less scientific vision of mankind, but they are not legal norms as the legal field is robustly understood as a set of commands issued by the sovereign power. To this extent, law is not seen as a mechanism used by the body politic to unveil the truth of individual interests and of political power, but the absolute structural limit to government's legitimate action. This situation is reflected in the development of the ideas of generality, abstraction, equality, and freedom. These ideas, within the context of natural law, are framing the contours of the legal discourse from the outside but not informing it. Individuals are equal and free in the state of nature, but these features are not transposed into laws that can still arbitrarily subjugate and constrain the subject insofar as they are consistent – at the broader level of social body – with the norms of nature. The laws and the rights of nature are general and abstract – in that they are derived from the study of the general and abstract theoretical object of mankind – but legal laws are not of the same sort as they do not apply to all without discrimination and do not necessarily regulate abstract behaviours. In other words, we see here that law has not developed yet into an apparatus that is capable of identifying the truth of individual interest. Human interest is conceived in static, metaphysical terms, and the government does not need to interrogate its subjects to operate in a way that is consonant with their interests, whose knowledge and truth have already been deducted through a logical scheme. Hence the paradoxical limit of political theories based on natural law: if the individual enters into society because she aims at protecting her natural rights, how is it possible that the sovereign, in commanding society, has an absolute power over the individual?

As a consequence of this deadlock, some questions were pushed forward and came at the centre of the investigations of later political thinkers: if political legitimation is a human matter, how can individuals actively shape the political contours of their society? How can the individual participate in government while being at the same time a ruler and a ruled? How can a citizen's will be weighed against others within the order of society? In the following historical period, law will become increasingly central in answering these questions, and slowly changed its nature, ceasing to be a simple emanation of sovereign power and instead becoming the fundamental generating mechanism within the discourse of political legitimation. This does not mean at all that the problem of sovereignty is expunged from the horizon of modernity. As Foucault remarked, in contemporary political theory we still have to cut off the king's head.[110]

The dilemma of democracy

As I turn to the political theories of Rousseau, Kant, and Hegel to explore how they reshaped the idea of law as a system of government based on the truth of individual interest, it is necessary to clarify that I do not mean to suggest that political theory did not make any relevant progress from the nineteenth century onwards. Far from it: the debate surrounding the nature and source of legitimation in modern societies has thrived and has been greatly enriched during this period. Nevertheless, it seems clear that the modern idea of political legitimation was born out of a break from the previous natural law philosophical era. Jürgen Habermas, among others, has made it clear that modern thinking diverges from that of earlier times because it generally rejects a metaphysical understanding of reality based on religion to embrace a post-metaphysical perspective.[111] This holds true for the discourse of political legitimation. The shift in the direction of natural law is the exemplar of such transformations as the legitimacy of the social organisation came to be assessed not from a heavenly perspective but by interrogating the rational norms of physical human nature.

Across the eighteenth and nineteenth centuries, however, changing social conditions, the powerful push of secularisation and the reopening of the public sphere as a place of rational confrontation[112] contributed to move political thinking away from the last metaphysical remnants and towards a full humanistic logic, paving the way for a more mature idea of democracy. It is within this context that the modern discourse of legitimacy has been framed. The ideas of Rousseau, Kant, and Hegel will be addressed not because they represent the whole of modern political thought – they certainly do not mark the end of political speculation – but because, in effect, they contributed to the largest extent towards drawing its boundaries and establish its horizon. By concluding my genealogical description with Rousseau, Kant, and Hegel's theories I therefore intend to trace the contours of the modern discourse of political legitimacy.

With these authors, we have the final emergence of a new vision of law that ceased to be seen as a simple command issued by the sovereign power and became a norm-based mechanism conceived to actively produce the truth of political power. Their writings address explicitly the role that the ideas of generality, abstraction, equality, and freedom played in framing the syntax of such new modes of law. Examining their theories, most importantly, will demonstrate how these four concepts, while providing the fundamental building blocks for the new legal order, at the same time reflected the logic of normalisation.

How did the political theories proposed by Rousseau, Kant, and Hegel contribute to this transformation? What kind of relationship did they envision between the individual, power and law? What is the syntax of law that constituted the legal field as a legitimation-producing mechanism? In a nutshell, the norm ceases to simply delimit law from the outside – as we have seen in the previous section – but becomes the paradigm by which law is internally articulated, relegating to the margins the role of commands. The discourse of legitimate political power consequently turns into a fully legalised discourse structured by a normalising logic. Hence, the role of law in modernity dramatically changes. Previously, law was just a means to implement the norms that ordered society. With the 'normalising turn', law became the mechanism through which the norms ordering society are generated by society's members themselves. The truth of their interest is the one that determines the legitimacy of the political order and guides the action of government, and it becomes apparent only through law. But in order to make this truth visible something else needs to take place. The individual needs to think in a certain peculiar fashion: she needs to express her truth through the paradigm of the norm; only once this happens does she become the subject of law and the legitimate source of political power.

With the aim of exploring the evolution of this phenomenon, I now address Rousseau's thought, where – as Foucault himself observed – the problematic relationship between a theory of sovereignty and art of government appears particularly acute.[113] The aim of Rousseau (1712–78) was, in fact, to imagine a system that would at the same time protect the fundamental freedom of the person while ensuring the legitimacy of a sovereign authority.[114] His concern was to build a theory of political legitimacy not as a theoretical reflection on the laws of nature but as a way of expressing the actual concrete relationship between authority and the people. In this perspective, he suggested that only a state that reflects the general will of its citizens is properly legitimated.

But what is the general will for Rousseau? How can we recognise it? A famous passage from the *Social Contract* (1762) is devoted to this problem:

> There is often a great deal of difference between the will of all and the general will; the latter considers only the common interest, while the former takes private interest into account, and is no more than a sum of particular wills: but take away from these same wills the pluses and minuses that cancel one another, and the general will remains as the sum of the differences.[115]

It is widely held that the general will can be identified with the common good,[116] or with what remains after all opposing particular wills have cancelled each other out.[117] More sophisticated interpretations have pointed out that the general will is the product of a specific tendency to equality[118] that has been instilled in the population through civic education.[119] From this perspective, and distinguishing between the general will and the will of all,[120] John Rawls has suggested that the general will is 'a form of deliberative reason that each citizen shares with all other citizens in virtue of their sharing of their common good'.[121] However, it can emerge only after we have eliminated, through the cancellation of the pluses and minuses of particular wills, the personal biases that, even unnoticed by ourselves, corrupt our perception of the common good.[122]

I would like to suggest an alternative reading of the formation of the general will that finds in the structure of law the crux of Rousseau's theory. I believe that Rousseau proposed to resolve the problem of the general will (the dilemma of how the subject dominated by individual interests can will the general will) by linking the expression of the general will with the forms of law. Rousseau, in fact, argued that law is a product of the general will; law, according to Rousseau, is the form in which the general will is expressed by the body politic.[123] He further argued that laws, to reflect the general will, must be both general and abstract in their object.[124] Consequently, it appears that the general will, to exist as general will, must always will in accordance with the logical criteria of generality and abstraction. In other words, only the citizen who frames the common interest of the society in general and abstract terms is actually expressing the general will.[125] In this way, Rousseau seems to resolve the problem of an actual commitment of each citizen towards the common interest, as the will of each will coincide with the general will if conceived in general and abstract terms. Rousseau's theory of the general will (and consequently of political legitimation) is thus best understood as a theory of a just constitution, supported by an ongoing democratic commitment and based on the rule of law.[126]

Asserting the principle of 'permanent existential justice of general will', Rousseau attempted to resolve the dilemma of a legitimate political organisation based on the material interests of its citizens without surrendering to a mechanical concept of the state.[127] Rousseau is thus able to closely link the content of law with the volition of the individual, giving a democratic substance to the rules that under natural law were for the sovereign to dictate.[128] Legitimation, in other words, does not rest in a fixed scheme that mankind has to follow (be it designed by God or nature) and that a sovereign is entitled to enforce, but is to be recognised as something that is created directly by the multitude of individuals. To this extent, we can see that the role of law changes dramatically in comparison with previous conceptions. Law is no more understood as a sovereign command generated by natural standards or norms; rather, it is the mechanism that legitimises commands through the paradigm of the norm. The norm, therefore, enters into the field of political calculations not simply as an external factor linked with human nature – as it occurs with the universal human standards set forth by the laws of nature in Grotius, Hobbes, and Locke – but as a mechanism internal to the structuring of politics itself. The originality of Rousseau's law lies precisely in such a functional shift prompted by the use of the norm: law ceases to be the mere manifestation of a sovereign order and becomes the very generative mechanism of the norms ordering society.

A closer look, however, reveals that Rousseau's political theory depends upon on a very delicate equilibrium. His theory can only work in a close-knit community, where social and economic differences are limited, and party politics are not present. Rousseau's political vision is only to be realised in such an idealised space, where the delegation of sovereign power by means of representation is minimal and where the sovereign (the people) can daily and actively participate in government.[129] It thus seems that Rousseau is able to resolve the dilemma of modern democracy only by eliminating the duality between sovereign power and its people in favour of a direct democracy. Law, in other words, is not sufficient in itself to guarantee the freedom of each citizen. In larger societies, the law will never be able to operate so as to sufficiently integrate opposing positions and will lead to undue coercion. It seems that, according to Rousseau, the general will is contingent with an actual community and can never be truly universalised. Consequently, legitimate law can be created only through a concrete communitarian relationship with fellow citizens, a condition which is hard to achieve outside an idealised small group. Perhaps unsurprisingly then, Rousseau denies, in relation to large populations, the possibility of constructing a shared political will that would reflect the interest of each citizen: in such situations the general will is very likely to conflict with the single will of a specific subject.

Immanuel Kant (1724–1804) offered one of the clearest visions of law as a mechanism establishing political legitimation through the use of the norm.[130] In contrast to Rousseau, Kant imagined law as a truly universal system capable of integrating the different wills of each single citizen, notwithstanding their substantial differences. Kant's starting point is that all individuals are equals insofar as they share an innate right to freedom.[131] Building on this idea, Kant conceives law as a tool protecting individuals and guaranteeing that they can develop according to equality and freedom while living in complex societies.[132] In order to do so, laws have to be promulgated so as to respect an individual's moral autonomy, providing her with space for action from coercion, but also to defend the autonomy of each citizen from the influence and intrusion of other citizens. Kant understood right – in the German sense of *Recht* – as 'the whole of the conditions under which the voluntary actions of any one person can be harmonised in reality with the voluntary actions of every other person, according to a universal law of freedom'.[133] But how can one produce laws that will ensure individual freedom? Kant's argument addressing this point sets out a theoretical approach that allows him to overcome the problem that prevented Rousseau from conceiving a modern democratic system.[134] Kant's suggestion is that we should not look into any metaphysically given idea of law, but that the latter should be created and made legitimate only through the use of reason and, more specifically, the application of the categorical imperative: 'the conception of freedom upon which [laws] rest does not admit of any theoretical deduction of its possibility, and it can only be inferred from the practical law of reason, called the categorical imperative, viewed as a fact.'[135] [136] In such a way, he suggested a solution to the problem of how it is possible to establish rules that, while retaining an external binding force, would not violate the autonomy of the individual.[137]

With Kant, more clearly than any other preceding thinker, the legitimacy of any social order is rooted in the efficacy of its laws that are designed to protect individual freedom. He suggested that a mutually enforcing relationship exists between the legal and the political field. For Kant the state is thus envisioned as fundamentally constituted by its laws insofar as they abide by the rational principle of right.[138] He saw law as being no longer a command that a sovereign power can legitimately impose in the name of some higher authority (be it God or nature) but as a logical system of rules generated by secular rational norms. To this end:

> Kant's law of right from reason is a universal formal law of the freedom of actions. Indifferent to all elements of content in human actions, it is concentrated solely on the question of the formal compatibility of the external freedom of one person with that of others, and thereby limits individual action within the boundaries of its possible universalisation.[139] [140]

Kant's system seems to overcome certain problems associated with earlier political theories. His reasoning is based on the principles of individual equality and freedom, and at the same time it focuses on the will of all the citizens.[141] He provides a method for the formation of such a will so that the latter would embody the position of the individual, but would also be common to all other subjects. The result is a sophisticated conception of a liberal republican state anchored in the rule of law.[142] It is interesting to observe how Kant's notions of equality and freedom come to inform the idea of law. They are 'as closely connected as the two sides of a coin. They are mutually definable. Liberty demands the legislation of the general united will; likewise, the principle of equality requires the rule of generally acceptable laws.'[143]

With Kant, we have reached one of the most robust conceptions of modern law as an apparatus: a process that links political power and individual truth through the paradigm of the norm. Political power is legitimate because it is rooted in the absolute truth of individual interest as unearthed through a rational process of universalisation enshrined by law. The problem of the relation between the individual, truth, and power is apparently resolved. Laws are elaborated as if they were created by individuals themselves and their fairness is guaranteed by their universal nature. Legal rules, in addition, have lost the metaphysical connection with heavenly orders and they are seen as purely instrumental for achieving society's goals. The individual, when conceiving legal provisions, should abstract from the contingent peculiarity of her own situation[144] and imagine rules that could be generally agreed upon by all other individuals.[145] Such laws are, in turn, general and abstract because, generated through a process of universalising rationalisation, they would apply equally to everyone and regulate in advance abstract conducts.

With Kant, we have a reconfiguration of the idea of political legitimacy, as he is responsible for a decisive break from political theories constructed along the lines of sovereignty. In Kant's vision, notwithstanding some inconsistencies,[146] the entity wielding sovereign power (be it a single person, or a representative political body or the majority of the population) is not superior to any other individual as everybody is subject to the rational principle of right. We see a shift in political thinking: the sovereign power does not create laws, but rather, law creates the sovereign power. Kant embraces what can be broadly defined as a logic of normality and applies it to the political field: political power is not founded upon a code of truth descending from a higher authority – as in the scheme of sovereignty – but rather stems from a rational system of norms that codifies an entirely social and practical truth.[147]

Within this context, the emerging syntax of law becomes a fundamental component of the political dimension. Kant's theory is very clear in this sense: generality, abstraction, equality, and freedom frame law from a dual point of view, ethically and functionally. As I indicated earlier, the idea of individuals being equal and free subjects leads to a situation where laws meant to defend the rights of equality and freedom so as to allow individuals to develop autonomously. At the same time, in order to create laws that would fairly implement equality and freedom for everyone, the individual needs to construct laws that imagine universal rules of general and abstract application. Consequently, and within a broader discourse of normalisation, generality, abstraction, equality, and freedom are, at the same time, central to processes that seek to democratically legitimise law and to structure the legal field. Kant's political philosophy, however, presented a high level of abstraction that creates some perplexities[148] and that can be summed up by Hegel's critique: trying to build a formal system of law based on human transcendent reasoning, Kant left his laws devoid of any substantive content and largely detached from reality.[149] The universalising method of thinking that should be the rational bond uniting society and justifying legal and political obligations, in other words, neglects to a very large degree the concrete articulations of the actual world.[150] [151]

Georg W. F. Hegel (1770–1831) addressed, in his political philosophy, the same problem that both Rousseau and Kant identified and tried to tackle, but whose solutions could be considered utopian or impracticable at best. Both philosophers suggested a theory for democratic systems legitimised by the wilful commitment of all individual citizens. Rousseau suggested a system that, by focusing on the contingent recognition of the *volonté générale*, could produce a state where political decisions would always be in tune with the feelings and wants of the social body (understood as a mass of individuals). Kant, on the other hand, by overcoming the restricted communal perspective of Rousseau's general will, linked the legitimacy of the legal and political structure of society with the idea of universal rational norms. These theories, trying to resolve the duality between the individual and the state, were not completely satisfactory in finding a balanced relationship concerning these two elements: Rousseau downplayed the autonomy of the state in favour of the independent free will of the individual; Kant overlooked the particularity of individual thinking in the face of his abstract deontological theory of rights.

Hegel attempted to resolve this duality and to resolve the discord between the individual and the state in a positive way.[152] In his work *The Philosophy of Right* (1820), Hegel developed a theory that fully integrates the single person within the state and that actually argues that the law of state should be the highest dimension of individual freedom.[153] Proceeding by means of his typical dialectical method,[154] Hegel in the *Philosophy of Right* does not provide a proper theory of law; rather, he attempts a holistic description of the relationship between the individual and the state in order to explain their mutual interpenetration. He articulates this picture in a series of 'moments' that supersede and encompass the precedent. Through these spheres (Abstract Right, Morality, and Ethical Life) the individual is progressively integrated into the complex structure of society and transformed from an undetermined person into a determined citizen in harmony with the state.

Hegel starts his account from the abstract right (§34) and the individual as bearers of rights.[155] In this moment, the individuals get in contact with each other only externally, as if in an instrumental way, without recognising each other ethically. The second moment is morality (§105), where the individual internalises previously external legal relationships. Finally, we reach the moment of Ethical Life, where the gap between individual and society is bridged. Here, the institutions of society provide a framework to support harmonious living or *Sittlichkeit*.[156] The individual is thus progressively integrated within her community, progressing from Family (§158), the most elementary social structure, based on love, to Civil Society (§182), which at the highest level is organised in Corporations, and, finally, to the state (§257), which is the final stage of mutual recognition between the individual and society and is divided into the Crown, the Executive, and the Legislature.

This is not the place to analyse in detail the complex dialectical passages that allowed Hegel to claim a profound unity between the individual and the state, but the central logic of this identification can be easily identified. Hegel, in the progression that leads from the private personal sphere of the single individual to the final public realisation of freedom that is the state, moves through a series of transfigurations in which the individual is translated from the orbit of one ethical system of reference (Family, Civil Society, and State) to another that includes and furthers the previous one. In these transpositions the individual is able to recognise herself in the higher sphere of society (and therefore to see it as her own reflection) by means of intermediary social bodies that operate as links between one social stage and the next.[157]

Hegel provides a description of the state that is at one and the same time a political, legal, and social theory.[158] Interposing a progressive series of systems of representation/mediation[159] between the state and the population of individuals, he is able to suggest a viable method of transforming the multiform will of individuals into the political will of the state.[160] To this end, the production of law (and consequently all the systems that allow the determination of such formality) is instrumental.[161] Law is understood as the nexus between the subjective and objective moments of freedom,[162] unifying both under a universal form. Law thus allows the individual to identify herself with society and its political structure on the one hand, and to produce political structure that can truly integrate the diverse wills of the citizens on the other.

Hegel explicitly recognises the role of law as the transformer that allows the individual to identify herself with the state,[163] envisioning an integral identification between the citizen and the state through its laws.[164] The state's relationship with the individual is therefore

> essentially reciprocal: it is only a final end for the individual to the extent to which its own end is his liberty and satisfaction ... [T]the state as 'concrete freedom' is the union of these two elements insofar as the individual is satisfied in recognising the universal as law and in taking the state as end.[165]

The positive enactment of law consequently becomes a central moment in the social expression of natural rights as it works as a 'transmission belt' that informs and connects at an ethical and practical level the individual and the state understood as an ethical and political community.[166]

What Hegel is pointing at, it seems to me, is the necessary interaction and integration between the individual conception and the social projection of what is right. Only in this second moment (§211 Remark) does law as a means of social integration come into existence and become able in turn to integrate the life of citizens. Not surprisingly, Hegel defines the state as a rational structure that unites subjective and objective freedom under the form of law and identifies the starting point of freedom not in individuality but in self-consciousness vis-à-vis society.[167]

Hegel's theory, at its face value, could fall under worrisome critiques, the most serious being the total subordination of the individual to the imposing power of the state and its bureaucracy.[168] His lack of development of the concept of equality is also generally considered to be problematic. With regard to the first point, many scholars have suggested a more progressive and modern reading of Hegel's philosophy,[169] but probably one of the best interpretations of *Philosophy of Right* is provided by Hegel himself. He argues that

> [t]he state is actual only when its members have a feeling of their own self-hood and it is stable only when public and private ends are identical. It has often been said that the end of the state is the happiness of the citizens. That is perfectly true. If all is not well with them, if their subjective aims are not satisfied, if they do not find that the state as such

is the means to their satisfaction, then the footing of the state itself is insecure.[170]

With regard to equality, his treatment of the subject in the *Philosophy of Right* is somewhat cursory, but only because he later addressed the problem in his *Encyclopaedia* (1830). In that text, Hegel suggested that equality before the law is only an empty tautology and what is really important is how law treats equal situations equally and different ones differently, a dilemma that is resolved only through the concrete articulation of the whole legal system.[171] Hegel, in other words, demonstrates that the state is not a formal machine for the recodification of the will and freedom of individuals. On the contrary, his philosophy of the state is a progressive dynamic of ethical recognition aimed at constituting a structure of political integration.[172] Private and political dimensions of the citizens are to a large extent coextensive and only a faithful projection of the private person through the prism of the legal system into the political arena can produce a truly legitimised community.[173] [174]

The problem of the rationalisation of multiple single wills into a singular political determination, that could not be resolved completely in the materialistic terms of Rousseau and was resolved only formally by the rational transcendence of Kant (resulting in a sterile exercise of deontology), is hence surpassed by means of an integrated and organic reading of the process of political will formation. This process is not only guided by procedural rules and personal spheres of freedom (i.e. the existence of abstract rights) but also leads to a deeper integration of the individual with his society through the formation of a substantive communal ethos.[175]

With Hegel, we have one of the most advanced accounts of a modern theory of the state.[176] [177] This is not to say that the state Hegel described in the *Philosophy of Right* has the same structure as modern ones, but, more simply, that Hegel saw the basic dynamic of modern democracy in the complete reflection of the free volition of the citizen in the legal, political, and institutional arrangement of the state achieved through a system of mediation based on law. We can see how Hegel's vision of modern society shifts the political field away from a discourse of sovereignty and roots it firmly in a discourse of normality. Political power, in other words, is no longer tied to the power of a specific individual but is seen as the expression of a rational societal order.[178] This order is achievable, according to Hegel, only through the medium of law. The latter, however, is not to be understood as the command issued by the unrestrained physical sovereign but as the set of rules generated by commonly agreed norms.

Hegel therefore reworks the syntax of law from a practical perspective. We have already seen that Kant's method, of elaboration of law was based on the qualities of equality and freedom and the principles of generality and abstraction. Hegel, in the *Philosophy of Right*, moves within the same boundaries delimited by these elements, but works out their mutual relationships in a more socially informed way, abandoning Kant's idealisations. While in the *Philosophy of Right* the treatment of equality is somewhat cursory, Hegel was concerned with the relationship between equality before the law and particular personal differences. In Hegel's vision, this dilemma is understood as the problem of the concrete articulation of a given community and is connected with the dilemma of freedom – that is, how to balance one's freedom to act with freedom from external coercion. Hegel's reflections on law can be interpreted as a thorough scrutiny of how, in the modern state, the dilemma of freedom – and hence of equality – has been addressed and resolved. Hegel suggests that the state is legitimated when the actual process of formation of law is a product of the ongoing ethical and political confrontation between all the members of a society.[179] Through a progressive series of systems of mediation (Family, Civil Society, and State in all its articulations) Hegel identified a method that, abstracting from the specific aspects of all individual wills, could lead to the formation of a democratic political will[180] and therefore resolve, procedurally and substantively, the political problem of freedom and self-determination. Generality and abstraction are hence set up in theoretical relationship with equality and freedom in a way not dissimilar from Kant's own: general and abstract laws are generated by free and equal individuals and in turn protect and shape individuals as free and equal subjects. The difference is that Hegel sees law as emerging from a dynamic dialectical tension within the community and does not rely on idealised thought experiments based on universalisation.

With Hegel we see that law is entirely framed within the terms of the norm: it applies to everyone, it divides society into discrete categories, and it represents the ordering principle of social reality. In this sense, the key social nature of the norm is clearer in Hegel's theory than in Rousseau's or Kant's. Political legitimation is constituted only through the medium of a law that is structured according to the paradigm of the norm. Law as a norm is distinctively seen by Hegel as a fully social construct that, in turn, shapes the societal order. The rules that regulate human conduct and that qualify individual actions in the world are no longer the projection of an absolute idea that is external to society, but, articulated along the paradigm of the norm, are conceived, at the same time, as the products and the organising principle of society's internal rationality.

With Hegel, we can also see clearly the last step in law's transformation into an apparatus that inscribes the subject within a triangle formed by power, knowledge, and truth. Rousseau's theory was the first to ideate a political system whose explicit function is to guarantee the individual's capacity to act freely and pursue her interests. Given the social nature of humankind, the theoretical problem becomes that of creating a mode of life that would reconcile the diverging interests of each person so that collective decisions would reflect individual volition. This impossible problem is – almost by sleight of hand – transformed into a solvable equation simply by assuming that the generality of individuals and the individual are the one and same thing and that these entities are conjoined by the truth of their will: only when the individual wills a will that is identical with that of the collectivity is she properly identifying her interests and therefore pursuing her freedom. Hence, the individual, in order to exercise of political power, and for political power to be created, must think according to a universalising scheme that – synchronising her volition with that of an abstract entity representing the collectivity – allows her to know the truth about herself. In other words, the individual must transform herself into a legal subject if she wants to live socially. Kant pushed this scheme even further. First, Kant is explicit in identifying the link between law and the knowledge of true volition that is only embryonic in Rousseau, indicating law as the generative instrument of political power, and not the compromise we need to accept for the benefit of social life; law is not the machinic surplus emerging from the transformation from individual to general will but the fundamental apparatus that makes the truth of individual will visible and enunciable at all. Second, there is no gap between what the individual wills as an individual and what she wills as a subject of law; the two entities become coextensive – only through law is the individual capable of knowing her own truth. Law thus emerges as that apparatus that makes the subject of interest possible. Through legal subjectivation she is made an active agent in the game of power and is hereby limited in her options; law provides her with a syntax that both makes her speak and silences her voice. With Hegel we can see the concrete subjectivating operations of such a dynamic at work. The legal discourse is depicted not as a mere thought experiment in universalisation but as the substantive, actual, practised subjectivation the individual must use to produce her truth as an individual and to generate political power. A double bind is established, firmly inscribing the subject within the triangle formed by power, knowledge, and truth. Law represents the apparatus that constitutes the subject and produces power out of her truth. Simultaneously, power–knowledge–truth feed back onto the subject through law, because law works as that apparatus that not only regulates how the individual is to know the truth about herself as a political subject, but interlocks her with a heterogeneous array of other apparatuses which will constitute her whole subjectivity as a living being (as a member of the family, of corporations, of the state, etc.). With this manoeuvre, law distinctively functions as an apparatus and the subjectivation of the individual along normalising lines is fully operationalised.

The features of a new politics

The aim of the present chapter was to describe genealogically how modern law emerges as that particular apparatus that transforms the individual by making visible and enunciable the truth of her political subjectivity. More precisely, I have explored how the secular interest of the individual is established at the basis of political power, and how law operates as a machine that enables the knowledge of the truth of such interests. In the previous pages I have tried to show that such mutation of the legal discourse takes place along the biopolitical shift between the discourse of sovereignty (a vision that recognises the ontological necessity of a relationship of supremacy between different individuals) and the discourse of normality. I have pointed out that law was progressively informed by the idea of the norm, arguing that the law functions less and less in accordance with the paradigm of the sovereign command and increasingly more in line with the norm: a rational standard that functions both as a principle of intersubjective communication and as an epistemological and ordering principle of reality. I have then attempted to delineate the syntax of this new mode of law by examining the evolution of the ideas of generality, abstraction, equality, and freedom in legal-political thinking, and its effects.

In the preceding analysis, it appears that the modern idea of democracy rests on the assumption that the population is formed by free and equal individuals. The story of the idea of modern democracy, in fact, reflects the complex passage that, from the metaphysical hierarchies of the Middle Ages, led to the idea that mankind was composed by a mass of equal subjects that could autonomously decide how to regulate themselves and pursue freely their own goals;[181] it is the story of how the individual ceased to be a little tile in the mosaic of the divine will and became a fundamental generative element of societal structure and dynamics. In general, the problem of freedom stood out, and became the defining characteristic of political thinking. There then emerged 'the belief in the natural, innate capacity of the human individual to regulate his own affairs in the light of a rationalistic interpretation of life'.[182] Locke, in this perspective, is often considered the founding father of the modern concept of the individual as a subject intrinsically entitled to a sphere of personal freedom rooted in personal interest.[183] We have seen how this claim to personal freedom subsequently came to the centre of the political discourse in Rousseau, Kant and Hegel. We have explored how it generated the question of how the individual could retain freedom while being at the same time subject to the laws of society, in other words the question of self-determination within a political community.[184]

The concept of the individual, the single person with an intrinsic worth that made her equal to everyone endowed with an innate right to freedom, came to be seen as the foundational element of legitimate political discourse. Laws, in order to be seen as legitimate, had to respect the individual as an equal and free subject; they had, in other words, to uphold the values of legal equality and liberty. At the same time, the working structure of democracy was provided by the production of laws that are both general and abstract in their object – thus protecting and co-ordinating all individuals within a shared framework of equality and freedom. General and abstract laws constitute the model of rule that regulates modern democratic society, but their importance was very limited in preceding systems based on claims of metaphysical legitimation. In medieval times, legal particularism and the existence of personal statuses and privileges denied the establishment of a set of abstract rules generally applicable to the whole population of a state. On the contrary, in modern legal systems general and abstract laws are paramount. They resolve the problem of linking the sovereign government and sovereign people by providing a procedural means of transforming the latter into the former, while guaranteeing a basic equality and freedom.

I have now outlined the relationship between law, the individual subject and political power, showing how laws based on generality and abstraction that implement legal equality and freedom are at one and the same time the product of and a guarantee for democracy, reflecting the lines of a normalising discourse. But how did democracy emerge institutionally and its central legitimising ideas of equality and freedom come to be translated into legal language? What is the historical evolution that led society to be regulated under general and abstract laws? How did the claims to legal equality and freedom overcome old legal paradigms and come to dominate the legal discourse of modern society? It is now time to turn to these questions and to examine how modern law was restructured as a machine capable of individuating the truth of the interest of society as a whole. To this end, the next chapter will be devoted to an exploration of this question by scrutinising the three historical revolutions that have ushered in the modern constitutional horizon: English, American, and French. At the end of the following chapter, we will have a more complete genealogical account of law as an apparatus, and we will be able to investigate more clearly its functioning within the broader context of normalising powers.

3

A Genealogy of Modern Law II: The Political Truth of Society

Introduction

With the aim of taking a further step in our genealogical account, it is now necessary to trace the development of the new syntax of law from the perspective of law as a mechanism to know the political truth of society. While the core of the previous analysis investigated the ways in which philosophers constructed the relationship between the legitimation of a social order and the individual, the following examination will focus more on some of the historical events and discursive practices that have led to the emergence of what we could call the constitutional horizon of modernity, that is, the generally accepted politico-institutional arrangement according to which governments should be limited in their powers by legal boundaries.[1]

If we take into consideration medieval times and, later on, absolutist regimes, we will be confronted with legal orders plagued by particularism.[2] General and abstract laws as we currently conceive them were simply lacking. There was virtually no rule that applied to everyone without discrimination and that set in advance, in a clear and binding fashion, the parameters by which to judge human conduct. Legal rules, in feudalism, were arranged according to personal agreements influenced by other external interferences and (often unknown to one of the parties) agreements, thus largely disrupting the possibility of having laws of general application. At the same time, feudalism was characterised by a highly hierarchical and fragmented structure of authority. Within such a context, society relied more on contingent commands than abstract laws in co-ordinating the community.[3] The idea of equality before the law as well was a largely alien concept for those times. The rights and obligations of every single individual changed dramatically in relation to the status of the other party and contributed to a highly fragmented and unequal legal order.[4] The concept of legal freedom was similarly unknown, at least in its modern incarnation as a sphere of personal autonomy and independence free from any external influence.[5]

In the present chapter, I will examine the passage from politico-institutional systems characterised by legal particularism to systems characterised by general and abstract rules where the principles of equality and freedom under the law are of central importance. To this end, I will focus on the three revolutions that can be said to have ended the fragmented legal orders of the *ancien régime* and framed the modern constitutional discourse: the Glorious Revolution, the American Revolution, and the French Revolution. By critically evaluating continuities and discontinuities between these events, I will show how, from this perspective, the modern legal discourse embraced the paradigm of the norm and how the relationship between law, society, power, and truth was reshaped in this passage.

Three revolutionary declensions of a paradigm shift

It is not my ambition to present here a fully-fledged historical study. My purpose is to identify in these three revolutions the seeds of our modern constitutional systems, or what we could call the constitutional horizon of modernity. Hence, I will not embark upon a comparative analysis of the development of constitutional law in each country or a detailed social account of England, America, and France at the time of their respective revolutions, but focus instead on delineating the legal discourse that developed through these events and how it is connected with our modern vision of law. Of course, these events were the product of a long and tortuous journey, and by focusing chiefly on them I run the risk of offering a flat account of a rich social, historical, and legal evolution. Conscious of this risk, I want to treat these three revolutions as turning points where various strands of history converged, as if in a knot, to diverge rapidly thereafter, thus offering to the interpreter the possibility of observing the interaction of various discourses, ideologies and concepts that tangled with one another at one point only to grow distant to each other in subsequent history. Before proceeding, however, some clarifications are necessary.

At the outset, I must acknowledge the relatively superficial and partial nature of the analysis I am going to offer: claiming to trace the rise of a new syntax of law and its key features by focusing solely on three events, important though they might be, could seem impressionistic at best and grossly misrepresentative for its minimalism at worst. Nonetheless these events make visible and map out the building blocks of a new mode of conceiving and practising law and government, powerfully establishing a legal-political landscape we can still identify as distinctively modern. Subsequent legal manifestations have clearly moved within that horizon. That is not to say that the principles set forth in those revolutions were immediately and fully implemented – far from it. However, it is undeniable that these revolutions and the debates that animated them served as a guideline and inspiration for the modern legal discourse like no others. Their genealogical role and influence in modern legal discourse is hard to deny. And while they might have left many promises unfulfilled for a long time, their ideological gravitational force is certainly immense.

In this sense, it is easy to argue that these three revolutions, together with their legal consequences, have decisively framed the constitutional discourse of modernity. As a consequence, a historically situated analysis of their occurrence will be adopted in order to help us draw the contours of modern law as a system of rationally interlocking rules. These events – reflecting a movement from the order of sovereignty to that of normality – were the first to speak of constitutional problems in a legal language that we are still using nowadays and that is framed by the paradigm of the norm. A study of those seminal moments will put into focus the inception of how such a discursive shift took place and how the legal syntax of normalisation emerged through it. I will thus show how the constitutional dynamics ignited by the English, American, and French Revolutions represented a blow to the logic of sovereignty, resting as it did upon the principles of interpersonal supremacy and exploitation. Adopting and – even if only to a limited extent – giving substance to the idea that society should be organised not in relation to command of a virtually unrestrained supreme entity but in accordance with rational universal norms, these revolutions translated the logic of normality into the legal-institutional dimension. Such a shift brought in a new mode of law that is, at least in its contours, distinctively modern and is based on a modern understanding of legal generality, abstraction, equality, and freedom.

Of course, it might seem rather problematic to group together the English, American, and French Revolutions in the same analysis.[6] These revolutions occurred in those nations at very different stages of their sociopolitical development and with widely divergent patterns, outcomes, and legacies. The three are certainly connected (the Americans claimed they were defending the rights secured by the Glorious Revolution[7] and the French Revolution to some extent was inspired by the American one[8]), but they are also at odds with each other: the Americans were revolting against the same political system that earlier had fought against Charles II, while France, America, and England were very unlike for social, legal and historical reasons. If we take into consideration the documents that framed the three revolutions, we could hardly face more divergent discursive structures and phraseologies. The Bill of Rights enacted in 1689 is akin to a legal contract which enumerates and secures a series of rights, the American Declaration of Independence is an act of denunciation of British infringements against colonists' liberties with a brief reference to natural rights, while the French Universal Declaration of the Rights of Man and of the Citizen is a programmatic text that sets forth the basic mode of production of laws for the forthcoming Republic. What is, then, the theoretical link that binds these revolutions and their outcomes? To what extent are we justified in grouping them together and claiming that they are all examples of the emergence of a new mode of law?

At a general level, the single most important feature that links the three revolutions is, quite obviously, that they were all fought to achieve democratic forms of self-government by breaking away from autocratic rule. To this extent, it is easy to suggest that these three revolutions moved away from the order of sovereignty to embrace that of normalisation. After all, the legal discourse that these events ushered in is one characterised by normalised public and individual powers; nobody is above the law, and therefore everybody is under it: tamed, regulated, limited by it. Neither public nor private powers can escape the gaze of the law and its reach. The common discursive problem that was tackled in the three revolutions, however, is not just that of limits to power but, most importantly from our point of view, also that of the production of the political truth of society and its implementation at the institutional level.

More specifically, we have seen how philosophers and political theorists have attempted to provide an answer to the question of what the truth actually is according to which society should be ordered – a worldly truth established through norms emerging from the materiality of individuals' interests. Lawyers and legal thinkers, on the other hand, tried to resolve the question of how to know this truth when faced with the multitude of individuals forming society and their conflicting interests, how it could be transposed from an ideal to a practical level, and how a legal system could be built that would properly express that truth.

Such a problem was articulated, as it were, through three different yet interconnected questions that dawned in turn. Which form of government is best suited to know and express the truth of society's interests? How should such a form of government be articulated to properly perform its truth-function and therefore produce truth? How should its actions be programmed so that they will always produce truth? We will see in the following pages how each country responded to those challenges and how, beyond the different answers that each revolution provided and the different constitutional arrangements that ensued, a clear shift towards normalisation took place and a new legal syntax rooted in the paradigm of the norm emerged.

More precisely, we will see that each revolution tackled chiefly a single one of these questions, offering to the subsequent ones a building block for the incremental move towards normalisation which becomes more clearly articulated with each event. This is not to say that eighteenth-century France experienced a stronger normalisation turn than England and the USA. Rather, I would claim that the shift towards normalisation – the reorientation of constitutional legal thinking – necessitated different levels of depths of theorisation across the three revolutions: the discursive shift that took place in France appears deeper and more theoretically structured than the one that occurred in the USA, and, in turn, that which took place in the USA was deeper and more theoretically structured than the one that occurred in England. This is nothing like the march of a sort of Hegelian spirit in the world, but the logical consequence that the rich transformations we are scrutinising encountered very divergent and peculiar social, political, and legal conditions which can be summarised (in a very crude way) thus: each revolution dealt with a different system of legal absolutism.

If we take absolutism as the last and most sophisticated form of feudalism[9] – and therefore of a legal system rooted in the language of sovereignty and founded upon the paradigm of the command – we can appreciate how much each country had to reinvent its constitutional discourse in order to finally abandon medieval legal and institutional structures (England barely experienced absolutism, while the American colonies were subject to the absolutist claims of a largely extraneous Parliament; France, on the other hand, experienced the most paradigmatic form of royal absolutism and, until the Revolution, was fully steeped in the *ancien régime*) through a shift towards normalisation. Hence, the reader should not be surprised that the four key features of generality, abstraction, equality, and freedom that were so constantly present in the previous chapter, will appear in their full form only when we will address the French Revolution. This last revolution was the one that needed the explicit (and theoretical) declaration of a syntax that, at a practical level, had already been developed but hardly spelled out in the previous historical events. The French

Revolution, having to act out a complete subversion of medieval legal and political forms, therefore represents a sort of denouement of a plot that took around one hundred years to be laid out in full and whose clearest expression was the Declaration of the Rights of Man and of the Citizen of 1789.

The long English Revolution: government as an institution

One of the most interesting remarks made about the Glorious Revolution of 1688[10] was made by Edmund Burke in his *Reflections on the Revolution in France* (1790):

> The Revolution was made to preserve our *ancient* indisputable laws and liberties, and that *ancient* constitution of government which is our only security for law and liberty ... [T]he ancient charter ... was nothing more than a re-affirmance of the still more ancient standing law of the kingdom.[11]

This comment is very interesting because it is at the same time a true and a false statement. It is true because the Glorious Revolution was based on several legal claims that relied on English constitutional history. Conversely, the Revolution (and the few decades that preceded it) was a veritable institutional rupture that irrevocably changed the political trajectory in England from a legal, political, and social point of view.

Among European realms, England certainly presented a unique example of constitutional evolution. It is generally acknowledged that, in contrast to the rise of absolutistic phenomena in Europe, England did not show a similar tendency, and was instead characterised by a longstanding tension between monarchy and the Parliament, which was eventually resolved in favour of the latter.[12] It is not that parliaments were unknown institutions in the continent, as they were present in many European realms; however, the British Parliament,[13] if paralleled with similar bodies,[14] had an unusual influence and authority not replicated elsewhere in the rest of Europe at the time.[15] One of the reasons for this anomaly was the presence of Commons in the Parliament, which made it possible for the so-called Third Estate to have participated in the political life of the kingdom and to have achieved an active role in legislation since the fourteenth century.[16] On the basis of a complex institutional arrangement, England showed from early on the characteristics of a constitutional monarchy, where the king is limited in his powers and there is a broader social contribution to the political and legislative processes of decision-making. The main consequence of this state of affairs was that the idea of a boundless authority in England was contested and the concept of the rule of law protecting individual rights and liberties from arbitrary power emerged earlier than in other European countries.[17] Burke's account of the emergence of English constitutional monarchy is therefore correct, and it echoes, as he himself underlined, Whigs' legal theories already proposed by Coke and Blackstone.[18]

On the other hand, there is much that Burke downplays in his depiction of the Glorious Revolution.[19] As has recently been observed,[20] the events of 1688 were both the consequence and the cause of a process of modernisation occurring in the English state, a country that was undergoing a swift centralisation of military, administrative, and legal functions.[21][22] The Glorious Revolution, within this context, marked a decisive turning point in the relationship between Parliament and monarchy, the latter eventually limited in its royal prerogative. The Parliament consecrated its pre-eminence over the King and the House of Lords in the practice of mixed government with the Bill of Rights and, henceforth, assumed a prominent role in the legislative process.[23][24] Viewed from this perspective, Burke's stance on the English Revolution was misleading as it understated the political innovation ushered in by the Glorious Revolution. The ambiguity surrounding the nature of the ancient constitution derives from the fact that the Glorious Revolution was the final outcome of a complex political struggle largely fought as much with physical as with rhetorical weapons, and it marked the beginning of an age of English constitutional history that definitely settled in favour of Parliament the problem of which institution was legislatively supreme in the realm.

In this struggle we find the first of the constitutional dilemmas that were resolved in a fashion that paved the way for the normalisation of the modern constitutional discourse. The question 'Which institutional arrangement is best suited to properly express legitimate political power?' had been discussed in England for quite some time by that stage,[25] and concerned the constitutional balance between a monarchy that was attempting to establish an absolutist rule and a Parliament keen on resisting such a change. Both parties agreed that England was to be ruled according to the constitution of the land,[26] but there was no convergence on what this constitution implied. It was widely acknowledged that the monarch had to rule together with the Parliament,[27] and it was largely agreed that the goal of the common law was to protect individuals and guarantee the well-being of the commonwealth,[28] but the crux of the English constitutional crisis of the seventeenth century lay elsewhere.

It was first characterised as a typically 'Schmittian' quandary (Who is the ultimate sovereign in times of emergency? When a crisis brings to a halt the established patterns of decision-making, what kind of mechanism is to be used to get out of the impasse?),[29] which then became a broader problem investing the ordinary dynamics of government (Who is the ultimate depository of the laws of the land and entitled to modify them when necessary? Which institution is better placed to identify the needs of the English people and to translate them into legal terms?). Both parties invoked the idea of the fundamental law of the land to advance their own agenda – the King referred to it in order to intimate that he had a duty to protect the kingdom from all dangers and therefore could not be obstructed in this task by any unruly assembly;[30] the Parliament invoked it for opposite purposes, that is to curb royal absolutist tendencies.[31] The most important English legal scholars of the time (Coke, Selden, Hale, Filmer, etc.) discussed the point incessantly with a wealth of historical and logical arguments. What is interesting to notice, from our point of view, is how limited in scope the controversy was. No relevant author, in fact, went beyond the issue of assigning final sovereignty to one institution over the other. The two other constitutional dilemmas that we have identified above and that delimit the constitutional discourse of normalisation, were largely ignored. There was neither discussion about whether the sovereign (be it the King or the Parliament) was subject to constitutional limits to its power nor any theorisation about how political power is to be formally expressed. England, in this sense, worked out in a revolutionary fashion only part of the constitutional problem of modernity (the most pressing part at the moment) and left the other two points aside for future generations to solve.

The sequence of events resulting from the stand-off between the King and the Parliament is well-known: the beheading of Charles I, Cromwell's protectorate, the Restoration and, finally, the Glorious Revolution. The outcome of the Glorious Revolution was the final victory of parliamentary sovereignty within a constitutional framework that, while maintaining the veneer of a mixed government, established the supposed absolute legal supremacy of an elected assembly.[32]

This dynamic might seem in direct contradiction to the shift-towards-the-norm thesis that has been so far advanced. After all, parliamentary sovereignty seems to point in the direction of the existence of an unbound institutional sovereign that can 'make and unmake any law whatever',[33] that is, a collective entity that operates through the paradigm of the command. Such a conclusion, however, would be mistaken for historical and logical reasons. As we have seen, very differently from its continental counterparts, the English Parliament was a collective body where commoners had a large and powerful representation. It was therefore an entity that expressed the diffused interests (which of course did not coincide with the interest of all) of a rather composite part of the English population (certainly not representative of the whole). Such a manifold entity, precisely because of its own social composition, could not express what we have described as sovereign commands.[34] Commands are essentially decisions taken by an entity that rests outside of their reach. Norms, on the other hand, are rules emerging from an entity and aimed at managing that very same entity. Such an entity is sovereign only in the political sense of being the highest-ranking institution, but not in the sense that it is above the logic of the norm. Hart, in this sense, was right in criticising Austin's command theory of law.[35] To the extent that a body is the expression of a multitude, and creates rules to manage that same multitude in a sort of self-reflecting manner, that body, even if sovereign, cannot be an 'uncommanded commander',[36] as its operations will always take place within the limit of the logic of the norm and subordinated to it.

An analysis of how, in the eyes of historical legal scholars, the Parliament came to prominence against the rule of the monarch will help us to unearth the logic of normalisation which slowly penetrated the English constitutional legal discourse. We have already seen that there was a widely-shared belief that England was a peculiar country because it presented a distinctive constitutional arrangement that, going back to Fortescue, was defined as *dominium regale et politicum*;[37] the English realm was therefore the realm of a mixed constitution where the King and the Parliament ruled together. Up until the seventeenth-century crisis it is difficult to assess the nature of the English constitution because it rested on the more or less pacific sharing of power between the King and the Parliament. It is known, however, that the true nature of things is discovered in times of difficulty. And therefore, when the apparent harmony of such an arrangement was perturbed by Charles I's attempts to move towards more absolutist forms of government, legal scholars were forced to investigate the balance of the fundamental law in order to determine which institution was the superior one, the King or the Parliament.

Sir Edward Coke (1552–1664) was one of the most prominent lawyers that addressed this issue. He is traditionally identified as the torch-bearer of the Parliamentarian cause,[38] but his thinking was more nuanced – or even contradictory – than that.[39] As a matter of fact, from an analysis of Coke's writing it appears that he thought of the Parliament as a sort of court of last resort that had to declare the law of the land[40] and was subject to the latter in the same way as anybody else.[41] To what extent the Parliament was under the law and did not have substantial powers to make new law is a matter of well-trodden discussion.[42] What interests us is the fact that Coke advanced the theory that the common law was an organic body of rules to be developed through reason and, in particular, the judicial procedure.[43] Coke relied very much on the historicity of the English legal system, how it presented one continuous line from the time of William the Conqueror to his day, but the intimation that law was also a creature of judicial reasoning, coupled with the idea that the Parliament was akin to a court, is of great importance for our genealogy. It demonstrates how Fortescue's vision of mixed government was here tweaked in a normalising fashion. The central point of Coke's understanding of common law is that law is a product of reason, that this reason must be produced by the community of legal minds, and that this collective mind is represented by the Parliament. Law is therefore not seen as an unbridled decision coming from an absolute and singular sovereign, but is a discourse that can properly evolve only under the taming – that is normalising – influences of history and collective legal reason.

The thinking of Richard Hooker (1554–1600) displays even more the underlying normalising logic that underscored much of English constitutional thought of the seventeenth century. Hooker did believe that the monarch should be under no man, but he rejected the idea that he/she was unbound by law. Within the context of a rather conservative vision of the English constitution – where the monarch ruled because of the original consent of the body politic – he introduced a distinctive normalising idea at its basis. When faced with uncertain situations (Is a given law good or bad? Should it be followed or resisted?), he argued that matters should be settled with reference to the collective voice of society because it would be impossible to achieve unanimous agreement.[44] Law, in other words, did not draw its force exclusively from an established and immutable social system;[45] its authority was more functional than historical: it was linked with the idea that law should be obeyed only when it is the expression of the truth about some fact of life established by society.[46] Such law is clearly marked by the paradigm of the norm. It does not creep up from some mythical past or descend from some metaphysical dimension. Precisely because history and God are often silent on very important matters, only society can know the truth about itself; only from within its core can correct judgements be made. Here lies the central case for self-government and for an idea of law that emerges from the necessities of society to regulate society itself.

The step towards the position that laws are a matter of the (normalised) consent of all persons interested and should be made through a (normalising) representative assembly instead of a monarch was a very short one. It is not surprising, therefore, that both John Selden (1584–1654) and Sir Matthew Hale (1609–76), in their later works on the English constitution, were not so much concerned with the immemoriality of the fundamental law (the static nature of which had little weight in their argument) as with the theoretical criterion of its change and functioning.[47] What mattered, in other words, was that laws were ultimately caused by the people's consent, and that people's consent, in turn, was expressed only through established constitutional patterns (hence the insistence on a vision of the English constitution as tripartite system – formed by the monarch, the Lords, and the Commons – that would mediate the transient will of the people).[48] What to do when the historical settlement breaks down, however, was a more dubious question[49] which was resolved only by Henry Parker (1604–52), who followed to its ultimate limit the constitutional theory of consent. In his thought as well, we find distinct normalising undertones, since he declared that in the event of conflict the Parliament should have the upper hand because it was swayed by no private interest (and therefore followed, in an almost necessary fashion, the common good) and expressed the will of the whole Kingdom.[50]

In seventeenth-century England, therefore, the Parliament was progressively identified as sovereign for theoretical reasons that were clearly rooted in the normalising logic. The Parliament was depicted as a constitutional mechanism for the correct representation of the will of the people, an assembly that, even if legally unbound, was not ultimately unrestrained. The Parliament could never err in its judgement, because it represented the whole population and therefore could never exceed the normalised limit imposed by the logic of self-expression. Once it is agreed that the truth of society's good does not reside in a transcendent dimension but stems from society's own interests, the mechanism of self-governance is faultless: one is always true when one desires one's own interests.

To sum up our analysis, we can schematise the outcome of the English Revolution in the following triadic terms. The shift towards the norm was initiated by reframing the idea of government along the three axes of structure, theory and function. The Parliament as an *institution* replicated society's dynamics. The theory of its structure was that the latter *repre-*

sented society's fundamental interests. The function of the Parliament, therefore, was to *reflect* in a naturalistic fashion the common good of society. This triad institution/representation/reflection had a double normalising role. Positively, it was capable of identifying the common good of society through the encounter of the variable interests of a population exemplified in the Parliament. Negatively, it tamed sovereign power through the operations of a representative assembly. In other words, conceived as a mechanism for identifying the truth about the common good of society, the English constitutional model worked (in the strictly normalising sense) towards the knowledge of such a truth, as well as working (in the sense of normation) as a system for imposing this truth.

The emergence of a victorious Parliament hence resolved the English constitutional crisis of the seventeenth century in a distinct normalising fashion. The limits of such transformation, however, must be stressed. Precisely because the English Revolution addressed only the problem of the locus of the expression of political power, the shift towards the norm in English constitutional history occurred in a slow progression linked more with the development of political participation and the extension of voting rights than with a clear legal change. Seen from this point of view, the English Revolution was not particularly revolutionary in itself. While imposing parliamentary rule, it did not guarantee, in the short term, a more democratic participation in political decisions, nor did it promote a more egalitarian community.[51] It did, however, represent a point of no return, and it ensured the continuous growth of a modern legal system with laws of general and abstract application defending the principles of legal equality and freedom.[52]

To be sure, in England the idea that laws should be general and abstract, and centred on legal equality and freedom, was never made constitutionally explicit. Its existence was more a matter of the political understanding of the nature of the constitution. The vision of law as an overarching system that tames power and co-ordinates society had already been present in the English system since the time of Magna Carta,[53] and it was at the basis of Parliamentarian claims against monarchical absolutism that reframed the English constitution.

English legal history seems therefore to show earlier signs of the passage from sovereignty to normalisation, which is only confirmed by the subsequent British constitutional history. Such a passage was a gradual phenomenon that was rooted in the peculiar development of the English legal systems and showed a more nuanced and progressive nature than the American and French experiences it later inspired. We can say that in

England, the shift towards normalisation in the constitutional discourse was something that occurred throughout history in an almost subterranean way.[54] The point of no return towards normalisation was sanctioned in formal terms by the Glorious Revolution with the underwhelming and somewhat subdued tone of the Bill of Rights of 1689,[55] which cast a retroactive light on past English constitutional history. Rather than the programmatic declaration of a new regime, it represented the confirmation of a supposed status quo that eventually developed into the British rule of law like the affirmation of a self-fulfilling prophecy.[56]

The American Revolution: government as a process

We have seen how, in seventeenth-century England, the constitutional discourse moved from the logic of sovereignty to that of normalisation. With the victory of the Parliament over the monarchy, a representative collective entity was put at the apex of the legal system. Such a body, because of its own highly representative nature and its reflecting function, operates according to the paradigm of the norm, understood as a rule almost statistically emerging from the interaction of society's needs and desires, and redirected towards society itself to manage and co-ordinate it.[57] This kind of arrangement, however, reflects the logic of normalisation only in a weak form, because it establishes no mechanisms to guarantee that the collective sovereign entity is effectively connected with the social body which it regulates. In other words, there was no constitutional mechanism in the seventeenth-century English constitution that ensured that the Parliament accurately reflected the totality of the population over which it ruled. As a consequence, the Parliament could always legislate as a despot, imposing its laws as though they were commands uttered by a detached sovereign upon whole sectors of society. This was exactly the cause that sparked the American Revolution and that framed the further step towards the logic of normalisation that characterised much of the American constitutional discourse. The Americans therefore addressed and resolved in a normalising fashion the second 'constitutional dilemma' we have identified above: how should government be articulated to properly produce legitimate political power?

As we have seen, one of the most enduring political interpretations of the Glorious Revolution was that the events of 1688 did not import a change in the British constitution but were a defence of it against monarchical prevarications. It could be said that the American Revolution was based, to a large extent, on a similar argument. Without focusing on the social and economic causes that generated the American rebellion,[58] we can see that from a legal and constitutional perspective the frictions between England and the colonies were based on a divergent interpretation of the constitution.[59] The point is that while the Parliament of Great Britain, after the Glorious Revolution, claimed it embodied the constitution and therefore that its deliberations were *eo ipso* lawful, American colonies saw the revolution of 1688 as a confirmation of the rights and liberties of the people that no authority could violate.[60] The worsening of this disagreement led to a harsh political confrontation. While the Americans invoked the upholding of the fundamental concepts of consent and representation in order to recognise parliamentary legislation as legitimate, the Parliament was denying them such privileges, claiming a supreme authority to legislate over the Empire.[61] In an ironic twist of fate, the Parliament of Great Britain was accused by the colonies of conspiracy against liberty[62] and charged with many of the same 'contractual' transgressions[63] that James II was accused of almost one hundred years before by that very assembly.[64]

But what, more precisely, was the object of contention? The first turmoil was occasioned in relation to taxation, but soon the conflict escalated to involve matters of fundamental constitutional importance. Many claims were advanced as to the cause of the conflict (the defence of ancient liberties, the need for consent to impose laws, constitutional restraint on legislation, rule of law as opposed to the arbitrary power of Parliament, the role of political representation, etc.), and their intertwined nature makes it difficult to distinguish them one from the other. But what, if any, was the common theme linking them?

At that time, a parallel was drawn between the events leading to the Glorious Revolution and those of the American Revolution.[65] The comparison, however, was not completely correct, as there was one fundamental difference. While in the Glorious Revolution the conflict was between the King and his subjects who were trying to participate in the legislative process, in the American revolt we are faced with a struggle that could be characterised as 'fratricide' as the colonists were rising up against that same Parliament that was supposed to rule for them and in their name.[66] This would lead one to find in the desire of self-government[67] the central issue that was fuelling the conflict. Self-government was certainly one of the claims made by the colonists against their motherland, but can it alone explain the revolt?

Such a solution does not appear completely satisfactory, as it does not explain why Americans did not see the Parliament as a legitimate government. The issue of representation, namely, the question as to whether or not the colonists were in fact represented in a Parliament that they did not elect, might then be recognised as central to the ideological conflict between Great Britain and America.[68] All things considered, however, this hypothesis does not resolve all doubts. Although it could be said that the colonies did not contribute to the election of Commons, the theory of virtual representation – which supposed the existence of a political representation[69] in the Parliament even for those who were not participating in the elections[70] – was meant to overcome precisely those very problems of actual representation. So why were the Americans not satisfied with virtual representation, which was otherwise peacefully accepted in the motherland?[71]

The answer lies in the failure to extend to the Americans the constitutional safeguards that accompanied virtual representation in Great Britain.[72] These safeguards were grounded in the doctrine of local interests and local knowledge,[73] the doctrine of shared interests,[74] and, most importantly, the doctrine of shared burdens.[75] This doctrine of shared burdens can be identified, in my opinion, as representative of the main source of discord between the British and the Americans. Its rejection essentially meant the collapse of the system of general and abstract laws upholding legal equality and freedom that had been secured by the Glorious Revolution and developed ever since. Imposing upon the colonist more onerous legal obligations than the British effectively created two classes of citizen that were not treated equally and to which were granted different spheres of freedom. The main point of friction between the two that led, in the end, to the revolt of the colonies against their motherland rested on the fact that many of the statutes passed by the Parliament (the Stamp Act and the so-called Intolerable Acts,[76] for example) represented a significant attack on the generality of laws, transforming the Americans into second-class citizens and into subjects of subjects, as it were.[77] While British laws still retained a distinctly abstract quality, their lack of general application undermined the very principle of equality before the law that they were supposed to uphold, with the result that the freedom of colonists was constrained.

As a consequence, the colonists sought to reinstate the basic rule of law, comprising above all else that principle of legal equality that was central to the political debate which eventually led to the Glorious Revolution. The Declaration of Independence was aimed precisely at achieving this goal by seeking to legitimise colonial grievances and to remind the British of the core tenets of their legal system.[78] If we accept this argument, the Declaration of Independence shows evidence for a more theoretical approach to the question of legality and law-making than does the Bill of Rights.[79] As such, the Preamble to the Declaration is probably the most important part of the document because it attempts to reinstate the legal model that was defended by the Bill of Rights, mainly with its reference to a natural status of equality.

With this in mind, we can appreciate how the colonists' claims, implicitly framed by the concepts of generality, abstraction, equality, and freedom, reflected a discourse of normalisation. The American Revolution was based on the premise that law should be articulated through norms instead of sovereign commands. The rejection of parliamentary sovereignty should thus be seen in this perspective: as a rejection of the idea of a political power operating beyond the limits of the norm and perpetuating the logic of sovereignty that reduces citizens to mere subjects. In this sense, the American Revolution was part of the natural progression towards the establishment of the paradigm of normalisation within the legal discourse, which first emerged in the English Revolution. However, as was previously remarked, while the shift towards normalisation was a subterranean and silent one in the English tradition, this passage had to be explicitly reinforced in the American case.

Faced with this problematic situation, American thinkers had to reconsider the structure of the government that well worked for the motherland, but failed to provide satisfactory results in the colonies. While, in England, the Parliament reflected quite accurately the will of the people whom it governed (and therefore adhered to the logic of normalisation), the same arrangement was unsatisfactory for the colonies, which were effectively ruled by an assembly acting as an external, detached authority operating along the lines of the logic of sovereignty. American revolutionaries, therefore, had to take a further step in the normalising shift in constitutional discourse as they realised that the establishment of representative government was not enough to guarantee self-government. The prevarications of the English Parliament had made it clear that the collective and representative nature of the supreme ruling institution of society was not enough to guarantee that government was properly reflective of legitimate political power. The idea that emerged was that the government should not just reflect, as if in a mirror, the truth of interests of the people, but rather that the government should be conceived as a mechanism structured so as to produce that truth. What was invoked, in other words, was a reframing of the idea of government as a process and not just as an institution.[80]

This way of thinking led to two very important consequences. First, the innovative call for a written constitution that would make explicit the conditions under which a government was to be considered an institution holding legitimate political power.[81] Second, the idea that for a government to be able to produce and not merely reflect the truth of the interests coming from society, it was necessary to structure it as a process, which in turn implied the notion of the separation of powers, and the vision of government as a mechanism guided by the principle of checks and balances.

This second point, in my opinion, is especially worthy of attention because it shows the double normalising transformation that marked the dawn of modern forms of constitutionalism, a transformation which was already begun with the English Revolution but whose contours are made more explicit in the American and French Revolutions. We have already examined how the constitutional framework established by the English Revolution had failed the colonies because, while its scheme of representation embodied in the Parliament worked well within the context of the motherland, that very same Parliament operated like an absolute sovereign for the Americans as it did not reflect their will as a people. Once independence was achieved, it was only natural that the chief preoccupation of the Founding Fathers was to avoid the repetition of this political corruption. The constitutional thought of Madison, Adams, Hamilton, and Jefferson is redolent with this concern. The thought of Madison, in particular, as expounded in *The Federalist Papers* n. 10 and n.51, is very clear on this point. Adopting an empirical stance, and setting aside normative positions,[82] Madison defended the American Constitution as the best legal arrangement possible precisely because it was meant as a mechanism which, separating powers, and instituting a complex system of checks and balances between the legislature, the executive, and the judiciary, was able to curb the factionalism that recurrently surfaces in society while leading to the supreme goal of the common good.[83]

The Federalist n.10 highlighted the instrumental nature of the new American constitutional system. Confronted with the democratic problem of factions developing into dangerous elites[84] – a problem that clearly echoes the accusations levelled by the Americans against the English – Madison suggested that the only solution lay in a republican form of government whose structure would multiply the loci of political interests and therefore avoid the development of one single faction into a dangerous elite.[85] In line with a long tradition of political thought, he believed that the presence in the government of different competing interests would be conducive to the common good. His intuition, however, was that the structure of government itself should be ideated in a manner that would – almost artificially, on the basis of different methods by which government officials in each branch of government were selected, their different terms of office, and their different powers – juxtapose divergent interests against each other.[86] Madison famously expounded his theory of separation of powers and checks and balances in *The Federalist* n.51. His conception of government is almost alchemical in its search for an optimal equilibrium that, through what we might call structural design, enhanced the powers of one branch while dampening another.[87] Other aspects of Madison's constitutional thought amply demonstrate that he was fairly unconcerned with the issue of democratic representation;[88] rather, he was trying to create a form of government that would operate as a mechanism that would be able to synthesise the common good out of the divergent interest of a population that was always under the danger of parcellisation, while protecting the population itself against its own sovereign excesses.[89]

The American constitutional settlement, therefore, had two main directives. In the first place, it limited the amount of power that each branch had vis-à-vis the others, thus structurally reducing the potential for any institution to take over and creep towards despotism. In the second place, the careful balance between the branches of government was intended to be conductive to the common good of the American people. The very structure of the American government, in other words, was meant to operate as a machine that would process the diverging and often conflicting and factitious interests of the people, so as to produce outcomes directed towards the common good. The American constitution as interpreted in *The Federalist Papers*, therefore, pursued a double normalising objective, a negative and a positive one. Negatively, it curbed political power by impeding its sovereign excess (normation). Positively, it was ideated so as to always produce a collective will in line with the common good (normalisation *strictu sensu*).

We can now see more clearly how the American Revolution took a step further towards normalisation when compared with the English system emerging from the Glorious Revolution. While the English relied on an *institution* that, because of its collective nature, would *represent* society and therefore *reflect* the truth of society itself, the Americans had found out the hard way that such a scheme relied upon a delicate political equilibrium which, in the wider context of an empire, could be easily derailed. To avoid these shortcomings, the Americans supplemented the English framework by understanding the structure of the government not just as an institution but as a *process* (integrating the divergent interests of society) that, thanks to the theory of *the separation of powers* and *checks and balances*, could perform the function not merely of reflection but of *production* of decisions in line with the common good. What we see, in the passage from the English to the American experience, is a reinforcement of the normalising logic in constitutional thought. Out of the English triad of Institution/Representation/Reflection the Americans developed the triad Process/Separation of Powers-Checks and Balances/Production.

While the establishment of a normalising dynamics seems clear, it must be stressed that constitutionalised signs of the syntax of modern law based on generality, abstraction, equality, and freedom were largely absent. As a matter of fact, whereas the American Revolution focused strongly on the issue of equality between colonists and British citizens[90] – and certainly the question of liberty connected with private property was a central one[91] – there was a remarkable lack of interests in the theoretical relationship between law and rights. The issue about how to protect rights, in other words, was not addressed from the point of view of the nature of law and individual entitlements, but rather from a purely institutional perspective. It is striking, in this sense, that in *The Federalist Papers* there is hardly any mention of legal equality and certainly no scrutiny of the fundamental features of law.[92]

Much like their British cousins, the Americans were part of a legal-constitutional shift whose massive consequences were far from clear at the time. The shift – to repeat – did not so much involve change in the ways in which law was to be conceived, but rather, generated a new conception of government that would yield in due course a new conception of law.[93] Original and innovative though the constitutional institutional arrangement that stemmed from the revolution was – the Americans were the first in history to produce a written constitution that originally established a legal order *ex novo* – the legal discourse it introduced was not so distant from that of the motherland. As a matter of fact, the rights of equality and freedom, so central in the Declaration of Independence, were contested claims in the political and legal practice of the USA, and the road towards their universal recognition through general and abstract laws had a very winding history, especially in relation to racial discrimination.[94] The causes of this contradiction are similar to those we observed in relation to England. The new syntax of English and American law did not develop from theoretical 'normalising' declarations – as we will see happened in France – because at a concrete level both institutional structures and socio-political dynamics were incubating the seeds of the paradigm of the norm through the idea and practice of self-government.

The French Revolution: government as a programme

We have seen that the English and American constitutional restructuring represented two waves, as it were, of normalisation in the constitutional discourse of modernity. Moving away from the idea that social order is determined by a metaphysical scheme where composite human interests have little part to play (a scheme embodying the logic of sovereignty), legal scholars progressively embraced the idea that society itself knows the truth about its common good (a scheme intimately connected with the logic of normalisation). The constitutional question of modernity therefore aimed at establishing a connection between the truth about society's common good and its institutional manifestation. Not any more 'What kind of order would replicate the heavenly plans of God?', but 'What kind of government would be able to make manifest the truth residing in body politic?'.

We have seen how the English and the Americans answered these questions. The English adopted a constitutional arrangement that centred on the Parliament as an *institution* that would *represent* the people and therefore *reflect* their common good at governmental level. The Americans had discovered that such an arrangement rested on a delicate and fragile equilibrium between a central institution and its people, and could easily fall back into despotism. As a consequence, they adopted a scheme that understood government not just as an institution but as a *process* organised according to the theory of the *separation of powers* and *checks and balances* so that it would always *produce*, as if by an alchemical procedure, the common good of the people. We have also seen how both arrangements followed the two sides of the normalising logic. Positively, these schemes were intended as mechanisms to make manifest the truth of society by extracting it as a regularity that emerges from the interaction of the divergent interests present in the population (normalisation *strictu sensu*). Negatively, they were conceived as frameworks that would enforce this truth by preventing government from swaying into sovereign excesses and ruling against the common good of society (normation).

While the constitutional discourse shifted towards normalisation, it is difficult to recognise in its full force the new syntax of law that was more clearly emerging in the philosophical discourse concerning the nature of political legitimation. Certainly this new syntax is clearly present in modern legal systems (as shown by Hayek and others), but its development is somewhat hazy in the Anglo-American experience. Previously, I have drawn attention to the exceptional status of Anglo-American legal history when compared to the history of the rest of Europe. The main difference between England and (*a fortiori*) the American colonies, on the one hand, and other European states, on the other hand, was the relative weakness of absolutist forms of government, and a kind of legal tradition that, while certainly very distant from modern standards in terms of generality and abstraction of laws, and equality and freedom before the law, was indeed more universalistic in nature. As a consequence, the new legal syntax that marks the modern discourse of law evolved in a subterranean fashion in England and the USA, mostly shying away from magniloquent proclamations.

While absolutism never fully took hold in England, it flourished in the rest of Europe, especially in France where the reign of Louis XIV is largely considered the epitome of such a system of government.[95] The passage from feudalism to absolutism was marked by a centralisation of political power: in principle, in absolutism the source of all laws is the king, who is, in turn, legally unrestrained.[96] The legal position of all entities, as well as individuals, was therefore determined by the supreme will of the monarch to whom they owed allegiance and deferred. Different sets of laws were applied to very different social groupings, whose members hardly had any opportunity for social mobility.[97] Estates, Orders, and Corporations were like cages that defined and preserved the legal status of their constituents.[98] In absolutism, in other words, we have a regime of privileges, with provisions that apply only to specific social groups whose members were bound to obey.

Hence, legal systems under absolutist regimes were very different from those that existed during feudal times because, although they retained much of the pre-existing legal forms and some of their rhetoric, they were characterised by a strong centralisation. The concept of legal status, which in modern legal systems identifies a fluid situation that the individual is able to modify according to a set of specific legal rules,[99] was, in the absolutist regime, an almost immutable situation that attached rights and duties to the individual according to her membership of a specific social group.[100] The only true universal element present in absolutism was represented by the figure of the sovereign, who embodied all privileges and from whom all privileges emanated.[101] In other words, laws were general only inasmuch as they pertained to the person of the king and his earthly expression of power, as he was the source of all laws.[102] Conflicts between individuals were not adjudicated on the basis of the legal relationship between two opposing parties, but, more subtly, on the basis of the special personal relationship that both happened to possess, to differing degrees, in relation to the king.

With this in mind, it could be said that, in continental Europe, modern law, with its features of generality, abstraction, equality, and freedom, progressively moved beyond this dual 'private' meaning of law: law as a rigidly personal legal status, and law as private concession of the king. From this point of view, absolutism represented a system suspended somewhere between sovereignty and normalisation. At one level, sovereignty was reinforced within the figure of the absolute monarch, but, at another level, normalisation progressively emerged as the overarching ordering paradigm of society and its citizenry.[103]

It is clear that absolutism cannot be conflated to one overarching phenomenon as it was articulated in very different ways across Europe. Nevertheless, French absolutism could be taken as the template for legal centralisation that occurred across continental Europe at the time. Building on this consideration, and given the role that the French Revolution and the Declaration of 1789 have had in shaping the concept of modernity,[104] I believe that the analysis of the historical context framing this event, together with a detailed interpretation of the Declaration itself, might provide a viable insight with regard to the path of legal evolution that occurred in continental Europe and, more generally, in civil law countries.[105]

Needless to say, it is beyond the scope of my argument to offer a thorough discussion of the causes and facts of the French Revolution or to engage with its socio-political interpretations.[106] The preceding brief summary of the structure of continental absolutist regimes has already highlighted key legal-political features that were particularly clear in France. First, there was no effective doctrine of separation of powers. Second, all powers were quite solidly in the hands of a small hereditary elite. Third, the legal regime largely reproduced the exclusion of the common people (in France's case the burgeoning Third Estate) from positions of power, and in general prevented social mobility. The combination of these conditions made the French Revolution the first modern upheaval that caused a complete change in the legal regime of a country. Neither the English nor the American revolutions, from this point of view, were radically revolutionary from a legal point of view or even a political one. As we have seen, they were perceived by their respective protagonists more as restorations of a broken ancient balance than a complete break with the past. The French Revolution, on the contrary, precisely because of the socio-political situation generated by the legal regime of absolutism, was explicitly aimed at turning the French regime on its head, stripping the King and the nobles of their legal and social prerogatives, and giving all powers to the nation.[107]

The French Revolution and the transformation that it ushered in, therefore, were much more radical in their scope than in the Anglo-American experience. It is for this reason that we can see more clearly here than in the two preceding examples how the constitutional discourse of modernity shifted towards normalisation and a new legal syntax based on the four pillars of generality, abstraction, equality, and freedom.

The years preceding the French Revolution were characterised by lively legal debates concerning the nature and content of the laws ruling the French government.[108] As I have pointed out above, at a superficial level there is a certain continuity between these debates and similar constitutional dilemmas that we have explored in the English and American context. What is the content of the fundamental laws of the land? Who is to enforce them? The king as the protector of the realm, or collective assemblies representing the population? The fact that France had had a tradition of absolutism, however, produced answers very different from those we have seen in England and the USA.

The initial bone of contention, unsurprisingly, concerned the fundamental laws of the realm. The way in which the dispute around this subject was framed, though, reveals an immediate difference between the French and the English context. Whereas in England the crisis had started as a conflict over which institution – the monarch or the Parliament – had the upper hand in case of emergency measures – and therefore the question about the locus of ordinary legislative power was set aside and only eventually seized by the Parliament[109] – in France the debate was oriented since the beginning towards the question of which institution could change the fundamental law of the land.[110] It was in fact clear that fundamental laws supervising the organisation of the body politic should be distinguished into two categories. On the one hand, there were 'natural fundamental laws', laws whose existence was almost a matter of logic and whose collapse would engender the dissolution of civil society.[111] On the other hand, there were 'positive fundamental laws' whose existence was a matter of contingent historical circumstances and tradition, and which therefore were open to change.[112] The historical conception of 'positive fundamental laws' generated a critical attitude about fundamental laws that was absent in England and the USA.

This attitude ran along two lines of criticism. In the first place, the content of fundamental laws was buried in the mist of time and therefore uncertain.[113] In the second place, the historical nature of 'positive fundamental laws' meant that they had been the product of specific historical circumstances.[114] Such criticisms shaped the whole subsequent legal debate that led to the French Revolution. The French system of 'positive fundamental laws' appeared to contemporary legal scholars as structurally flawed. Being historical, 'positive fundamental laws' were constrained by an 'enumerative logic',[115] binding the organisation of the body politic to age-old traditions whose contents were deemed both unsatisfying and insufficient by legal scholars.[116]

As a consequence, French scholars undertook a restructuring of the country's legal system which, while falling into the same path as the English and American experiences, is also much more profound and far-reaching in its theoretical aspects. While the English and American experiences were framed in a conservative rhetoric of preservation of ancient rights against political corruption and personal ambition, French lawyers were facing the more complex task of delineating the new foundations of the fundamental laws of society. Whereas in England and the USA the constitutional discourse was focused on finding constitutional mechanisms of defence against the return of despotism, France was struggling with the forward-looking question of how to think a new legal system altogether. From this point of view, it is interesting to see how the reference to natural law and rights had different meanings in the American and French Declarations.[117] The former was a document conceived to restate the right to preserve the natural dynamics of societal evolution, and law was seen as a limit to the government's corrupting meddling with human affairs; the latter, conversely, was trying to provide the government with the instruments which would allow society to revert to its true nature, a nature that had been perverted by centuries of political corruption.[118][119] While, therefore, the American Declaration had a conservative perspective,[120] the legal ideal set out in the French Revolution was deliberately conceived in an innovative way with respect to the past, and its purpose was to demolish the *ancien régime* and move towards a better future.[121] In the French Declaration, therefore, law acquires a more prominent role than in the Anglo-American examples. Instead of invoking a mythical and misty legal past, the French were concerned with the almost 'scientific' enterprise of theorising a wholly new system where society could 'bootstrap' itself out of the miseries of medieval abuses.[122]

Central to this enterprise is the third 'constitutional dilemma' that we have mentioned at the beginning of the chapter, the answer to which constitutes the third and final normalising wave of the modern constitutional discourse.[123] While the English and the American Revolutions respectively answered the questions 'Which form of government is best suited to reflect legitimate political power?' and 'How should government be articulated to properly produce legitimate political power?', the French Revolution was concerned with an even more foundational problem: how should government actions be programmed to properly express legitimate political power? Given the French situation, it was not a matter of providing the institutional 'hardware' that would connect the government with the truth of the common good already present (however contradictory and coarse its form) in society, but of how to delineate the 'software' that would interlock the art of government with the truth of the common good, so as to always cause the truth of the common good to appear in the actions of government.

Anticipating the conclusions of the subsequent analysis, the answer to this problem is that legitimate political power can only be expressed through the language of law as delineated by the French Declaration – namely a law characterised by the legal syntax framed by generality and abstraction, and legal equality and freedom. The third (and most theoretically complete) normalising constitutional arrangement emerging from the French Revolution presents, then, a new triad: the government must work as a *programme* that will *express* the truth of the common interest through a specific new *legal syntax*.

In the French debate we can see roughly the same elements discussed in the English and American Revolutions. The train of thought is a familiar one: the natural goal of political societies is to serve the interests of the individual, which coincide with the interests of all – the common good – the knowledge of which must be extracted from the multitude of the people. While in England and the USA the central notions of such reasoning (common good, will of the people, the people, etc.) were hardly explicitly discussed or problematised, and their existence was accepted almost as a natural fact, in France we see how the same substantive notions were thoroughly dissected and brought to light through a sophisticated 'legal constructivism'. These notions, in other words, while recognised as the basic natural elements of any political associations, became visible, as it were, only when expressed through a legal language.

In France, as in England and the USA, personal interest represents the cornerstone of political authority. In France, however, personal interest becomes relevant only when it expresses the general interest of all.[124] It must immediately be noted that there is an important difference between the Anglo-Saxon *common good* and the French *interet générale*. The 'common good' is normally conceived as an individual interest that is shared by the majority of the people and, as such, is taken as the paramount good of the community. The common good, therefore, emerges out of a sort of majoritarian or probabilistic rule where the majority of the population – naturally following their instincts – is by definition right. The notion of *interet générale*, on the other hand, is artificial and represents the interest of the single individual who imagines her own interest as being that of society as a whole.[125] It is not a natural occurrence, but requires a social commitment from the individuals. The *interet générale* emerges as the expression of the *general will* of the nation. Also in this case, we are quite distant from the naturalistic inflection of the *will of the people*. While the latter assumes that the aggregate of individual wills constitutes the will of the whole population – again following an implicit (and rather crude) majoritarian rule – the former is a peculiar construct that comes to light only through the language of law. The nation, in fact, is not just a people or a multitude, but the regulative form that these collectivities acquire through anthropomorphisation.[126] The nation, in other words, is the form which a people takes on its path towards maturity, and which makes it able to think itself.[127] The product of such thinking is the *general will*, which is not the mere accumulation of all the particular wills of each individual in the population; rather, it is a special kind of volition that is directed at the common interest of society, a volition that forces the individual to think about the good in universalistic terms.[128] In this mechanism – linking political power, general interest, common will, and the nation – legicentrism is key.[129] What is central, however, are not positive laws but the logical rules that are at the basis of their formation. The nation, in fact, is recognised as an absolute power, even above fundamental laws or the constitution,[130] and could theoretically turn into a despot. However, the very way in which the legislative concatenation is conceived prevents this from happening. The pronunciation of the nation, in order for it to exist as such and not as the dictate of a despotic majority, must follow certain syntactic rules which will always ensure the pursuance of the common interest through the expression of the general will. These rules, in other words, form the logical necessity of any positive law and represent the operative horizon of any political association. But what are these rules of law (understood as *droit*) standing above the law (understood as *loi*)? The French Declaration of 1789, its nature, its place in the constitutional framework, and the text of its articles, give us an enlightening answer.

First of all, it must be noted that the deputies of the *Assemblée nationale constituante* – who on the night of 4 August 1789 had abolished the feudal order in France, thus making a *tabula rasa* of privileges and paving the way for a new legal regime[131] – debated whether a universal declaration of rights should precede or follow a new constitution for France.[132] This was not a minor issue, because it demonstrates that the deputies, by discussing and drafting the Universal Declaration before any subsequent constitution, were pursuing two goals. Firstly, the Declaration was intended to be a 'new catechism' for the nation.[133] It was supposed to work as a kind of blueprint that would both inform the people about the foundations of the new French society and instruct them on how to 'think' about political power within the new socio-political setting. Secondly, the drafting of the Universal Declaration before the constitution implied that the rules established by the Universal Declaration had a peculiar nature. Being conceived and issued before any constitution, the Universal Declaration does not concern the substantive legal order but the theoretical premise of its existence.[134] As a consequence, the declaration is both a legal and a non-legal text. It is legal to the extent that it purports to establish the limits of every conceivable legal order by delineating their necessary syntax, but it is non-legal precisely to the extent that it functions as a logical and not a positive limit.[135] Here we can see the last normalising concatenation – after the English and American ones – that finally interlocks law, society, political power, and truth. The nature of the Declaration makes clear that this seminal document was intended to constitute the *programme* that would make possible the *expression* of the truth of the common good through a new *legal syntax*.

The French Declaration, therefore, is a text that is chiefly focused on law-making as a mechanism ideated for the self-managing of society. The French document sets forth a series of provisions regarding the nature of law and the rules of its production that have no direct equivalent in the English Bill of Rights and American Declaration (or, for that matter, with subsequent constitutional documents adopted in those countries). In this regard, the language and structure of the French Declaration help us to understand more clearly the role that generality, abstraction, equality, and freedom played in framing the constitutional discourse of modernity.

It must be noted that the Preamble performs an important discursive function that immediately differentiates the French from the American Declaration. Both Preambles mention natural rights, but while the American Declaration is founded upon natural rights and not concerned with their declension – their infringement is mentioned as a cause of discontent but they are neither delineated nor defined – the Preamble to the French Declaration, through its reference to natural rights, establishes a certain horizon to subsequent legal acts, a horizon of 'ideal right' that will be set out in the Declaration and actualised subsequently by the constitution and positive laws.[136] With this manoeuvre, the French Declaration performs an important operation: it creates a junction between the last remnants of natural law and positive law.[137] It establishes two concurring and mutually supporting ideas. On the one hand, by announcing the existence of certain 'natural, unalienable, and sacred rights of man' it identifies a category of individual entitlement that is not socially created but, rather, socially ingrained. It is no coincidence that there is only an anodyne reference to a metaphysical dimension ('under the auspices of the Supreme Being'). The notion of natural rights in the French Declaration is a fully secularised one: natural rights are the outcome of the choices of a society ruling itself rationally. They are something immanent in society and waiting to emerge from the complexity of its folds. On the other hand, as we will see in a moment, the Declaration makes these rights devoid of any substantive content as it creates a formal system that will allow for its production. The emerging picture is that of a matrix: ideal fundamental rights found society at its most essential level, but they acquire substance only when produced according to a certain logical framework and within its limits.

This matrix embodies a legal discourse that has embraced the paradigm of the norm as its core. Law as a norm becomes both a rule of judgement and a means of producing that rule.[138] Within this context the references to the nation in the Third Article, and that of the general will in the Sixth Article, represent together a crucial pillar as they make explicit the entirely secularised and socialised status of rights and law, and their normalising nature. All legislative decisions can be taken exclusively in the name of the nation where the whole of sovereignty resides (i.e. the nation is the source of all law). Legislation, however, can only be expressed as a general will, as the will that takes as its object the whole of the nation. What emerges is a self-referential autopoietic system: the positive legal field enables society to speak the truth about its own interests and to manage itself accordingly.[139] The relationship between right and law, between some overarching, foundational entitlements and their actualised articulation, is hence resolved as an instrumental relationship where only the new structuring syntax of law will allow the political society to properly make manifest those rights and duties – those norms – which govern its nature.[140] This is far more than a procedural approach to the somewhat mystical dimension of fundamental rights where formal guarantees ensure the abstract fairness of legislative outcome; this is almost a scientific process of chemical synthesis through which we gain access to the objective core of human nature so that society can manage itself according to that nature.

The mechanisms delineating the operational possibilities of the system are established by the subsequent articles of the Declaration. The phrasing of the First Article ('Men are born and remain free and equals in rights') indicates the structure of a revolutionary vision that is explicitly based on a conception of equality and freedom as fundamental entitlements that are made socially visible through legal articulation.[141] This is further confirmed by the wording of articles Four and Six of the Declaration.[142] Article Four defines freedom in a purely legal sense as the limits to liberty are determined exclusively by law; article Six, on the other hand, presents the right to equality as one connected with the existence of laws that are applicable to everyone without discrimination.

Equality and freedom are therefore constructed from a purely legal point of view rather than relying heavily on a metaphysical reference to the state of nature as designed by God. There is no reference to ancient liberties, nor to any historical status of equality as in the Anglo-American experience. Quite the contrary: equality and freedom are notions that will be determined entirely by law. It is therefore interesting to note that freedom has no positive definition. Liberty is, in fact, described mainly in negative terms – freedom is whatever law does not prohibit. As a consequence, law is always delimiting freedom as a void, as a space that is unknown to law itself but that law makes manifest. Equality, on the other hand, is specifically conceived as equality before the law. It is therefore a concept that has to be constructed exclusively from a legal point of view. Compared with the phraseology used in the Bill of Rights and the Declaration of Independence, equality and freedom are not conceived as two substantive, historically grounded concepts, but instead as two ideas that can be articulated only through law and can be construed as existing solely within the legal dimension.

To this end, the features of generality and abstraction are instrumental. A very small parenthetical phrase clarifies their role in the system outlined by the Declaration. In article Six it is said that law must be 'the same for all'. This seems to mean that laws should be not only general (i.e. address all individuals or, as Rousseau suggested, address the population as a single body) but also abstract (with regard to the kind of action they are called to regulate).[143] Only through these qualities does it seem possible to build a system that produces legal equality because it treats individuals as undifferentiated subjects and, as a consequence, ensures freedom as defined in article Four.

In view of the preceding analysis, we can see how political power eschews to the largest extent the logic of sovereignty to embrace that of normalisation, as its actions will always be framed by the four key features of generality, abstraction, equality, and freedom. In other words, we have a system that, no matter what kind of decisions it will allow, will always have all its subjects acting according to the rule of law.[144] By setting forth the contours of a new syntax of law, the French Declaration imposes upon everyone, even upon the sovereign power, the logic of a legal system that embraces all individuals, notwithstanding their social differences. It delineates a structure where equality before the law is inherently connected with the generality and abstraction of rules, and where freedom is therefore protected and yet legally defined.

In the French Declaration, the shift of the legal discourse towards normalisation is delineated in its clearest theoretical form. Again, similarly to the English and American experiences, we can appreciate the double direction of normalisation understood as normalisation *strictu sensu* and normation. Legitimate political power emerges as the interest of the whole of society is made visible thanks to the new syntax of law. At the same time, legitimate political power cannot escape the limits of the language of law now deeply intertwined with the logic of the norm. Hence, the norm replaces the command as the legal paradigm governing society. Law, understood in such a normalising sense, is both the expression of power and a constraint on its reach. The new syntax of law represents the form through which power is supposed to constitute its very being.

The normalising constitutional horizon of modernity

The analysis of the three revolutions that have established the constitutional horizon of modernity illuminates how the modern legal discourse progressively shifted towards the logic of normalisation. While in the second chapter we explored the emergence of a new normalising legal syntax as a source of political legitimation, in the present chapter we have studied how the new legal syntax emerged in the restructuring of the relationship between political legitimation and its institutional manifestation. More precisely, once it was established that the truth of human society was not to be found in sacred books and heavenly plans but in the very interest and good of society itself, the question was to ideate a legal system that would allow the truth about society to emerge and to be actualised through an institutional system. This almost necessarily imposed the abandonment of constitutional settlements that granted power to a few individuals who could decide on their own what the common good required and the conceptualisation of frameworks that would be able to see the truth of society as a whole beyond the particularistic egoism of single individuals. We have seen how each revolution represented a step away the logic of sovereignty and towards constitutional arrangements embodying the logic of normality, each contributing to the building of a system that not only limits power under the paradigm of the norm but, most importantly, makes power manifest through the paradigm of the norm. These passages addressed the problem of government at once ontologically (what should a government be?), functionally (how should a government operate?), and theoretically (what principles should a government abide by?).

In England, the constitutional crisis of the seventeenth century was resolved by rejecting monarchy as a system capable of protecting the common good of the people while establishing the Parliament as a collective *institution* that would almost naturalistically *reflect* in its decisions the truth about the common good of the people because of its *representative* structure. In the USA, the failures of the British system pointed towards an understanding of the government as a *process*, that would *produce* the truth about the common good of the people thought the *separation of powers* and *checks and balances*. Finally, in France, we see the most radical and dramatic of the revolutions prompted by the need to subvert the old *ancien régime* and the socio-legal hierarchies of absolutism. In that case, government is set up as a *programme* that would *express* the truth about the common good of the people through a new *legal syntax*. The French Revolution, therefore, more clearly than the English and American examples, demonstrates how the new normalising vision of law is crucial in the production of societal rules. With it, we can see at its clearest how a mode of law rooted in the paradigm of the norm in modern times stands inextricably interlocked with power as its only vehicle of existence.

This is not to say that the logic of sovereignty fades away completely from history. As it happens, the problem of sovereign power as something that can ultimately go beyond the boundary of the agreed norm is still very much present in our day, and its persistence tells us that the orders of sovereignty and normality stand in an uneasy and unresolved relationship. Nonetheless, is difficult to deny that sovereign power, within the modern legal discourse, is conceived akin to a mythical sleeping dragon, quiet and hidden until the sound and fury of the world awakens it. In our everyday life we are safely surrounded by the humdrum of legal normality. And its order is founded on a specific conception of law – law as a vehicle that is both a limit to power and the sole means to bring legitimate power into existence – which the English, American, and French revolutionaries, through their disparate efforts and sometimes conflicting visions of the world, have brought into light within the short span of less than two hundred years.

4

The Normalising Complex and the Challenges of Virtualisation

Introduction

In the previous two chapters I have offered a genealogical analysis of modern law, exploring its role as a *sui generis* apparatus of subjectivation. On the basis of my reading, modern law emerges as an apparatus of subjectivation focused on the political truth of the subject, understood both as an individual and as a member of society. More precisely, modern law appears as a discourse that establishes rules of formation that concern, at the same time, the knowledge of the political truth of the subject and the production of said political truth. On the one hand, modern law makes possible the recognition of a truth that is supposed to be resident in the materiality of the life interests of the subject, while, on the other, it stipulates the structure through which the subject can properly think and articulate said truth. As Foucault intimated, there is no hierarchical or causal relationship between knowledge and truth; rather, they are the two sides of the same coin: we know truth and, at the same time, we make true knowledge through the same set of rules of formation.[1] Modern law, therefore, functions as a machine that links truth and knowledge in a mutually supporting relationship through a fundamental syntax imbued with the paradigm of the norm. Having completed our genealogical analysis, we can now move forward in our study, and examine modern law within the broader context of normalising dynamics of power and the changing contours of our societies. To this end, I will proceed as follows.

First, I will offer a more detailed account of the generative syntax of modern law by showing its normalising effects of subjectivation. Modern law thus transpires as a discourse that inscribes the subject within a scheme of intelligibility which is informed by the logic of normality while, at the same time, it takes the subject as the main mover and propagator of said scheme. The result of such dynamics is a universalisation of the legal subject that transforms the individual into a normalised entity through the immediacy of an illocutionary act.

Second, I will examine the peculiar relationship between the discourse of modern law and others apparatuses of subjectivation (both disciplinary and governmental). In that perspective, I claim that modern law has two main functions: it performs an original act of normalisation by codifying the subject as the universal legal subject, and it establishes the general field or environment of power by legitimising and co-ordinating all other localised and specialised normalising apparatuses. Accordingly, I propose that modern law and discipline/governmentality circumscribe the subject within a self-supporting normalising concatenation. On the one hand, modern law makes possible the workings of discipline/governmentality by prohibiting social divisions and creating universal subjects upon which biopolitical strategies can be efficiently enforced. On the other, discipline/governmentality constantly recodify the subject in a standardised fashion, thus concretely producing a normalised population which can be reflected in the universality of law.

Third, given the landscape I have outlined, I examine the challenges that modern law is facing in what has been recognised as the contemporary biopolitical passage from the regime of normalisation (based on universal standards and generalised norms of behaviour) to that control (based on an individualising paradigm that focuses on the specific characteristics of each single person). More precisely, I will suggest that the contemporary restructuring of social ties is affecting of our changing conception of the self. Building on Bauman's description of our times as a 'liquid modernity', my study indicates that we are moving towards an understanding of the individual as a 'virtual' entity, which is at odds with the normalising paradigm that informs modern law. This is a dynamic, I contend, that began with normalisation's inherent allusion to Otherness as what lies beyond the norms, and that is supported by the logic of the syntax of modern law. Paradoxically, that Otherness has started to progressively erode the image of commonality upon which universalistic claims of liberal legalism rest – a phenomenon accelerated by the rise of control society.

Finally, I posit that the emergence of control societies, linked as they are to a new virtual understanding of the individual, has brought us to the absolute limit of the normalising complex. This vision of the subject as a virtual entity indicates a growing awareness of the presence of an existential uniqueness, or Otherness, in everyone's life that challenges the attempts at conceiving the social body in terms of normality. This has important implications for our current legal system which, as I have intimated, developed genealogically in relation to the dynamics of normalisation. The nature and scope of these implications, together with their potential effects on the future of our legal discourse, will then be addressed separately in the conclusions.

The illocutionary effect of modern law: the creation of the universal subject

It is probably true that, in the modern age, we 'live in and by the law'.[2] Compared with previous historical phases, modernity is certainly characterised by an unprecedented expansion of the reach of law, its presence and force extended over a number of fields as never before. Modern law, however, is not, quite mythically, a 'brooding presence in the sky',[3] as its ideal ubiquity is counterbalanced by law's self-imposed limitations, guaranteeing individuals a rather rigid sphere of independence from external influence. Our actions, therefore, are not just restrained or dictated by law, but law also empowers individuals with a certain degree of autonomy vis-à-vis the interference of other individuals, and private and public entities. This platitudinous picture of modern law, which, as anyone can see, stands at the basis of the common idea of the modern legal phenomenon, becomes quite interesting when seen through the lens of the Foucauldian theory of power. As we have already observed, Foucault rejected a vision of the relationship between power and freedom as a zero-sum game; instead he interpreted their bond as coextensive, creating the general framework for all potential actions.[4] Seen in this perspective, modern law appears as the idealisation of the Foucauldian conception of power: a framing discourse that makes possible the field of action of the subject by defining, articulating and ultimately protecting a particular regime of freedom.

So far, we have reconstructed the modern legal discourse genealogically, demonstrating that it is characterised by a specific syntax which is rooted in the paradigm of the norm. We will turn now to a more detailed conceptual analysis of the functioning of the syntax of modern law in order to examine what kind of regime of power/freedom it engenders, and delineate its functional possibilities. To this end, we will explore the logical relationship between its core tenets (generality, abstraction, equality, freedom), with the view of unearthing its normalising effects.

The (already mentioned) distinction Hayek makes between commands and laws appears particularly useful for this task because it exemplifies the general difference between a legal system based on the paradigm of commands and one based on the paradigm of the norm.[5] Commands (even general commands) apply to a single occurrence that is contingent in nature. In general, when one issues a command the objective is to transform reality 'right there' and 'right now' and not to provide a framework for future action.[6] The latter is law's primary goal. We know that when a law sets forth a provision it never refers to an actual scenario. Instead, a legal provision tries, in principle, to regulate a potentially infinite number of cases for a potentially indeterminate period of time. In order to identify such a set of cases, law needs to define their common elements.

Therefore, according to Hayek, modern law's intrinsic function is to protect personal freedom, to ensure that a sphere of liberty where the individual could not be unduly coerced is created and preserved.[7] General and abstract laws, that are mindful of and respect the right to equality before the law, have as their main goal the creation of a space of liberty that would allow the person to lead her life and pursue her interests without being subjected to someone else's will. But how does the syntax of modern law ensure this ideal result? In which way does law as norm frame subjectivity differently from law as commands? What is the precise logical relationship between generality, abstraction, equality, and freedom?

In the first place, we need to distinguish between the levels of applications of these tenets. Generality and abstraction represent the theoretical preconditions of modern law while legal equality and freedom represent its material conditions. Generality and abstraction identify the theoretical relationship between law and its object: they require that law considers its object as a non-singular entity; law, in other words, must relate to its object through universal categories of individuality (generality) and action (abstraction). Legal equality and freedom, on the other hand, are the material conditions determined by the preconditions of generality and abstraction. Once law regulates actions and individuals in a general and abstract fashion, subjects will be equal and free before the law, as there will be no discrimination on the basis of a personal status (equality) and no arbitrary interference in singular conducts (freedom). Once we have clear the two different level of application of the four tenets, it is easy to see a correspondence between generality and equality, on the one hand, and abstraction and freedom on the other. The first dyad delimits the topological field of law, while the second pertains to its temporal field.

The case for a correspondence between equality and generality in law seems pretty straightforward, but it begins with a puzzle: how can law be truly general? When are people treated equally? In reality, very few laws can be absolutely general, and these few laws normally pertain to fundamental human rights. More specific laws are, on the other hand, what forms the majority of rules of any legal system. Laws are specific in this sense because they refer to a special category of persons or actions (e.g. rules of conduct for police officers or regulations of financial transactions). To this extent, different groups of people are always treated differently and laws incessantly and purposefully discriminate between different situations. A curious dilemma, therefore, may be found in any legal system that adopts laws of general application and embraces the principle of equality before the law: what does it mean to adopt one general law (and therefore embrace the principle of legal equality) if laws normally apply to a specific group of individuals or actions, negating by this mere fact both their general application and the equality of all before law's dispositions?

The solution to this apparent paradox is simple. To say that a legal provision is general is to say that it has to be applied to the general public of legal subjects. This means that whosoever (or whatever) falls within the conditions set forth by a certain provision will be subject to that provision regardless of her individual specificity. The feature of generality, in other words, is meant to identify the potential set of people that will be subject to a given legal disposition. What makes a law general and what defines generality in law, therefore, is a potentiality, or the possibility, that the law could be applied to all individuals indiscriminately. From an organisational point of view, it makes perfect sense to limit and specify the field of application of legal provisions and apply them only to the restricted group of individuals that embodies the characteristics set forth by the law. Law does not cease to be general for this reason only.

On the contrary, law is general exactly because there is the distinct theoretical possibility that anyone within the population could be part of the group for which some provisions apply and others do not. It should be clear, then, that a specific condition must be present to make effective any claim of generality in law. This condition resides in the possibility that any individual could, at least in principle, migrate from one 'legal group' to another. Only when an individual can move among the different legal categories in which community is divided can a claim of the generality of law be made, as the provision is theoretically applied to the nameless 'potential subject' of law. Such a condition is that of equality. Legal equality, therefore, should be understood in this perspective. It does not entail an actual equality before all laws, but, more subtly, the equal potentiality of all of being subject to all laws. The principle of generality in law therefore delimits the absolute *field of application* of all laws, its topological space, as it inscribes all society's members within the potential scope of laws.

Freedom and abstraction, on the other hand, represent a second dyad in the structure of modern law. The central role of the right to freedom in modern legal history is undeniable, and it has already been pointed out that some authors interpret the entire history of liberal democracy in terms of a struggle for freedom.[8] Curiously enough, though, when it comes to its definition, no document or legal text seems able to offer a satisfactory account of it, and most modern constitutions enumerate a series of rights correlated with the right to freedom such as rights that purport to manifest a certain particular aspect of freedom (freedom of speech, of movement, of religion, etc.), avoiding any specific, substantive, characterisation.[9]

Why is this, and, most importantly, what does this imply for the modern legal discourse? The answers to these questions are interlinked and show the importance that abstraction has in the modern legal system. No definition of freedom can be given, because the substantive content of freedom must be found within the legal system, through the complex interactions between laws, principles, and statues. *Legal* liberty, in very simple terms, is the faculty of doing whatever is not prohibited by laws. A complete definition of freedom within the boundaries of a legal system, therefore, will perfectly coincide with the entire legal system itself because it is the whole intertwining of laws that defines what one can or cannot do, which can otherwise be described as one's sphere of freedom. As to what this implies, that is an altogether more complicated matter. What could be the significance of a freedom that is to be found, on a case by case basis, in the depths and contradictions of an entire legal system? What is the meaning of the claim to freedom that all liberal democracies purport to possess, if this freedom changes dramatically from system to system, from year to year? In other words: what is the invariant function of freedom under the rule of law? And more importantly: how are freedom and abstraction connected?

Going back to the distinction Hayek makes between commands and laws, we will remember that modern law's primary function is to regulate a potentially infinite number of cases for a potentially indeterminate period of time. We have already seen how generality/equality addresses the problem of the infinite number of cases. Abstraction/freedom, on the other hand, addresses the temporal side of law. Under the logic of modern law, a fact to be regulated is identified in legal terms only if law considers it in abstraction from all its correlative factual incidents, which law itself does not include as relevant in its dispositions. Referring to an abstract conduct, law acquires the quality of being infinitely repeatable, its fixed provisions seamlessly and ceaselessly regulating reality. Law refutes the contingencies of command because its main goal is to extend its reach beyond the paralysing, unrepeatable conditions of each single occurrence. Given these premises, we can directly address the main question: what is the structural relationship in law between abstraction and freedom?

It seems clear that abstraction generates a kind of freedom that liberates the individual from a situation where unfathomable, arbitrary, and erratic commands reign unchecked. It creates a safe space of independent action for the individual while simultaneously submitting her to the continuous gaze of authority.[10] When the first article of the French Declaration of 1789 solemnly stated that men are born and remain free in rights a powerful logical principle emerged: men will be freed from the contingency of decision to the extent they will be subject to the abstract, all-encompassing, seamless web of law. Freedom and abstraction, in other words, determine the *mode of action* of law, which, detached from the contingency of a personal command, will be applied countless times following a predetermined path.

Indeed, generality and equality create a legal subject that can move within the whole field of legal provision, while at the same time freedom and abstraction unfetter the person from the yoke of personal, contingent orders. However, this new dimension of freedom also has the effect of enveloping all individuals within the reach of law, regulating a significant part of their lives to an unprecedented extent and with unprecedented efficiency. Freedom is therefore also linked with a particular kind of 'unfreedom' that tends to homogenise all subjects within its orbit and limit the forms and intensity of their interpersonal relationships. The individual, in other words, is free to the extent that she is continuously subject to the gaze of law and to its regulating function.

The temporal and topological dynamics just described represent what we could call the 'framing effect' of modern law, which surrounds all potential acts of the subject within a very peculiar grid of power/freedom. The syntax of modern law also produces what we could call 'transformative effects', affecting subjectivity from the point of identity. Simply stated, while under the logic of sovereignty the identity of the subject was fixed to a certain status which determined her spectrum of life possibilities, in modern law the subject experiences power and freedom as an unspecified legal subject, an interchangeable and independent single entity. Also in this case we can see that the core features of the syntax of modern law work in dyads as logical operators.

The first dyad is formed by abstraction and equality, and concerns the performative side of subjectivity. A subject whose actions are considered in the abstract and judged in an equal fashion is indeed a subject faced with a specific framework of power that she can navigate in order to construct her own freedom. Such a framework, however, comes into existence at the cost of the dampening of individual subjectivity, of removing her actions from the specificity of her personhood. The result of such dynamics is that the subject of modern law is a *flat* subject. Seen through the prism of law, no gesture properly reflects the individuality of its concrete author; the subject of law acts only insofar as her gesture is the sanctioned gesture of the idealised subject of law.

While the dyad abstraction/equality transforms the subject into a flat entity, the dyad generality/freedom produces a different outcome, as it allows the subject to develop her own life plan. As a general subject, she is not any more under the yoke of a predetermined legal status and she has before her a seemingly infinite set of life choices which are articulated through her legal freedom. Provided that she moves within the limits provided by law, nothing, in principle, can stop her from autonomously deciding her existential path. In this perspective the subject of modern law is a *loose* subject among other loose subjects, a single independent discrete entity whose choices, however, are constantly channelled by the legal framework.

The syntax of modern law therefore produces framing and transformative effects that map human subjectivity within a grid of intelligibility elaborated in accordance with the paradigm of the norm. The primary and most important impact of modern law on the subject therefore is simply this: her construction through norms as a universal subject. This is a quite unsurprising conclusion. The universalistic claims of the modern legal discourse are commonplace. My hope, nonetheless, is to have shown how these claims are genealogically and logically informed by the paradigm of the norm. My analysis intimates that all the major dimensions of human experience – time, space, action, identity – are recast through the use of norms in a universalistic mould that is supposedly common to every subject and makes every subject common, closely following the double line of normalisation *strictu sensu* and normation that is typical of the normalising regime.

If we compare the system of personal domination that was typical of the Middle Ages with legal systems based on equality and generality, freedom, and abstraction, the latter seem *prima facie* liberating, upholding an inviolable personal autonomy of the subject as such. Upon closer inspection, however, it is possible to appreciate that medieval personal domination, which was typical of the Middle Ages and was so oppressive in its manifestations, existed mostly in a contingent, intermittent, episodic, and casual fashion. The presence of law in the hands of a few powerful individuals was activated only on the occasions when those powerful individuals actually commanded something of the common man. The rest of the time, law simply dissolved in the background. With modern legal systems the situation is almost the reverse. The intensity of the manifestation of law has decreased – the limits to the power of the authorities are posited in advance and cannot be surpassed, and there is no longer any absolute sovereign – but its presence is now almost endless and all-encompassing. Law never leaves the individual alone, as its manifestation is not linked with the contingent will of a powerful subject but is connected with an impersonal, perpetually present, will.

It is in this perspective, given the preceding discussions on generality, abstraction, equality, and freedom, that we can appreciate the logic of normality embedded within this new syntax of law. Law is no longer enacted in the name of the sovereign and his commands but instead it indicates the set of rules rationally developed out of certain basic norms. Modern law appears as a system of interconnected regularities that channels the fluxes of power, and organises society and human conduct. Law is no longer the simple expression of the will of the single powerful individual, and nor does it possess the simple repressive effect which is generally associated with a command theory of law.[11] Quite the contrary: modern law purposively uses individuals' own autonomy to favour certain societal patterns over others. Being at everyone's disposal, law displays a capillary nature that mimics the effect of internalisation typical of normalisation: it uses each single person to expand its dominion; the more its rules are used by people, the more society is enmeshed with its discourse, permeated by its logic.

The universalising impact on subjectivity produced by modern law literally provides the absolute co-ordinates outside of which human life cannot be conceived, as it radically interlocks subjectivity with an ideally inescapable specific grid of power/freedom. It must be underlined, however, that this operation is performed in a purely discursive dimension. What we have examined so far is purely the illocutionary impact of law on subjectivity. As such, modern law has clear limitations because by and in itself it cannot change the materiality of subjectivity. The specific syntax we have explored so far works specifically at an ideological level.[12] The universal subject constructed through norms, in other words, is not necessarily reflected in the material subjectivity of individuals and populations. However, modern forms of power operate on individuals and populations by manipulating their living bodies through disciplinary and governmental apparatuses (prison, army, factory, school, hospital, etc.). The relationship between these apparatuses and the apparatus represented by law has been the focal point for all those scholars who have endorsed in one form or other the so-called expulsion thesis. We are now in a position to address this matter directly and to show that modern law, *pace* the supporters of the expulsion thesis, is not a discourse that is incompatible with discipline and governmentality, but is actually part of a broader normalising complex.

Law and other apparatuses: the normalising complex

We have already seen how Golder and Fitzpatrick and Tadros respectively suggested a way out of the expulsion thesis by proposing that modern law is not incompatible with biopolitical forms of power, but rather works alongside them. While I agree with their general intuition, I have criticised their solutions, arguing that their lack of a genealogical approach to the discourse of modern law prevented them from seeing law as an apparatus of subjectivation *sui generis* and thus from offering a convincing explanation of the relationship between law and other apparatuses of discipline/governmentality.[13] Now that I have described the internal workings of the discourse of modern law, I can explore the effect that such peculiar discourse produced on society as a whole in relation with other apparatuses.

Briefly put, my argument is that the legal normalisation of the individual established a functional concatenation with the subjectivating normalising apparatuses represented by disciplines and governmentality. Legal distinctions between individuals being mostly eliminated, few obstacles remained to the enveloping application of a normalising discourse to the entire social body. Under the domain of modern law, the whole population came to be composed of the same set of subjects that could be moulded and managed in accordance with the rationality of the sciences and technologies.

More specifically, I would argue that the shift towards the norm in the legal discourse had two main effects in relation to non-legal discourses and practices. In the first place, law inscribes the subject into a totalising panoptical horizon where a potentially infinite number of discourses and apparatuses can penetrate human life to an unprecedented extent. In the second place, law operates as a 'transmission belt' among different apparatuses, translating the subject from one apparatus to the next.

With regard to the first point, it is important to notice that the normalising effect of modern law on the legal subject and on power formations in general creates a specific social environment whereby social differentiations are (in principle) erased and there is an equivalency between individuals. This transformation, however, does not mean that the new normalised subject is absolutely protected from power; quite the contrary, the universalisation of the subject opens its life to the scrutiny of competing discourses of knowledge and apparatuses of power. In theory, modern law can regulate any aspect of social life, and in fact, compared with earlier legal systems, the aspects of human life that have come under the scrutiny of legal provisions have increased immensely, englobing the subject since the moment of her birth in an encompassing web of legal provisions that monitor and regulate her existence.[14] Law, however, is significantly ignorant about what is to be done with human life and it must look for detailed rules of management somewhere else. The universalisation of the subject, therefore, conjures the proliferation of an endless array of discourses and practices that focus on specific dimensions of subjectivity and whose intervention is possible only within the limits of the legal discourse. Law, in other words, enables power to surround and penetrate human life by sanctioning the multiplication of planes of visibility of the subject and authorising the operations of numerous and diverse apparatuses of discipline and governmentality. In addition, law, being the discourse of power that overdetermines all other power discourses, expands coextensively with those, penetrating in the individual and society as deeply as those practices that it legitimises. If in the biopolitical age human life becomes a political problem that must be addressed by scientific means, then law is both the master key that has opened life to the gaze of scientific discourses and the supplement of power that through these discourses insinuates itself into life.

Disciplines and governmentality, as a consequence, had the opportunity to function with a newly discovered and stronger intensity that was increasingly focused on the individual as their norms were integrated into the legal discourse. Even today, when criminal courts refrain from pronouncing a judgment pertaining to a mentally disabled person, when social services are assessing the quality of children's care, when decisions of life and death are delegated to medical personnel, when one's technical knowledge is measured according to a public qualification, such actions are certainly taken following legal rules, but law itself, by referring to the rational paradigm of a scientific discourse, is actually enforcing the normalising gaze of a very specific apparatus of power/knowledge. The universal subject of law, so different from the colourful, yet shackled, medieval legal subject,[15] was, in effect, the pellucid object that disciplinary and governmental apparatuses swiftly scanned with their inquiring gaze and directed with their scientific rules.

Modern law not only inscribes human life into a totalising panoptical dimension, but also participates in the machinations of discipline and governmentality in a more concrete way by operating as a kind of conveyor system between normalising apparatuses. In this sense, it can be said that modern law, by normalising the subject and power, adopted an orchestrating role, 'intervening in the social construction and government of the modern subject'.[16] We have seen how law creates the general environment of power by offering a set of rules that both produce and tame power. From this point of view, modern law represents the matrix of power. No power relationship in modern society can exist without establishing itself within the contours dictated by law. Positively, every discourse in normalising societies ultimately needs to be founded in law if it wants to be backed by its authority and forcibly overcome competing claims. Negatively, no discourse can openly operate in contrast with the standing legal order without incurring the sanctions of the legal regime itself. 'Illegal' discourses can exist only at great cost or temporarily: either they take place clandestinely, avoiding the gaze of the legal system, or they attempt to legitimise themselves by changing the legal regime from the inside, accessing legal institutions and making use of legal rules. This is not to say that every discourse in modern society must *at all times* be legitimised by law. Some discourses can well exist without entering into contact with the legal dimension (it is easy to imagine an aesthetic ideology that takes hold of collective imaginary without recourse to legal means and without legal consequences). The reach of these discourses and their connected apparatuses, however, will necessarily be limited: as they will rely exclusively on their own persuasive force for propagation, they will face a continuous struggle to impose their authority.

Disciplines and governmentality, therefore, aspire to legitimise themselves with the authority of law and to make use of its force. The other side of such attachment, however, is that law is called to establish the performative limits of every discourse or practice that aims at imposing its logic on human life. Law allows or prohibits the actions of knowledgeable subjects and regulates the sphere of influence of each apparatus: presiding over the boundaries of every discourse, it is law that assigns the subject to one or the other, sanctioning the reach of one discourse vis-à-vis the other. Law bridges the gaps between discourses and distances the operation of different fields of knowledge so as to ensure, to the largest extent possible, the absence of conflicts and the smooth co-operation of various systems; it literally operates as a machine of translation in the double sense that by providing a common language of power it puts into communication the various aspects of subjectivity made visible by knowledge discourses and moves the subject from one apparatus to the next, overseeing all the permutations and transformation that the subject will experience in life.[17]

Here we can address directly the crux of the expulsion thesis that has beleaguered Foucauldian studies (or at least the acceptance of Foucauldian studies) for too long. Borrowing a concept from Science and Technology Studies (STS), and from Sheila Jasanoff in particular, I would intimate neither that law has been colonised by disciplines and governmentality nor that it is impermeable against their influence, but rather that the two are linked by a dynamic of co-production. In the words of Jasanoff:

> co-production is shorthand for the proposition that the ways in which we know and represent the world (both nature and society) are inseparable from the ways in which we choose to live in it. Knowledge and its material embodiments are at once products of social work and constitutive of forms of social life; society cannot function without knowledge any more than knowledge can exist without appropriate social supports. Scientific knowledge, in particular, is not a transcendent mirror of reality. It both embeds and is embedded in social practices, identities, norms, conventions, discourses, instruments and institutions – in short, in all the building blocks of what we term the *social*.[18]

Our further step in our analysis makes clear how much law and other discourses of power/knowledge are interlocked in such a relationship. I have claimed several times that law represents the overarching discourse of power in modern societies, but I have also stressed that specific sub-discourses of power/knowledge are constantly carving their own sphere of competence and establishing themselves as machines of truth in circumscribed fields.[19] In in these cases, the gravitational centre of authority is relocated as law sanctions the existence of a discourse which claims the knowledge of a truth which was previously invisible to law. When this happens, law is transformed into a framing tool which provides the structure of the intervening discourse by setting both (sometimes fluid) spheres of competence and mechanisms of compensation between different discourses.[20] At the same time, law also recedes into the background, offering deference to a new discourse of knowledge with rules of formation different from the legal ones and whose own authority deeply affects the legal discourse.[21]

As several authors in the field of STS have convincingly argued, the representation of the natural world by scientific discourses is a way of intervening in it.[22] As a consequence, law's legitimation of scientific discourses allows sciences to produce a reframing of the human life which necessarily feeds back on the very object that law is supposed to regulate, causing a local adaptation of law itself to the new environment within which it is situated in a self-feeding loop.[23] The result of this interaction is precisely a complex dynamic of co-production – radically distant from the relationship between law and sciences as a zero-sum game as implicitly portrayed by the expulsion thesis – where law and other discourses mutually influence each other while reshaping the subject and the social environment.[24][25] Their concatenation, multiplying the layers of meaning in human life, signifies a fuller encirclement of subjectivity and yields a thicker environmental space for power than the one provided solely by law.[26]

My investigation thus far has shown how law historically developed as part and parcel of a distinctive normalising *complex*. The legal normalisation of the individual granted her a sphere of autonomy unexperienced in precedent legal orders while embedding her within the discourse of power to a much larger extent than before. Recognising a typical Foucauldian paradox, we could say that the person, transformed into the legal subject, fell irredeemably into the seamless web of a normalising dynamic precisely because she took active part in it through the means of law. The single person, being recognised as the generative unit of the social order, was at the same time perpetually subject to the gaze of power as no particular status, no peculiar situation, could subtract her from its grasp. Law in normalising societies, far from losing importance, was instrumental in this mechanism. It potentially enveloped all societal phenomena, thus enabling a ceaseless normalising process. The individual who contributed to the creation of law was also subject to a wide range of power discourses that minutely shaped her identity and granted her the mark of normality.

The illocutionary act of subjective legal normalisation intrinsic to the modern syntax of law – that is, the creation of the normal legal subject – was thus 'plugged into' normalising *dispositifs* that aimed at creating a normalised concrete subject. The result was a 'swing-by' effect whereby the subject was caught in a normalising circuit: the individual is normalised through a legal universalisation which opens up the gates to additional normalising apparatuses operating on the subject. Normalising apparatuses, on the other hand, reshape the individual so as to provide the legal regime with docile subjects. In modern societies, therefore, the subject is inscribed within a totalising assemblage of capture formed by these two dimensions as they create a concatenation that circularly enables the normalisation of the human being and accounts for its own legitimation. Modern law and biopolitical strategies of normalisation work symbiotically, and law itself functions as a normalising apparatus, insofar as practices of normalisation are capable of creating a seemingly homogeneous social body upon which the discourse of law can be in a position to legitimately inscribe the universalism of the modern legal subject. To the extent that modern law presumes and produces the existence of a universal legal subject, its functioning is made possible by the normalising recodification of the social body through disciplinary and governmental practices.

A brief reference to the nature of nationalist ideologies might be useful in order to clarify my argument. Nationalism is commonly recognised as one of the pillars upon which the early modern state developed, as it offered to the post-*ancién regime* society a new ideological centre upon which to build the new identity of the citizen once the status-based order had disappeared.[27] It also served, broadly speaking, as a legitimating gravitational field for sovereignty. As Habermas also recalls,[28] laws, at least at the beginning of the liberal project, could not be relied upon solely on the basis of a bond of communicative rationality, but needed a more sanguine, even mystical foundation. It is well-known, however, that the idea of the nation has hardly any substantive connection with historical consistency or ethnic purity (two of the most common tropes in nationalist thought).[29] On the contrary, it is a socially constructed notion that was inculcated in the population mainly through public education and propaganda.[30] Given these premises it is easy to see how nationalism was the projection at a politico-ideological level of the normalising ideal and provides a perfect example of how the normalising continuum worked. Does not nationalism, which basically equates the state with the supposedly homogeneous and original community of the nation, legitimate the participation of the individual in the sovereign dimension of power on the basis of her introjection of a 'normal' national identity which is created through the accurate workings of the normalising complex ('Of course you are a full citizen, but only insofar as you share the nation's language, culture, tradition, etc. . . . only insofar as you are part of the socially "normal" group of individuals within the country')? On the other hand, were not disciplinary and governmental apparatuses legitimised in the application of their normalising tactics by the sovereign power of national parliaments and governments?

It is hoped that at this point I have offered to the reader an original interpretation of modern law that challenges more classical liberal readings and avoids the expulsion thesis trap. Whereas the liberal narrative sees modern law as an instrument that allowed the affirmation of individual freedom, I have pointed out that law should be understood in a more historically situated way and that its mechanisms can be fully comprehended only if contextualised within a broader biopolitical dynamic. Following this line of thought, I claimed that law worked as part of a normalising concatenation. Law, in other words, had 'traction' not simply because it had an intrinsic communicative force but also because it enabled a recodification of the individual within discrete commonalities sharing substantive common traits. In this context, modern law worked as a system that co-ordinated and regulated societal functions along the lines of a self-legitimating normalising continuum.

Compared with the liberal canon, my analysis might offer some fruitful insights with regard to the current problems of law. Whereas liberals struggle in identifying the nature of law's contemporary difficulties because of their ahistorical understanding of law, I would recast these difficulties in the light of a shifting biopolitical correspondence. I have in fact argued that modern law and its related ideas (universal rights, democracy, constitutionalism, etc.) developed mainly in conjunction with normalising societies founded upon the concept of the norm. But what happens to our society if the normalising regime crumbles, if the very concept of norm withers away? How can law and democracy as we know them adapt? How can mutual recognition survive? These are indeed pivotal questions. Before I address them and investigate them in the context of the future of our law and society, I have to establish a case that normalising societies are in fact dissolving, and identify what paradigm is slowly supplanting that of the norm. To this task I now turn.

Liquid modernity and the biopolitics of control: a tale of virtualisation

I have so far evaluated the role and function of modern law within the contours of the normalising dynamics. I have claimed that modern law was part of a normalising complex insofar as it was concatenated with practices of subjectivation that disciplined the individual and the population as a whole. Does this picture grasp the true nature of our contemporary socio-legal situation?

It seems that, from the point of view of the structure of law, little has changed. My description attempted to provide a general, yet accurate picture of the modern legal dimension. On the other hand, can we take normalising societies as a satisfying description of our contemporary times? Is it correct to argue that nowadays society and the individual are framed by a normalising discourse? This question, which has an important value in itself, also carries a fundamental impact in relation to law. It has been an integral part of my thesis that law must be read within the context of a broader biopolitical discourse. As a consequence, the identification of a contemporary biopolitical shift from the discourse of normalisation to another regime will necessarily be very significant for law and therefore must be scrutinised closely. In the remainder of the present chapter, I will try to offer a description of the current predominant biopolitical discourse, with the aim of analysing law's mutation within its context in the following chapter.

Zygmunt Bauman provides a fascinating – yet dismal – account of our contemporary times through the metaphor of liquidity. Bauman opposes 'solid' and 'liquid' societal forms. Drawing from physics, Bauman points out that 'solid' forms are characterised by a static structure that is stable in time and in principle resistant to external forces, whereas 'fluid' forms are defined by an absence of fixed structure as they present an ever-changing configuration that adapts to external conditions but, at the same time, is able to penetrate into the smallest spaces. While solids tend to erase the variant of time and are defined by the space they occupy – their structure being the same at two different moments – liquids are almost exclusively identifiable by their temporal frame, as the shape of the space they occupy changes constantly.[31] Solid and liquid societal forms are therefore defined by opposing qualities: heavy versus light; condensed versus capillary; systemic versus network-like.[32]

Solid and liquid forms are both modern. But while the first represented a recasting of old traditional structures (e.g. the estates, the corporations) into an improved, more efficient, version of solidity, the latter mark a new stage in the process of modernisation, a final dissolution of previous forms.[33] Namely, the difference between solid and liquid modernity rests in the collapse of the modern illusion of a *telos* in human progress and in the deregulation and privatisation of the modernising tasks and duties.[34]

This has led to an unprecedented process of individualisation, which Bauman does not see as straightforwardly liberating, but as a problematic strategic situation that leaves the subject open to a challenging and unsettling social complexity. Borrowing a phrase from Ulrich Beck, he suggests that 'how one lives becomes a biographical solution to systemic contradictions'.[35] Bauman's argument is that the modern state has proclaimed and established a *de jure* (legal) autonomy of the individual which does not correspond to a *de facto* (factual) autonomy. This has led to a gradual corrosion of communal ethical bonds and hence to a melting of world views and an increasing normative incommunicability among subjects.[36] As a consequence, 'a gap is growing between individuality as fate and individuality as the practical and realistic capacity for self-assertion ... Bridging this gap is, most crucially, *not* part of that capacity.'[37]

Facing a rapidly changing social environment, the individual has at her disposal an almost infinite selection of living chances, but such freedom to be anybody (which anyway has to confront the practical possibilities that one has to invent one's own life) has its drawbacks:

> the becoming bit suggests that nothing is over yet and everything lies ahead, the condition of 'being somebody' which that becoming is meant to secure portends the umpire's final, end-of-game whistle: 'you are no more free when the end has been reached; you are not yourself when you have become somebody'.[38]

Within this context it is possible to see that the whole question of identity – of what one is as a subject – becomes problematic. The individual is constantly called upon to redefine her self within a fluid society. This confers on the individual great opportunities, an unprecedented responsibility, but also a sort of irresolvable enigma. On the one hand, she is urged to be really herself, while on the other, her self is pulled apart by multiple conflicting narratives. An individualised identity turns out to be a chimera that tries to stop the flow of liquid modernity, but at the same time must be flexible, adaptive, liquid,[39] facing different practical conditions and situations. The substantive subjective commonality that represents the glue holding society together in the normalising paradigm is made unstable by the very conditions of liquid modernity as described by Bauman:

> The task of self-identification has sharply disruptive side-effects. It becomes the focus of conflict and triggers mutually incompatible drives. Since the task shared by all has to be performed by each under sharply different conditions, it divides human situations and prompts cut-throat competition rather than unifying a human condition inclined to generate co-operation and solidarity.[40]

Bauman's differentiation between solid and liquid modernity seems to be a perfect metaphor for historical changes in biopolitical regimes. Solid modernity aptly describes the reorganisation of society under disciplinary standards.⁴¹ It captures the qualities of a biopolitical regime that extended its gaze over to the whole population, reframing identity in a normalising fashion. The biopolitical regime that seems to be emerging in recent times, by contrast, is very different and it has distinct liquid traits. While Foucault never explicitly articulated this biopolitical passage of modernity, the latter has been openly addressed by Gilles Deleuze.

Deleuze, identifying the societies arising from the new discourse of power as 'societies of control', describes the dynamics of 'control' in the following terms: 'control is a modulation, like a self-transmuting moulding continually changing from one moment to the next, or like a sieve whose mesh varies from one point to another'.⁴² The insinuation of control in our life is therefore carefully shaped upon every single individual, picking out her personal characteristics. The strategy of control does not constrain the individual to conform to a general, 'normal' standard. On the contrary: it uses a potentially limitless, more variable, set of standards to impose domination, those standards being different and specific and very personal but, at the same time, generated by the same matrix. Power is thus much more pervasive than before, an omnipresent and inescapable presence that shapes us in ways that were previously unknown. While in normalisation the standard is identifiable and applied through coercion (not necessarily physical), control is more dispersed and disguised, and takes on a greater variety of forms. This is the key passage from normalising societies to control societies: the individual no longer has to be introduced into a structure of control because control has fully penetrated the individual.

Normalising societies set one 'normal standard' to which the individual has to conform: the person is forced into a re-forming machine that conducts her to the desired ideal of power. Control, on the other hand, is fragmented into a multiplicity of relationships. It refutes the static nature of norms in favour of the mobile multiplicity of the real:

> In control society . . . the key thing is no longer a signature or a number but a code: codes are passwords, whereas disciplinary societies are ruled . . . by precepts . . . We're no longer dealing with a duality of mass and individual. Individuals become 'dividuals' and masses become samples, data, markets or 'banks'.⁴³

A common matrix generates our personal digit – different from all the others but created by the same source – that infiltrates individual life through a never-ending process of control that shapes our very being.

Every single biographical configuration becomes, in this perspective, 'the standard' to deal with. The differences between normalisation and control one are striking, resembling closely those between solid and liquid modernity.

In normalising societies the paradigm was represented by enclosed spaces with their own internal rules. The individual was introduced into their ganglia and reprogrammed through their practices. The subject, under the gaze of normalising apparatuses (the factory, the prison, the army, the asylum, the family, etc.), was firstly repositioned within the plane of reference of the apparatus itself (the subject became in turn a worker, a criminal, a madman, a father, a mother, a son, etc.) and then normalised according to its rules and standards. Within this scheme, the individual had to go through a process of normalisation that had a start and a definite ending. There was, so to speak, a progression that led the individual from the lower to the highest ranks of the disciplinary structure.

Control societies, on the other hand, work on a liquid principle of osmosis. There is no definite structure where the individual is enclosed. Quite differently, the individual 'surfs' through different stages and she is put into a dimension of perpetual formation. There is no final rank to reach, no highest status to hold. The individual always has to reinvent herself within the realms of work, of society, of family relations. General standards are abandoned in favour of flexible and personalised codes of conduct that can take advantage of societal fluidity. As Deleuze pointed out:

> In disciplinary societies you were always starting all over again (as you went from school to barracks, from barracks to factory), while in control societies you never finish anything – business, training and military service being coexisting metastable states of a single modulation, a sort of universal transmutation.[44]

Given the above picture, we can attempt to recast the problem of identity as posed by Bauman and analyse in more detail its dynamics. We have seen that liquid modernity represents an unprecedented era for the person who has been dislodged from traditional solid structures and thrown into a sea of competing, multiple life possibilities. The dynamics of the burgeoning biopolitics of control press on towards a liquid society of personalised life regimes, where power confronts each individual as a distinct singularity. To this extent, the individual is increasingly at odds with older normalising forms of self-identification that imply a static homogenising status,[45] epitomised in the political realm by the figure of the 'generalised other',[46] the legal subject. There is no norm in control, no master standard applicable to everyone. The subject, in other words, is facing a new understanding of the self that revolves around an ever-changing personal strategic situation, infinite existential configurations, and a never-ending process of self-creation. While the individual in normalising societies could be pinned down along the spectrum of normality, her nature evaluated and monitored within the contours of a normality spectrum, in control societies there is no longer a benchmark of normality, and every subject tends to be seen as a kind of her own. In this perspective I would like to suggest that we are progressively abandoning a concept of identity based on static norms (which are fixed, universal, 'solid'). Quite differently, the dynamic of subjectivation that characterises modernity could be better understood in the terms of an increasing 'virtualisation' of the individual.

I am using the terms 'virtual' as developed by Deleuze and, more recently, by Pierre Lévy[47] and Brian Massumi.[48] With the term 'virtual' I am referring to the potentiality present in any entity, its multiple abstract dynamics that can be actualised. Contrary to common usage, therefore, the virtual is not opposed to the real. As Deleuze was suggesting, in fact, 'the virtual is fully real in so far as it is virtual'.[49] The virtual, quite differently, is opposed to the actual. If the virtual is the full set of potentialities present in an object, then its opposite pole is the actual understood as the crystallisation within space and time of such potentialities, its contingent occurrence.

Bruce Braun explains this very aptly: the virtual is 'material yet real, abstract yet concrete, a future to come that is already within us, but which remains ungraspable'.[50] The virtual is entirely part of the real, it is one of its 'unequal halves' along with the determinations of the actual.[51] As Lévy points out, 'the virtual is a kind of complex problematic, the knot of tendencies or forces that accompanies a situation, event, object, or entity, and which invokes a process of resolution: actualisation'.[52]

Every real object is, in effect, made up of two unequal halves: the actual and the virtual. The actual is the contingent identity of an object, what differentiates it within reality from all other objects. It is the crystallisation, the still picture, of all the potentialities of an object within a specific time and space. Virtuality is the other half of the real object and represents all its potentialities, its manifold becoming. Between these two terms a complex relationship exists. In the first place, the actual is not simply the stable part of the object opposed to its ever-changing virtual counterpart. The actual is static but not stable. Reality is not a stable thing because both the actual and the virtual change at every moment.

The actual, echoing the famous argument from Democritus, ceases to be at the same moment it exists and, as a consequence, the virtual that is connected with it changes accordingly. Any situation, in fact, is like an individual dot in space producing in time an array of virtual multiplicities, and the minimal movement of this dot creates a new set of virtualities.

In the second place we see that there is no hierarchical relationship between the actual and the virtual but, more properly a mutual co-genesis. Lévy argues that actualisation

> appears as the solution to a problem, a solution not previously contained in its formulation. It is the creation, the invention of a form on the basis of a dynamic configuration of forces and finalities. Actualisation involves more than simply assigning reality to a possible or selecting from among a predetermined range of choices. It implies the production of new qualities, a transformation of ideas, a true becoming that feeds the virtual in turn.[53]

At the same time:

> virtualisation [proceeds] from a given solution to a (different) problem. It transforms an initial actuality into a particular instance of a more general problematic, one on which the ontological accent is now placed. Having done so, virtualisation fluidises existing distinctions, augments the degrees of freedom involved, and hollows out a compelling vacuum [*vide moteur*].[54]

A certain thing, a given situation, therefore, is at the same time virtual and actual. We live, according to this picture, in a world that is made real by endless processes of actualisation and virtualisation. More specifically, in our times we are moving from a society focused on the actual side of reality towards one focused on the virtual. In this perspective it seems that control is bearing a progressive virtualisation of our understanding of subjectivity, a burgeoning problematisation of actuality and its normalised, static identities.

If we pay heed to this account, and turn back to the interpretation of modern law given in the previous chapter, we must investigate the consequences that this biopolitical shift from normality to control might have for our legal landscape. To what extent can the normalising complex survive within the context of liquid societies populated with virtual subjects?

The collapse of the normalising complex?

Given the preceding discussion, modern law's functioning appears problematic: if law worked in concatenation with normalising practices, what is its role now within control societies? If law had traction because it recodified individual subjectivities in such a way that they would be aligned with the normalising paradigm, what is its strength in an era of virtualisation? More generally, in what ways does the dislocation of the normalising complex challenge modern law and its subjectivating operation of inscription of the individual within a triangle formed by power, knowledge, and truth?

In order to offer some answers to these questions, I will try to resolve a preliminary problem that cannot be overlooked: why did the order of normality break down (or why is it breaking down)? If the normalising complex was so efficient in recodifying reality according to its paradigm, how did its crisis emerge?

At the outset, it is necessary to recognise that normalisation, encompassing and efficient though it proved to be, has never been completely capable of a totalising recodification of the social body – this was also recognised by Foucault, who, even at his most pessimistic, never failed to recognise the possibility of resistance vis-à-vis the operations of power.[55] This incapacity, in my opinion, is not due to a given contingent deficiency in normalisation itself but is rooted in the very logical limit of normalisation. This logical limit is represented by the fact that concrete individuals can always present some characteristics that challenge the inscription of the subject within a normalising scheme. The idea of normality presupposes the measurability of something in accordance with a given standard and implies the possibility of translating a piece of the real into an element pertaining to a theoretical set.[56] Normalisation, through its norms and apparatuses, works smoothly insofar as it is possible to understand reality (a concrete situation, a specific individual) in accordance with its own standards and to subject it to its influx through individual self-regulation. There is, however, on certain occasions a gap between theory and practice. Sometimes the translation of a substantive object into a theoretical framework is too impractical or even impossible because that part of the reality that is scrutinised in order to be pinned down along the spectrum of measurability (normal/abnormal) defies categorisation. The real world, in other words, sometimes presents us with entities that cannot be properly inscribed within any received discourse. This challenges our customary understanding of reality, creating fissures in its fabric. Within the context of the normalising complex, such fissures have produced particularly unsettling consequences. I have shown how modern law and discipline/governmentality mutually reinforce one another, placing the individual along a normalising continuum. Such an operation, however, cannot be successfully implemented when the mechanisms of power are confronted with something unforeseen by their epistemic grid, an object that does not fit within their predisposed schemes. In all those cases, the normalising complex 'jams' and comes face to face with its own logical limits: how is it possible to normalise something that falls beyond the boundaries of a recognised spectrum of normality/abnormality? How can one apply a standard to something that is not comprehensible in the terms of such a conceptual model?

An example demonstrating the limits of normalisation is provided by a criminal case analysed by Foucault himself. In 1825, Henriette Cornier, a housemaid, killed a nineteen-month-old infant without apparent reason.[57] Foucault was interested in this case because, according to his reading, it showed how psychiatric power came to constitute itself as a domain of knowledge necessary for the exercise of juridical power.[58] The legal intricacies of the case were quite unusual. Article 64 of the 1810 Napoleonic Penal Code established that there could be no crime if the accused was in a state of madness at the time of the action. The judges, in evaluating the case on the basis of art. 64, could therefore follow two distinct routes. Either they could decide that Cornier was not mad at the time of the action – and therefore she should have suffered capital punishment given the nature of her crime – or that she was insane and therefore not indictable. Since it was difficult to determine whether Henriette Cornier was mad at the time of the action, the judges had to resort to the counsel of psychiatrists to determine whether or not, in accordance with art. 64, they could exercise their punitive authority. This very interrogation, in Foucault's understanding, was a clear example of how diverse forms of power/knowledge penetrated the juridical system, effectively creating a new hybrid regime of infra-penality which combined law and disciplinary practices.[59]

The distinguished psychiatrists called to examine Ms Cornier were, in fact, unable to establish the nature of her mental state at the moment of the crime. While her behaviour under clinical scrutiny did not provide elements that could lead to a declaration of insanity, the doctors could not exclude the possibility that she was actually under a spell during the homicide. Their reports were, to all intents and purposes, inconclusive:

the patient escaped the grid of psychiatric normality/abnormality and therefore these 'judges of discipline' could not decide whether or not she was mad when she killed the infant. The incapacity showed by the psychiatric power/knowledge to assess Cornier's state properly put the judges in an awkward situation. Faced with the sibylline response of psychiatry, the penal discourse could not properly function. As Foucault himself noted, the 1810 code embraced the idea of a penal system that is able to respond 'normally' to crimes, establishing a table of correspondence between the criminal act and the punishment that was quite different from the scheme of criminal punishment under sovereignty regimes:

> crime is measurable, and ... it is therefore possible to match it with a measured punishment, the possibility of punishment is fixed and determined ... by uncovering the underlying interest of the criminal and his conduct ... The crime's rationality, thus understood as the decipherable mechanism of interest, is required by the new economy of punitive power, which was not at all the case in the old system of an always excessive and always unbalanced expenditure of torture and execution.[60]

The impossibility of finding an intelligible rational motive behind Cornier's act, and the doctors' inability to diagnose her madness, however, prevented the application of such linear correspondence between her crime and her punishment. The court's final decision is quite telling, in that the judges had to try to resolve the conundrum they were confronted with and failed to do so, as they could not interpret her case in accordance with the very legal discourse they were meant to upheld. The sentence reflected this contradictory situation: Henriette Cornier was condemned to life imprisonment with hard labour. She was recognised as being responsible for her actions, but premeditation – which clearly emerged from all the factual evidence available and was explicitly admitted by the defendant – was excluded from consideration in the sentencing.[61]

The case of Henriette Cornier is an example of how the normalising concatenation between law and disciplines can 'jam' if confronted with an object falling outside its spectrum of normality. Since Cornier's behaviour could not definitely be ascribed by psychiatrists to either madness or sanity, it was similarly impossible to locate her actions within the field of law: the sentence that condemned her was the recognition that she was neither criminally punishable nor unpunishable. Both systems – law and psychiatry – were only partially capable of reaching a conclusion as to the meaning of her behaviour and could neither declare their authority over her nor announce their indifference towards her case.

What is important here is to note how the mechanisms of normalisation reacted before an exception that had the effect of undermining the foundations of their established discourse. Faced with a foreign element that challenged its supposedly panoptic gaze over the individual, the normalising complex experienced a blockage that derailed its otherwise smooth and predictable functioning. Such is the logical limit of the normalising scheme: when the reality of the subject defies the neat categorisations conceived by the prevailing conception of normality, reality itself escapes the obsessive surveillance of the order of normality by presenting it with an undecodable entity.

This foreign element, this unknown object, has a well-known name, and has been at the centre of much recent (and not so recent) philosophical, political, and legal debate: the Other.[62] The Other represents the limit of a discourse of normalisation and challenges its efficiency by continuously rewriting the boundaries of its own existence. While the normalising concatenation continuously tries to mould society along the lines of a regulated, understandable continuum, the existence of the Other transforms its efforts into a Sisyphean enterprise. As soon as the mechanisms of power rearrange society according to its ordered standards, the vision of the Other reappears, challenging the seamless domination of norms.

Here we are facing not only the limit of the normalising discourse but also its intrinsic paradox: the order of normality for the first time makes the Other visible. The rise of the normalising paradigm reassembled the social order of medieval society, dismantling the sclerotic metaphysical hierarchy that structured and underpinned it. In the Middle Ages, the position of each individual within the social body was strictly fixed, forcing the subject to adhere to what we could call a 'static identity', a mode of being that rigidly designated the existential horizon of a whole segment of the population.[63] The change in the biopolitical discourse and the emergence of a new mode of law erased the ontological categories that divided society, moving it towards a restructuring that produced a more homogeneous social body, more fluid but also more amenable to the machinations of disciplinary and governmental apparatuses: a phenomenon I referred to as the creation of the normalisable subject.

It does not seem untoward to claim that the redefinition of the subject in the terms of 'normality' is therefore intimately linked with the appearance of the Other. The very concept of Otherness can be delineated only with reference to a field of normality and represents the residue that lies beyond the boundaries of that field. As the Other emerges out of normalisation, it should not then be characterised as something completely alien to the discourse of the normal itself, but as something that floats at its limits, an object that is external to it but that, at the same time, can still be articulated in the language of normality. The case of Henriette Cornier is once again a good example of such a figure – the disturbed woman who does not fall within the spectrum of normality/abnormality and yet is still subject to its punitive authority. One could also mention the idea of the Other in the field of gender or cultural studies.[64] Here, there is always a constitutive relationship between the normal and the Other in the sense that the first term poses the condition for recognition of the second and strives to colonise the latter with its hegemonic discourse. The Other, therefore, is an object that is external to the field of normality, and yet it is still normalisable and, as such, can potentially be included by its discourse.

In this perspective, it is important to note that the idea of Otherness is almost unthinkable within the conceptual framework of sovereignty societies. According to that schematic, society was rigidly divided into ontologically different existential categories. As a consequence, certain groups of people, such as villeins, could be literally treated as inert objects of property, excluding virtually any meaningful idea of universal human recognition. The discourse of normality, on the other hand, characterised by its tendency to subject everyone to its all-encompassing gaze, creates the Other as the object that is out of its reach but that can nevertheless be subject to its authority. The Other thus exists only in relation to the field of the normal that defines her term of reference and aims at recodifying her subjectivity. Hence the paradox I referred to earlier: the discourse of normality, while having the effect of homogenising society, at the same time makes the Other visible for the first time by offering her recognition.

This structural paradox of normality is accompanied by another, that we could tentatively define as a 'phenomenological paradox' since it manifests itself only through the historical unfolding of the normalising mechanism. It can be described as follows: the discourse of normality not only made the Other an object of possible recognition but, paradoxically, also endowed her with the tools to challenge and subvert the discourse of normalisation itself. I have explored at length how, in the modern era, the individual was recodified according to a normalising concatenation. One of the typical aspects of normalisation is that the individual is constantly under the gaze of a panoptical power and, most importantly, that the subject tends to internalise accepted rules of behaviour. Such internalisation, produced by the social penetration of normalising practices and apparatuses, made the discourse of power more efficient and all-encompassing than ever, as it transformed the single individual and the multitudinous body of the population into the means of its own propagations, as they were its 'reproductive organs'. This, however, also has the effect of making the individual participate in the very genetic moment of such power. The great efficacy of the normalising regime is due to the fact that the individual, through internalisation, speaks in the language of and acts out the discourse of power, thus reproducing her own subjectivation while simultaneously propagating the established order of power. At the same time, however, she is also empowered as she can articulate her claims through the learned language of normality. As Ewald suggests, 'the norm . . . is a principle of communication, a highly specific means of resolving the problem of intersubjectivity'.[65]

I have examined this dynamic when I explored the conceptual, secularly oriented, framework supporting modern law: political power in particular, in that context, is created through the (constitutionally established) synthesis of the various individual interests present in a given community where the individual is both a ruler and a ruled. A similar dynamic is present in the scientific discourse informing the rationality of disciplinary and governmental practices. The scientific discourse derives its authority not only from its capacity to govern reality efficiently but also, and most importantly, from the fact that it is an open rational discourse in which anyone, in principle, can participate. It can thus be argued that legal-political power and scientific power are internalised by the individual because the individual is, in principle, an agent integral to their formation: the single person becomes at one and the same time both the active subject and the passive object of the power/knowledge nexus.

The normalising complex, therefore, has a strongly inclusive nature that tends to surround as much as possible the individual, who is understood both as a source and as a target of power. The normalising complex, however, in order to be capable of efficiently directing society through its disciplinary and governmental apparatuses, also has to harbour within its very mechanisms the seeds of a possible subversion of its own dynamics. Normalising societies, in other words, posit the individual at the centre of their machinations with a potentially contradictory end result: the single person is transformed into the main object of biopolitical operations at the cost of establishing her as the limit of the operations of power itself, as she can challenge from the inside the very discourse of power to which she belongs.

This inherent tension in the discourse of normalisation has grown stronger in time and has had important practical consequences for the relationship between the normal and the Other. Its development can be seen as acting *within* the discourse of modern law, and it is well represented by the distance that, for a long time, separated (and to a certain extent still separates) the theory and practice of modern law and democratic constitutional *dicta*. I have already mentioned this problem at the end of Chapter 3, where I pointed out that the universalistic declarations contained in the earliest examples of democratic constitutions rarely corresponded to the actual socio-political situation. As I have tried to show, law, within that context, was made possible by the implementation of a normalising process that was aimed at cementing the population around certain substantive general standards.[66] At the same time, however, law provided the enabling framework with which to challenge the normalising complex from within: it not only delineated the contours of a universal discourse of mutual political recognition, but it also offered a space of resistance to minorities and oppressed groups alike. The idea of fundamental rights that helped the expansion of a normalising dynamics was also instrumental in undermining and partially dismantling the latter.[67]

In modern history, people have used their legal rights with a certain efficacy to counter the apparatuses of power, preventing that movement of recodification towards substantive general standards that was central to normalisation. In this context, the rise of the Other was as gradual as it was inevitable. Insofar as law was bringing within its reach marginal subjects with a view to including them in the terms of the normalising concatenation, it was also incorporating them within its own discourse, empowering them to subvert it and undermine their recodification in the terms of the normal.[68] The dramatic social and political struggles that have characterised modern society and challenged the contours of its normality are impossible to conceive outside the discourse of modern law and have, in fact, been mainly framed in legal terms (it is almost superfluous to mention the feminists' struggle, the battle for civil rights, gay movements, and so on). In this sense modern law works in an ambiguous way: it can both foster autonomy and also support and undermine normalisation, suppress the Otherness in the social body, and help its resistance and recognition.

Given this background, the thesis I wish to posit is that the advance of virtualisation in our age has brought us to the absolute limit of the normalising complex. The progressive vision of the subject as a virtual entity expresses the recognition of a fundamental Otherness in everyone's life that presents a very significant challenge to the possibility of thinking about the social body and human existence in terms of normality.

I have already explored the differences between the regime of normalisation and that of control. While the former relies on the panoptical enforcement of a single optimising standard upon the social body by sorting, training, and disciplining the population, the latter adopts a completely new approach that focuses on individualisation and emphasises the unique potentialities and limits peculiar to each person. Within the order of normality, the Other is a residue that incessantly questions the validity of universal standards. It is evidence of a fissure within a system that is not capable of accounting for an element external to its field. Control, on the other hand, elevates the Other at the centre of its logic. The Other is no longer the sign of a systemic failure; rather, it is the reference point for a new dynamic of power that is entirely constructed around the uniqueness of every single individual. What is at stake here is a paradigm shift involving two different logics of discourse: the idea of a single order is opposed to the order of singularity. That is to say that the idea that there is a universal ordaining principle upon which to found society is opposed to the idea that there is no such thing, universal principles being at odds with the protean nature of reality.

The effects of such changes on the discourse of normalisation are easy to grasp: it will not be feasible to conceive of human life through the lenses of normality as it will become more and more difficult to identify any relevant common standard by which to sort and classify the social body. The solid structures of society connected with the order of normality will therefore prove unworkable and melt away into the virtual flows of a new liquid modernity. The subjectivating function of modern law is therefore made impossible. The subject resists law's interpellation as a universal entity, as law is unfit to extract any common political truth from her, her vitality escaping along infinite lines of flight. The transmission belt that, through law, linked subjectivity, knowledge, and truth to power is irredeemably interrupted, the legal discourse that supported the biopolitical social structure of modernity falling into unsalvageable disarray.

It is at this juncture that we perceive in its full force that tension between the legal discourse and liberalism that Foucault mentioned but never entirely articulated.[69] The dream of liberal government is that of being the mirror image of society, a system of management following the regularities of the social body so closely as to disappear within its fluxes. The punitive side of law, which Foucault saw as a remnant of a fading era, is in the ideal of liberalism a sort of necessary excess, the price we have to ensure the permanence of law or restore a natural equilibrium that is external to and precedes law. If individual interactions were not obstructed by the social sedimentations accumulated through history, if people were perfectly rational, the ideal goes, law would not be needed, as society would be able to regulate itself. But such a vision rests on the assumption of a baseline of human normality which was always and only a liberal fantasy. Its existence was, in fact, forcibly internalised through disciplinary practices and institutions, by imposing the matrix of normality upon the fluidity of reality. Ironically, it has been law itself which, in the course of fulfilling its promise of individuality and autonomy, shattered the dream. Granting a modicum of individual protection against the very same powers it operationalised, law allows, for the first time in history, the virtual side of life to emerge. Cracking the mould of normality that has shaped modern society, law is showing that normality is not a natural feature of humankind but a utopian diagram whose universalisations run against the grain of the real. By doing so, however, it also irredeemably undermines its own normalising foundations, proving itself a paradoxical apparatus now outgrown by the multitude of human life.

The normative and functional crisis of modern law

The push towards virtualisation ushered in by liquid modernity forces us to question the implications of these changes for modern law. Framing this dilemma within the contours of my biopolitical reading of law, I can now put into focus the gist of the problem: on the one hand, we see the dissolution of one limb of the normalising complex represented by disciplinary and governmental practices recodifying the individual at a substantive level, while, on the other, the basic structure of law appears unaltered. I have argued how modern law was concatenated with certain practices of subjectivation, thus creating normalising dynamics. What is the role of law now that this chain is breaking down and the subject is no longer adaptable to a normalising mould? I would like to suggest that law is facing (and will increasingly have to face in the coming future) two interconnected problems: a normative one and a functional one.

The normative problem pertains to the properly ethical and political dimension of modern law. I scrutinised in detail how law provided a mechanism of ethical recognition and political integration for modern secular societies, and I suggested that such a task was made possible to a large extent by the workings of subjectivating normalising practices. Modern law itself was based on the assumption that, at a certain substantive level, individuals were 'normal', that is, equal (be it cognitively, morally, biologically) and free (i.e. reasonably responsible for their ideas and actions). This assumption was propagated by means both of theoretical ideas (such as that of the nation) and of subject-constituting practices (e.g. the proper disciplinary/governmental dimension represented by the carcerial system, the industrial system, the familial system, etc.). How is this dynamic going to change now that the normalising recodification is increasingly inefficient and inefficacious?

In analysing this dilemma, it is interesting to address the allegedly inclusive dynamics of classical liberalism. Confronted with the fragmentation of modern society, the standard liberal response is a renewed commitment towards the liberal project itself. The mechanism of ethical recognition and political integration supported by modern law can, in effect, be aptly summarised as the constant striving towards 'the inclusion of the Other'.[70] But what does the inclusion of the Other mean, and, most importantly, what is its significance within the context of control society?

First, we must understand that the 'inclusion of the Other' formula does not represent only the constant tension of modern law in its attempt to recognise and integrate the different subjectivities present in the social body, but may also be read as the expression of a fundamental normalising drive. I have already pointed out that the relationship between the normal and the Other is one of colonisation, the normal continuously trying to rework its standards so as to accommodate and to tame the challenge represented by Otherness. Behind the liberal project of including the Other an inherent normalising logic looms large.

Secondly, and building on the above considerations, I wish to avoid the temptation to believe that the failure of a normalising subjectivation of the individual represents the true completion of an inclusion of the Other, the final recognition of her radical difference. On the contrary, the extent to which any discourse about the inclusion of the Other within the context of control society is doomed to fail should be apparent. We should also not forget that the Other is the product of normalisation itself. It exists only as the residue of the normal, as a fissure in its order: the Other is constituted only against a given normal, as its dark, unexplored side. From a conceptual point of view, it is therefore necessary to clarify that the approaching final dismantling of the normalising complex does not signify a clearer perception of the Other and its final recognition and integration but, again paradoxically, it signals its coming demise.

Lacking a stable point of reference, it is impossible to determine what pertains to normality and what to Otherness. This double withering away has a particularly relevant consequence for society as a whole. I have just reiterated that the relationship between normality and Otherness has been characterised by a tension towards recognition: the order of normality strives to include the Other within its field, while the Other struggles to find its own space within normality. This scheme of recognition is possible only because it is hierarchically oriented: the inclusion (or the potentiality of inclusion) within the discourse of normality marks the successful recognition of the Other. The absence of a reference point caused by the withering away of the discourse of normality, however, sabotages this mechanism. The consequence is that our modern democratic system of recognition and integration may be placed in jeopardy and lose its normative appeal. What I am suggesting is that, in a society where a normal baseline has faded away, to talk about the Other – which can be understood only in a negative relation to such a baseline – makes little sense. The proliferation of Otherness, in other words, by slowly pushing the discourse of normality towards its final deconstruction, introduces within the social field a new, more radical Other: the Xenos (the ancient Greek word for 'alien'). But while the Other was such in relation to a normal term of reference (thus dividing society into two co-produced fields – the Normal versus the Other), the figure of the Xenos represents all individuals. The Xenos is an absolutely single individuality in the era of control as the unifying dynamics of normality cease to arrange the social body into discrete collective groups. Within the contours of a biopolitics of control, the virtual side of human life progressively emerges and it becomes increasingly difficult to find meaningful and stable shared traits capable of establishing a communal identity. As a consequence, it becomes harder to find a reflection of ourselves in our neighbour, whose life, instead, turns into something alien to us, an extraneous dimension to which we cannot relate. The only common element is that there are, paradoxically, no elements in common.

The consequence is that our communities, based as they are on a well-established discourse of normality, seem to struggle when approaching a radical diversity through a liberal framework. The crisis of disciplinary and governmental apparatuses, unable to present to the legal discourse a social body recodified along the pattern of normality, has left the political mechanism of inclusion of liberalism without a substantial subjective anchor. Control societies force liberalism to face its unsurpassable limit: there is only so much inclusion the system can withstand before the line between what is normal and what is Other dissolves and all individuals are transformed into absolutely alien subjects, all different from each other. In this sense the fact that our post-national societies are plagued more and more by exclusionary tendencies, in opposition to the inclusive logic of liberalism, can be read as a symptom of the political crisis that the passage from normality to control bears.[71]

Built along the discourse of normality, the political structure of modern democracies is now facing the rise of a new life form – the Xenos – that undermines the most basic foundations of normalising societies. Confronted with this unsettling tide, the regime of normality is forced to retreat into itself since it cannot regulate a xenomorphic social body. In order to protect its own existence, the discourse of normality attempts to deny the Xenos any possible recognition and casts her out from any dynamic of inclusion. It seems, therefore, that there is a striking difference between earlier exclusionary politics and those being re-enacted today. The former manifested themselves as strategic discourses employed to expand the regime of normality to the greater part of the population and to divide it into manageable groups,[72] while the latter appears more as the reaction of the discourse of normality against the emerging dynamics of control. The foreclosing of the mechanism of political inclusion in favour of the supposedly ethnic or cultural unity of a social body appears in this light as the attempt to salvage the oppositional logic of normality versus Otherness. The liberal ideal of modern law, within this context, seems caught in a troublesome contradiction. On the one hand it provides a technical universal system of recognition of difference, but on the other, it does not seem to offer a sufficient ethical and moral drive capable of pushing us beyond the crisis of the discourse of normality. This forces us to question the suitability of modern law to work as a mechanism of integration within the context of the emerging biopolitics of control.

The functional problem is probably simpler to state from a theoretical point of view, but it is certainly no less consequential in its effects on the contemporary legal landscape. The question can be formulated in the following terms: can modern law efficiently regulate our contemporary society? Modern law provided societies with a more sophisticated and effective means of organisation and management than earlier legal regimes. The new syntax of law proved successful because it was directed towards a population that at a subjective level was continuously recodified within the paradigms of normality. This success cannot be solely ascribed to the new structure of law, but was in fact due to the particular concatenation that law formed with disciplinary practices and governmental policies. The result was a continuum that surrounded the individual and recodified the population as a whole in accordance with the normalising paradigm. Disciplinary and governmental practices, in other words, operated on the individual so that she would embody and embrace the behaviours and beliefs of a given normal persona, creating at a substantive level a general and abstract subject that could reflect herself in the general and abstract character of the legal subject. The smooth functioning of this mechanism, however, is challenged in the contemporary context owing to the shift in the biopolitical discourse from normalisation to control. Thus, it is necessary to ask ourselves: how are our legal systems, genealogically linked with the structures of a solid modernity, reacting with an increasingly liquid society? How will modern law – capable of regulating a normalised population – be able to govern societies that will be progressively composed of fundamentally different subjects whose basic commonality is heavily disputed?

With the rise of control and the virtualisation of subjectivity the functioning of the normalising concatenation appears untenable. On the one hand, we still have a law that is developed from a syntax marked by a universal model, while, on the other, we have a subjective dimension that is characterised by a virtuality that, emphasising the unique potentialities of each individual, undermines any substantive commonality within the social body. Therefore, while in normalising societies we had an isomorphism between the syntax of law and forms of subjectivity – the normal subject paired with the general and abstract universal legal subject – we are now experiencing a growing dysmorphism: the universal subject of law is confronting the unique and concrete virtual subject.

The expansion of the virtual perception of subjectivity cannot but exacerbate this problem and intensify its magnitude. The more we are conceived as individuals endowed with a unique bundle of potentialities, the less laws of general and abstract application can provide effective solutions to our problems. The manifest specificity of each single individual will represent a challenge that the syntax of modern law seems unable to meet, our legal system being confronted with a completely atomised social body. When the process of virtualisation of the individual reaches its apex, modern law's atrophy will be complete as universal legal rules will have to face the lack of their traditional object: the normal subject.

Taking into consideration in a broader perspective the functional problem that I have just analysed, it could even be said that such a problem represents an invariant issue within the modern legal discourse that the rise of control has simply pushed to its absolute limits. This appears to confirm the hypothesis that control is exploding the normalising complex from the inside. Modern law was characterised from its inception by the idea of stability and predictability – that is, by an inherent firmness in its structure that would ensure, quite fittingly, the rule of law over the rule of men. It is precisely within the framework of the rule of law that we can identify one of the most distinctive features of modern law in comparison with earlier legal modes: its positivity. The fact that law is posited in advance by certain legitimate secular authorities and enacted following certain official rules is both an innovative and a qualifying element of modern law which, to a large extent, is recognised as central by modern legal scholarship.[73] This characteristic converges with the biopolitical dynamics of normalisation. Positivity ensures the establishment of a system of rules that, being laid out in advance and in principle calculable in their effects, allow the recodification of society along a predictable normal pattern: society is governed and individuals interact on the basis of shared legal standards that aim at excluding and mitigating the effects of the occurrence of exceptional circumstances.

Observing this scenario, however, one cannot but notice a curious conceptual conundrum. What is the role of discretion in all this? If law is to be posited as existing, how can the system tolerate the fact that certain entities (judges, but also administrative authorities from the government up to the policeman on the beat) are recognised to have a certain degree of latitude in their legal determinations? The identification of positivity as a core feature of the modern legal system has generally been accompanied by the recognition of a dimension of discretion at the level of implementation. The perfect example of what we could call 'the discretion paradox' is to be found in the jurisprudential attitude embraced by Hart. How is it possible that Hart, one of the foremost modern legal positivists, argued emphatically in favour of the conceptually necessity of judges' discretion?[74]

One possible explanation for this paradox is that modern law, while contributing to the formation of normality, at the same time necessarily evokes the existence of a yet-to-be-known Otherness. This might also explain the increase in the incidence of exercise of judicial discretion in the nineteenth and twentieth centuries.[75] The creation of a positive field of normality necessarily yields the emergence of a field of Otherness that defies its inscription within the former. Modern law, working as an integral part of the normalising complex, embodies this very logic. On the one hand, positive law functions by identifying in advance the parameters for its functionality, but on the other, it has to necessarily embrace a certain degree of discretion in order to allow the rigidity of the legal system to adapt to the complexity of real life situations and the continuous emersion of instances of Otherness. The primacy of legislative power was therefore understandable in this perspective, as general and abstract laws were dealing with a society subject to the seamless workings of a normalising gaze. Control, liquidity, and virtualisation, however, force this scheme to face its own limitations. As the field of Otherness expands to the vanishing point such that it no longer can be absorbed by normality, the stability and predictability of universal laws may increasingly leave space for the modular effectiveness of executive discretion.

Given this picture, I am tempted to suggest that the normative and functional problems I have just reviewed are best seen as two sides of the same coin. The combination of the normative and functional problems, in fact, poses a very troubling dilemma that puts into jeopardy the whole modern legal discourse: if it does not make sense, under the functional point of view, to use universal laws to regulate a radically xenomorphic social body, then also from the normative point of view there is no appeal in subjecting all to universal laws, since subjecting the Xenos to universal categories necessarily means unjustly constraining her into a set to which she does not belong.

Conclusions

The current status of legal theory

At this stage, I have to confess that any analysis of the forthcoming development of the discourse of law will necessarily be hypothetical in nature. The present work is intended to offer a fresh critical perspective on the legal landscape of our age, and, as such, has the nature of a preliminary exploratory endeavour. Further research will be needed to imagine in more detail our legal and political future so as to offer effective proposals to tackle the crises we are facing and to prepare for the ones that may loom ahead. In this context, I can offer only some diagnostic remarks.

Broadly speaking, it could be said that the current state of the debate on legal and political theory can be divided into two opposing camps. On the one hand, we have staunch defenders of the liberal project (such as Habermas) who believe that liberalism, notwithstanding certain worrying problems and inescapable dysfunctions, is the project that is best placed to light the way forward even in the face of an increasingly virtualised and globalised society. On the other, we have the critics of liberalism as a legal and political ideal, the lively followers of postmodernism (whatever that is) who unflinchingly denounce law's inconsistencies and injustice as inherent characteristics built into the discourse of modern law.

Taking into consideration this landscape, my suggestion is that we are facing a sort of blockage in legal and political thinking. I would like to argue that, ultimately, and for all their differences, liberal and critical scholars seem both to cling tightly to the form of modern law that I have criticised as increasingly unfeasible for our times. Modern law appears to be taken, at least in a certain discursive sense, as an unquestioned 'black box';[1] the politics of law are increasingly questioned but the syntax of law itself, and its functional relationship with changing biopolitical forms of power, is left untouched. This seems to me the most important point neglected by both liberal and critical analyses of law. In order to articulate my claim more fully, I will first address the liberal position by taking Habermas and Held as two prominent (yet very different) of its standard-bearers, and subsequently turn towards current critical approaches to law and rights.

The blockage of the liberal camp

Habermas proposes a sophisticated liberal interpretation of modern law. He has suggested that modern law is constituted by a normative and a factual dimension. Law is, in fact, a set of commands backed by sanctions and at the same time a series of rules of action that demands compliance on the basis of its legitimacy.[2] This tension, according to Habermas, was already present in Kant but was resolved solely on metaphysical and moral grounds.[3] That kind of reasoning is of very limited use in our contemporary society, which is characterised by secular thinking and moral relativism.[4] Habermas, trying to overcome these limitations through the application of his theory of communicative action,[5] attempts to provide an interpretation that would be both normatively attractive and sociologically sound.[6]

The central foundation for such an ambitious project is represented by Habermas's discourse principle, which states: 'Just those action norms are valid to which all possibly affected persons could agree as participants in rational discourses.'[7] The application of this principle to the legal context would lead to a situation where 'only those [regulations] may claim legitimacy that can meet with the assent of all [parties] in a discursive process of legislation that in turn has been legally constituted'.[8] This system provides a powerful scheme of legitimation, granting the parties a space of communicative freedom where they would be able to co-ordinate 'their action plans on the basis of a consensus that depends in turn on their reciprocally taking positions on, and intersubjectively recognising, validity claims'.[9]

In order to make possible such a dynamic, every democratic legal system must work out a basic system of rights that would guarantee the equal and fair participation of every citizen in the legal and political discourse.[10] Every single citizen would, in this way, have the possibility of actively participating in the construction of democracy. The political discourse would be supported by a broad, inclusive, spectrum of reasons,[11] bringing within the public arena citizens' actual interests and values. The outcome is a communicative power that 'has a real impact on formal decision making and action that represent the final institutional expression of political "will'".[12] In this context law has the fundamental function of a transformer that picks up the political directions signalled by society and, through the administrative system of the state, organises society according to those very directions.[13]

To fulfil this task, law will have to endorse a system of rights understood as a minimal but absolutely necessary constitutional structure for any democratic state.[14] Negative liberties, membership rights, and due-process rights guarantee the private autonomy of the individual. Rights of political participation and social-welfare rights, on the other hand, guarantee the formal and substantive aspects of public autonomy. These rights do not stand in any hierarchical relationship and each side is indispensable to the other. They are, in other words, *coextensive* and form the conditions of existence of deliberative democracy.[15]

Under these conditions, law will be valid from a dual perspective: a formal one, since there is a fundamental sphere of autonomy that cannot be invaded by law itself; and a substantive one that stems from the fact that law becomes a reason for action once it has come about through a democratic process of opinion and will formation that 'justify the presumption that outcomes are rationally acceptable'.[16] According to this vision, the rule of law, basic rights, and constitutional restraints play a crucial role in channelling a democratic practice, while also being supported by a substantive practice of ethical and political communication and interaction. Law and democracy – the very characteristics that I have earlier used to define the modern state – are thus interpreted as mutually reinforcing and interdependent. As a result, they are capable of reaching a dual goal: on the one hand, they stand out as a mechanical tool for social co-ordination ultimately backed by coercive sanctions, while on the other, they operate as a vehicle of political integration for they are instrumental in achieving a meaningful rational understanding and acceptance between diverging normative positions.

Habermas's description of law appears at first sight to be a more accurate account of the modern legal-political situation than that suggested by Foucault. However, a closer look will demonstrate that the above liberal picture presents certain inconsistencies that a Foucauldian approach seems better suited to grasp. It is generally recognised that, upon the emergence of the modern state, liberal theory was in itself insufficient to create a framework of ethical recognition and political integration. Habermas himself, among many others,[17] showed that, historically, constitutional rights guaranteeing private and public autonomy were not enough to hold together the new socio-political communities of modern states. The idea of the nation[18] was necessary for the formation of a common identity for the whole population. It helped to create a sense of belonging, thereby overcoming social, cultural and economic differences between citizens beyond the (too often solely formal) rights of equality and freedom under general and abstract laws. As such, the notion of national identity is both a modern object and an artefact-object. In this regard Bauman observes:

> The idea of 'identity', and a 'national identity' in particular, did not gestate and incubate in human experience 'naturally', did not emerge out of that experience as a self-evident 'fact of life' . . . *The idea of 'identity' was born out of the crisis of belonging* and out of the effort it triggered to bridge the gap between the 'ought' and 'is' and to lift reality to the standards set by the idea – to remake the reality in the likeness of the idea.[19]

On the basis of such considerations, we can immediately draw a first observation. As we have amply seen, the emergence of modern law did not only shape dynamics of power and ushered in democracy but also operated at the level of individual subjectivity, shaping personal identities and ingraining them within its mechanisms. Therefore, as the case of the rise of modern states shows, a historical account of law, democracy, and state cannot neglect a careful analysis of practices of subjectivation. Any interpretation of the development of the liberal complex must be accompanied by a thorough description of how the deep interstice between the general and abstract legal subject and the single, concrete individual has been filled by the substance of common, artefact identities. National identity was certainly one of the most important versions of this connective substance, but what about other practices? What about all of the other dynamics of subjectivation that through the decades and the centuries have told the individual how to act, live and think? The national sentiment seems just one of these dynamics, and a careful scrutiny of law attempting a holistic understanding of its workings cannot be satisfied by this dimension alone. Quite the contrary, it has to address the various powers, discourses of knowledge, disciplines, norms, and institutions that have animated the subject of liberalism and helped shape and channel her concrete subjectivity. This is something that a liberal understanding of law appears to neglect, but it is, nevertheless, central to a Foucauldian analytical framework.[20]

The need for an alternative take on law, that would treat the question of subjectivity more seriously, emerges even more clearly when viewed in relation to the looming problems of our contemporary multicultural times, which are proving testing for the whole liberal legal-political structure. Tackling this issue head on, Habermas – again taken as one of the most sophisticated interpreters of liberalism – suggests that the ideas of nation and nationalism are not tenable any longer. He presents in very lucid terms the immense transformations that society is undergoing at the present time, and he is also aware that the traditional legal and political structure of the nation state is at odds with an economic globalisation that conjures the image of 'overflowing rivers, washing away all the frontier checkpoints and controls and ultimately the bulwark of the nation itself'.[21] More precisely, Habermas sees that globalisation threatens the existence of three pillars of the modern state: territorial sovereignty, democratic self-determination, and democratic political legitimation.[22] Nonetheless, against the gloomy visions of postmodernists and neoliberals, he rejects the 'end of politics' in favour of a renewed effort towards political normativity.[23]

Within this context, the progressive development of the European Union as a supranational democratic environment has long represented for Habermas the (problematic) embodiment of his political ideal. Taking the European Union as an example of democratic regimes to come, he suggests that in order to create a new politics that would go beyond national borders, what is needed is not a technocratic institutionalisation of economic markets but the fostering of a new civil solidarity. Such solidarity, once limited to the national dimension, should 'expand to include all citizens of the union, so that, for example, Swedes and Portuguese are willing to take responsibility for one another'.[24] Against the so-called 'no-demos thesis',[25] Habermas argues that the old social and cultural artefact of national identity – that made possible the establishment of solidarity among the citizens of the newly established states – is not needed any more.[26] Quite the contrary: in a multicultural society 'the solidarity of citizens is shifted onto the more abstract foundation of a "constitutional patriotism"'.[27]

This is certainly an enticing prospect. Nevertheless, one cannot help but notice that, according to Habermas, during the first phase in the development of national states, the construction of a fictional identity that could unite a population restructured in comparison with medieval times was something necessary. In the globalised dynamics of our contemporary world, however, Habermas seems to be forgetful of the role that identity formation plays in our society. Calling the modern citizen to a discursive endeavour, he is implicitly taking the modern subject as an unencumbered self. For example, the problem of an ethical communitarian bond that would unite the citizens of the state is simply neglected or reframed into a pan-European optimistic perspective.[28] In our times, Habermas sees the idea of the nation as a worn-out carapace that has outlived its usefulness for a community of individuals who have reached normative, political, and communicative adulthood, and who are engaged in a pure rational mutual understanding. Certainly the idea of the nation, once considered essential for the working of the state, is fading away in terms of its status as a fundamental term of reference for individual and collective identities, notwithstanding certain recurring ethnic regurgitations. But Habermas simply *assumes* that this demise (together with the emergence of a universal system of rights) has set free the rational nature of modern individual and to a large extent *disregards* the contemporary issue of identity: how is identity formed? What are the power discourses that impinge on it? Why should the question of subjectivation, which, as Habermas himself acknowledges, is so fundamental to our understanding of the political history of the last 300 years, be abruptly abandoned in our day?

Habermas, by fully embracing the paradigms of Enlightenment, treats nationalism as a historical epiphenomenon of the rational discourse of modernity, an instrumental occurrence with no substantive meaning of its own. The issue of identity and subjectivity has a similar contingent and transient character if compared with the 'march of communicative power' in the world. Confronted with the challenges of globalisation and modernity's unfulfilled goal of integration, Habermas candidly suggests a renewed commitment towards the 'unfinished project of modernity'. It is unclear, however, why we should finally assume that socio-political recognition and integration could be based on law and rights alone, and disregard the thorny issue of how the subject is shaped and channelled. It is far from proven that the understanding of democracy and the state can now proceed solely via consideration of law alone (constitutional patriotism being our social glue), without any inquiry into the actual concrete existential condition of the subject. It seems thus that the liberal vision of modern democracy as a framework that exists beyond the reach of systemic crisis and that can self-referentially work out its own problems is unsubstantiated.

The result of such unfailing – and to a certain extent naive – support for the classic edifice of modernity causes Habermas to be quite cursory in his treatment of the particular dynamics of power insisting on the individual. When he argues in favour of renewed commitment towards the project of modernity as enshrined in constitutional patriotism, his view seems little more than a normative cry and still less a reflection on the future of politics, as he does not substantiate his assertion with empirical study or evidence. The resurgence of nationalist movements across the globe,[29] the blighting of the public sphere of deliberation represented by the state in favour of opaque transnational dynamics of power and regulation,[30] the enduring inability of institutional experiments such as the European Union to achieve a true social and political cohesion,[31] appear to directly contradict Habermas's hypothesis. Habermas, in sum, while being able to provide a convincing description of the theoretical principles and dynamics of modern law and democracy, seems to fall short in accounting for some of their most troublesome and dangerous dilemmas and potential crises. He stops short of explaining why, after a first successful period of inclusiveness and integration, liberal democracy is now increasingly plagued by conflicts, pulled apart by centrifugal forces, and generally wanting in legitimacy.[32]

In Habermas's vision (and in the liberal vision more generally), law is meant to guarantee co-ordination between subjects through communicative action, but one must recognise that communication itself occurs between individuals who have already been touched and shaped by power. Habermas's line of argument disregards the influence of various discourses of power on the formation of the (supposed) pre-political individual. As Habermas himself suggests, the identity of an individual is not something spontaneous or natural. It is, instead, a complex object that is largely shaped by a dominant societal narrative.[33] Within democratic systems and in the context of laws centred on generality, abstraction, equality, and freedom, such a narrative has been greatly reshaped when compared with the Middle Ages.[34] In that era the concept of the individual was rigid, fixed, reflecting a metaphysical order, but such a vision was completely transformed during the following centuries, pointing towards a more egalitarian idea emphasising the free agency of the individual.

Nevertheless, we have seen how this transformation was far from having an absolute liberating effect on the self. The rigid identity typical of the Middle Ages had a very 'thick' substance, a viscous condition from which it was almost impossible to escape. The belonging of an individual to a particular segment of the community – such as the peasantry – fixed her role within society from both a legal and an existential point of view; it greatly limited her development as a human being and to a large extent determined her way of thinking and being in the world.[35] This thick identity was slowly replaced through the centuries at a political level by a more 'thin' one, that apparently left the individual freer than in earlier times. Habermas has shown well[36] that in modernity the reframing of the conditions of participation in the public and political discourse of society have prompted the creation of more inclusive frameworks and dynamics. But this liberation of identity was a legal one, and it would be wrong to claim that it led automatically to the emergence of an unencumbered existential personal self.

The question of how the individual has been subject to a cultural and intellectual reshaping at the substantive level of identity must be taken into consideration if we wish to achieve a satisfactory understanding of the modern legal phenomenon. We cannot assume that, since the legal subject became freer (and we must remember that it did so in a slow and contradictory way), this was also the unqualified case for the concrete person. Quite the contrary: we must focus on this decoupling between the legal and concrete subject. It is necessary to realise that in modernity there are these two levels of identity and that law cannot be studied in isolation from the concrete and existential dimension of individual life.

What we need to take into consideration, in other words, is that in modernity the separation between the substantive concrete individual and the universal legal subject should lead us to understand that law is part of a *concatenation* that includes specific dynamics of subjectivation. In this perspective a Foucauldian perspective seems best suited to investigate these assemblages. Focusing on the ways in which modes of subjectivation shape the individual, it certainly seems a promising framework for investigating how the concrete subject is modelled by discourses of power/knowledge. It shows how the discourse of law, operating as an apparatus, is always in a dialogue with other discourses, how the legal subject can never be taken as an unencumbered self but, on the contrary, is always to be seen as connected with a substantive individual whose mind and body are continuously under the gaze of power. The whole work of Foucault could be read in this sense, as an open-ended research concerning how the individual is continuously and silently subject to the reshaping panoptic gaze of socially embedded power dynamics.

This blind spot in Habermas's theory wrongly leads to the conclusions that the scheme of private and public autonomy that is at the base of constitutional patriotism (and, according to Habermas, resides at the core of liberal democracy) arguably still retains its force as a discursive principle of rationality capable of connecting different and distant normative frameworks. Modern law, in this sense, is ostensibly a very appealing idea in times characterised by virtuality. Since it is, in principle, an open discourse, modern law can be used as a neutral ground for developing new lines of integration and recognition. Modern law would therefore represent a working framework receptive to transformation and subversion. Is this not exactly what has happened in the history of Western states? Were they not, at the beginning, socio-political spaces marked by exclusion, racism and discrimination which eventually, because of and thanks to the syntax of law, mutated into self-reflective organisms and flourishing democracies where political dialogue (notwithstanding the difficulties and dangers they have to face) has an unwritten future? Were not the struggles for justice, emancipation and tolerance that marked the modern era fought and won within the very structure of law, demolishing, bit by bit, hegemonic ideologies and oppressive practices?

As a matter of fact, the more we move towards a modular existence characterised by virtuality, the more the liberal ideal appears appealing: is not liberal law, with its fundamental rights, its structural recognition of the claims of the individual, its categorical defence of the communicative subject, the ready-made solution to our (post)modern problems? If control implies a deflagration of the unity of subjectivity, what better tool, then, than liberal politics and law to reaffirm the possibility of a constructive encounter between radically different subjectivities? Put in this way, one must recognise the strength of the liberal discourse and its impressive flexibility and adaptability. Recognising the importance of the public/private autonomy nexus, liberalism qualifies as an open language that requires as necessary only the structural conditions of its perpetuation. Seen in this light, liberalism appears in the rosy tones of a progressive project of integration and hope.

One prominent herald of such a view is David Held.[37] Held is a strong advocate of cosmopolitanism, suggesting that it

> can be taken as the moral and political outlook that offers the best prospects of overcoming the problems and limits of classic and liberal sovereignty. It builds upon some of the strengths of the liberal international order, particularly its commitment to universal standards, human rights and democratic values that apply, in principle, to each and all.[38]

This approach is proposed both as a normative standard – drawing on the idea of justice as theorised by Rawls[39] – and as an actual direction in which our society is proceeding.[40] It aims to surpass the traditional configuration of nation-state sovereignty in order to build a different and more reliable system of legitimation. It thus seeks to provide an answer to the post-Westphalian order by focusing on the dignity of the individual.[41]

The modern version of cosmopolitanism is based on three principles which are clearly an evolution of the liberal project.[42] The first is the 'principle of egalitarian individualism', which rests on the assumption that 'the ultimate units of moral concern are individual human beings, not states or other particular forms of human associations'.[43] It is

> the basis for articulating the equal worth and liberty of all humans ...
> Its concern is with the irreducible moral status of each and every person
> – the acknowledgment of which links directly to the possibility of self-determination and the capacity to make independent choices.[44]

The second principle is the 'principle of reciprocal recognition', which emphasises that 'the status of equal worth should be acknowledged by everyone [requiring] to respect all other people's status as a basic unit of moral interest'.[45] The third principle 'stresses that equality of status and reciprocal recognition require that each person should enjoy impartial treatment of their claims – that is, treatment based on principles upon which all could act'.[46]

These liberal visions are sound and even appealing in the light of their bona fide call to an inclusive rationalistic discourse that would be respectful of autonomy, freedom, dignity, and mutual recognition. However, if we were to embrace these suggestions, we would face yet another paradox: why are liberal politics and liberal law in crisis today in an era where they should, in fact, be flourishing? The implicit answer to this question that the propounders of modern liberalism (ranging from Habermas to Held) advance is that liberal politics and law, in fact, are not in crisis. Only the institutional structures and social dynamics historically germane with the liberal project are straining under the pressure of a diverse and interconnected (globalised) world. The classical liberal state, in other words, is in crisis, not, certainly, the liberal project as such. Hence the powerful appeal exercised by liberal theories that insist on a dimension that goes above and beyond the territorial state, such as constitutional patriotism, cosmopolitanism, and global constitutionalism: they embrace the working dynamics of liberalism while suggesting that the ballast of its now-obsolete institutional by-products should be dropped.

This seemingly straightforward line of reasoning immediately presents us with one corollary and one shortcoming. The corollary is that there is nothing to be fixed if we look at the contemporary syntax of modern law. Everything has to be played out at the level of political democratic debate within the language of liberalism, but liberalism as such needs hardly any adjustment. The shortcoming is easy to identify: how realistic is it to invoke in the face of the growing biopolitics of control systems that have shown troubling weaknesses within the more limited borders of nations? And how realistic is it to decouple the structural logic of law from the political-institutional dynamics that are synonymous with liberalism itself (e.g. political representation, separation of powers, rule of law, fundamental charters, etc.) and that have made possible the transformation of masses of individuals into a single political subject? Faced with this dilemma, liberalism seems an answer that has been given too soon, since the ongoing virtual revolution' – our individual differences as our sole common trait, such that no group claim can be favoured over another and we will all be (frighteningly but equally) alone – is far from being realised completely. Are we really ready to accept humanity as the Xenos, to see ourselves as the Xenos, to build a legal system capable of questioning the central universalising drive of modern law? To this extent, liberalism represents a hope to pursue, but hardly an innovative way forward.

The blockage of the critical camp

Against the liberal camp stand, very broadly speaking, critical thinkers. Moving from different philosophical premises and adopting various methodologies, critical scholars nonetheless form a generally coherent front in contesting the orthodox liberal narrative about rights and freedom, recognising that law is often instrumental in establishing ideological hegemonies which suppress diversity and force identity homologation. I want to argue that, notwithstanding their originality and vigour, the conclusions of the critical camp are, in the end, not so dissimilar from the liberal ones. Notwithstanding its sophistication and complexity, it seems to me that much of critical theory does not seem to go beyond what can be described as somewhat circumscribed tinkering with liberal legal tropes, with the consequence that critical scholars have been unable to create a true viable alternative to the liberal canon in the legal field, both in terms of narrative and in terms of subversive tools.

While liberals and critical thinkers move from widely divergent premises and methodologies, therefore, they reach practically similar conclusions; the use of rights is indeed the central instrument for the affirmation of new and different spaces of freedom. Such conclusions, I believe, are the product of what I would call the 'heterotopia illusion'. The term 'heterotopia' was introduced by Foucault in a famous article entitled 'Of other spaces'.[47] In it, Foucault argued that in societies we can always find some spaces which are neither imaginary nor ideal (like utopias) but are 'something like counter-sites, a kind of effectively enacted utopia in which the real sites, all the other real sites . . . are simultaneously represented, contested, and inverted'.[48] While the concept has been extensively used in various fields, its application to law has been limited. This is deeply surprising: is not law the heterotopia *par excellence*, the space where reality is continuously 'represented, contested, and inverted'? Law, in this sense, can be seen at the same time as a space of domination, of struggle, of resistance, and of change.[49] Both liberals and critical thinkers implicitly embrace the idea of law as heterotopia. Beyond their differences, both take law as a (problematic) transformative space where identities can be remoulded and changed, and new forms of living have the opportunity of becoming. After all, is this not what modern law has always (allegedly) been about, a supple instrument through which we can explore ourselves both individually and collectively, a tool with which to construct our social environment, a machine linking truth, power, and knowledge in an ungrounded potentially endlessly open agonistic dimension?[50]

My genealogy pointed exactly towards this reading, but it also had the not less significant import that modern law necessarily recodifies the protean excess of Otherness into a normalising mould. Conceived within a normalising logic, modern law cannot but reiterate its normalising function, transforming all kinds of subversive invocations into a set of manageable permutations which cannot challenge on their own terms the limits of the legal discourse. This is precisely the problem with heterotopias. They necessarily mimic the very spaces they are supposed to evade; they can only distort the image they reflect without truly transforming it in an act of radical re-creation. Curiously enough, Foucault himself was aware of this conundrum even as he did not explicitly connect it with the concept of heterotopia but with the problem of political tribunals. In a discussion of popular justice and political tribunals with two 'Maoists' who would later become two of the most representative *nouveaux philosophes*,[51] he pointed out that the very invocation of the tribunal form in popular justice would have the effect of replicating those bourgeois dynamics and apparatuses that popular justice was meant to subvert and crush. His more general preoccupation was that no matter how hard one tries, preceding discourses, and in particular the juridical one, exert such a gravitational pull that all transformational practices, if not sufficiently detached from those, will inevitably reiterate their basic structure or dynamics. While liberals are apparently satisfied with the reproduction of the current legal discourse (at least in its core principles), critical thinkers are vocal about the constrictions imposed upon subjects by modern law, but they fail to offer a viable alternative. This runs through both the politico-philosophical foundations of critical theory and its more practical legal implementations.

To address this problem, I will first turn to the ideas of Judith Butler as an emblematic figure in the field of critical studies,[52] and then tackle

Golder's recent proposal for a Foucauldian politics of rights.[53] I will scrutinise these two authors as a sort of complementary dyad. While Butler represents the politico-philosophical side of the critical argument, Golder applies critical insights more directly to the legal field. By assessing their proposals in conjunction, I aim to unearth in more general terms the theoretical shortcomings which are currently limiting the critical approach to law, and to zero in on what I see as their main cause: the lack of a genealogical analysis of modern law which exposes the unsurpassable structural limits of the modern legal discourse.

Butler proposes a performative turn as a means of attempting to escape from the dominating discourse of liberal politics given her dissatisfaction with what she sees as its false promises of liberation.[54] In order to counter the pervasive power discourses and to explore the infinite existential possibilities of the individual, she theorises a perpetual reinvention of the self. Worried about the sclerotising consequences that any stable language might induce (such as that of gender or even that of law), she instead argues for the liberating effects of a 'protean' style of life where 'parody' would be turned into a political action. She understands clearly, in relation to the contemporary problem of Otherness, that any time the Other enters into law (as a Woman, a Homosexual, an Outcast, etc.) she is hypostasised and becomes an icon; the Other becomes crystallised, losing its fluid quality, it becomes a totalising general and abstract 'we'.

Such a position, which seems at first sight promising in terms of the infinite existential possibilities it opens for the subject, does not, however, seem to engage at a positive level the problems that appear to affect modern law in an era of virtuality. Butler's suggestions provide a stimulating roadmap for political practice, but say nothing about the crucial problem of a new mode of law. In a similar way to Foucault's, Butler's analysis, so compelling in its criticism of liberal politics, in fact presupposes and even embraces the modern legal paradigm where fundamental rights are instrumental in allowing the individual to express (performatively) her unencumbered self. Of course, the possibility of being oneself within society is something that Butler questions as something attainable in absolute terms.[55] According to her view, the discourses through which we come to be formed do not just prevent us from being able to access a supposedly original core of selfhood through mechanisms of foreclosure, but ultimately testify to our impotence in articulating one's identity – of giving an account of oneself – without reverting to a language that is essentially external to us.

Echoing Lacan, but also Levinas, she thus argues that the deepest strata of our existence are partially constituted by a lack that no signifier can express, and that we learn what we are and critically reflect on ourselves through the lens of a system of references that precedes the subject and structures it from the outside. Such a realisation, far from implying a sceptical attitude towards a meaningful idea of selfhood, opens the way to new possibilities for self-interrogation and self-assertion. The subjection to a varied range of discourses – each with its own rules, prohibitions, and limits – which is necessary for the articulation of identity and social life becomes, in Butler's theory, the basis for a practice of subversion: the individual who participates in the dominant discourse by playing by its rules is urged to use those same rules to explode that very discourse from within, finding within the intricacies of its norms unexpected spaces for self-liberation and self-determination.

This is true for any kind of discourse that performs a mediating role between the apparatuses of power and the individual, including the legal one.[56] So, for example, with reference to human rights – which for a long time have been deaf and blind to the question of minorities, homosexuality, and queerness – she suggests that their invocation in a critical vein can offer new avenues to rewrite and rearticulate the human.[57] In this perspective Karen Zivi has argued that rights claiming within Butler's theory functions as a *perverse reiteration*:

> If the 'human' of the human rights traditionally excludes lesbians, gays and women, if the 'human' is defined through the very exclusion of these groups, then, when using the language of rights, such groups are not simply suggesting that they are human in the way that we usually conceive of the human.[58]

This subversive usage of human rights is challenging us to rethink the meaning of precisely what it is to be human by exposing the limits of our very conception of the human. Law, according to Butler, functions thus as a language that can both forcibly frame the individual within certain given, figurative identities that reflect a certain arrangement of social paradigms and serve the purposes of resistance to the point that law itself, by means of enacting rights, seems able to establish a field of agonism where subjectivities and personhood can be negotiated, reframed, and re-formed.

Such a potentiality assumes even greater importance against the background of contemporary forms of sovereign power that tend to establish a direct hold over individual life. Building on Agamben's ideas about the state of exception, Butler argues that the colonisation of social norms by sovereign commands in the name of flimsy constructed security needs remoulds the contours of liveability to an unprecedented and unacceptable extent.[59] In the name of the sovereign – an entity that is performatively constituted at the moment of the declaration of a supreme emergency – the space of agonism that law can guarantee is shut and the possibility of subversion and liberation inherent in its discourse dramatically foreclosed. Butler clearly sees this problem in the Bush administration's handling of terrorist suspects' 'indefinite detention'. The suspension of one's fundamental rights on the basis of an arbitrary decision that defies the limits of law signifies the absence of a 'definitive prospect for a re-entry into the political fabric of life, even as one's situation is highly, if not fatally, politicised'.[60] The need for security gags the individual, denying her the chance to defend herself effectively and use her voice to challenge the order of power. In this sense the perverse 'graft' of sovereign command on the administrative structures of a governmentalised society has the effect of creating 'populations that are not regarded as subjects, humans who are not conceptualised within the frame of a political culture in which human lives are underwritten by legal entitlements, law, and so humans who are not humans'.[61]

In the face of such dangers, Butler invokes the idea of legal rights and, especially, the rule of law as the ultimate bastion protecting the possibility of questioning the contours of our social life and hence of creating new forms of subjectivities. Butler is clear in explaining that she is not interested in the rule of law *per se*, but rather in exploring how the rule of law could limit the perverse effects of state sovereignty.[62] Under this light, as Elena Loizidou argues, law would be able not only to passively protect the individual from undue intrusion by an oppressive form of sovereign power, but also to actively 'take up the task of the translator – to translate ... rather than interpret our irreconcilable differences when we make demands for life *per se*'.[63]

Such a line of reasoning is fascinating but also problematic. The discourse of law and the language of rights only partially resemble the ordinary language game upon which Butler is able to found her politics of parody.[64] The structure of the discourse of law is, in fact, much more static that ordinary language and cannot fully accommodate the protean nature of one's subjectivity. I explored this problem at length when I outlined the intrinsic normalising traits inherent in the very syntax of modern law: the recourse to the discourse of universal rights in order to allow individuals to articulate their subjectivity creates a mechanism by which the multifaceted and fragmented object that is the person is continuously recaptured within the rigid framework organised by the discourse of law. The features of generality and abstraction, and the principles of equality and freedom translate the person into a universal subject who is, by definition, at odds with the particularity of her individuality. Seen from this perspective, then, modern law can be liberating only to the extent that it oppresses and homogenises the particularities of each single identity; it constitutes a discourse that always moves in the direction of the norms, imposing certain standards that, at the same time, allow us to express ourselves intelligibly but also shackle us to a given and restrictive discourse.

In other words, while Butler is suggesting some imaginative ways towards a different kind of politics, her apparent reliance on the modern discourse of law seems nonetheless to undermine her whole project. Butler's theory (which can be taken as a representative example of the postmodern school of thought) is subsumed within the liberal discourse; liberal rights are a necessary precondition for her theory to function: how else would one be able to express oneself, freed from dominant overlapping societal discourses? Her suggestions therefore carry along with them a paradox. Her critique of liberal politics does not seem to be accompanied by a thorough assessment of modern law's structural discursive shortcomings in the face of the protean and incomplete nature of the self, and in the end we are left wondering how it is possible to build a radical political project within the hollowed-out shell of modern law.

The projection of this problem in the legal field proper can be seen in Golder's most recent attempt to propose a Foucauldian politics of rights. Golder, building on many of Butler's ideas, as well as other critical thinkers ranging from Wendy Brown to Jacques Rancière to Emilios Christodoulidis, has recently suggested a tactical use of rights as subversive counter-conducts, delineating a Foucauldian politics of rights that has both a positive and a negative side.

Positively, Golder intimates a usage of rights as a tactical tool to achieve a strategic aim. More precisely, he advocates rights claims as a means of making local and circumscribed (tactical) advances in specific fields so as to achieve a deeper and more general (strategic) goal. Golder analyses this approach in detail with regard to the 'right to die', which has been sponsored both by liberal theorists and Foucault alike, albeit with very divergent trajectories in mind. With regard to the liberal stance on this problem, Golder makes reference to the *amicus curiae* brief[65] written by a group of liberal philosophers (Ronald Dworkin, Thomas Nagel, Robert Nozick, John Rawls, T. M. Scanlon, and Judith Jarvis Thomson) in support of the legalisation of medically assisted suicide in the 1997 Supreme Court case of *Washington v. Glucksberg*.[66] The (ultimately unsuccessful) philosophers' argument, Golder observes, rested on a close collaboration between medicine and law, subordinating the pleading for assisted suicide by suffering patients to medical authorisation. In doing so, the liberal argument implicitly reinforces medical power's authority in determining what kind of life is worth living and what kind of death is acceptable, thus leaving unquestioned 'the powers of law, state, and medicine to regulate not only one's exit from life but the character and quality of that life itself'.[67] Foucault, on the other hand, offered a completely different approach.[68] According to Golder, Foucault imagined a right to die that would not simply strike a balance between the interest of the state in keeping a body alive and the desire of the individual to end her suffering, but would make of death a moment of aesthetic creation, a space of self-appropriation where the individual can rethink her own life and displace her own subjectivity.[69] Hence, in Golder's reading, when Foucault theorised about the use of rights he was not veering towards the classical liberal understanding of rights as an end in themselves, the enunciation of power protecting some individual or collective freedom. Rather, he was pointing towards a tactical use within a broader subversive strategy. Rights are then conceived as a medium whose invocation could open up the political and bring to light alternative ways of living and becoming that would challenge current subjectifying impositions.

Negatively, Golder supports a tactical retreat from the use of right as part of a broader strategy against certain pervasive discourses or apparatuses. In this case he takes his cue from Foucault's stance on the death penalty. Foucault discusses the problem of the death penalty on several occasions, but, in doing so, he never invokes a right to life against the penal machinery of death. Golder suggests that Foucault chose this stance because he knew that any framing of the death penalty in terms of individual rights would do nothing but reaffirm the general validity of the broader context within which the death penalty is inscribed: the penal system.[70] The death penalty was, for Foucault, just the 'triumphant apex, the red and black tip, of a tall pyramid'[71] constituted by the penal system and its sovereign right over the life of the individual. In this context, it appears futile to fight for the abolition of the death penalty when the whole apparatus that supports it – and of which capital punishment is only the most visible excrescence – remains unchallenged. The risk is to legitimise the system or acquiesce to its ordinary operations.[72] The solution is therefore to abstain from a tactical use of rights that would address a single (albeit abhorrent) issue and to direct a more encompassing critique against the general problem space that has generated the issue in order to subvert it in its entirety.[73]

Both approaches, notwithstanding their sophistication, ultimately fail to break away in a significant fashion from the liberal canon and to offer a radical rethinking of the legal field. Golder's positive approach, while fascinating, falls in line with the classical liberal narrative. Golder suggests that rights, when used tactically, should not be seen as an end but as a medium for creatively reshaping one's life and escaping established mechanisms of subjectivation; what matters, in other words, is not the destination but the journey. Such a transformative vision, however, presents some interconnected problems that gravely weaken its strength and appeal. First, Golder's rights journey inevitably starts from the platform of liberal law. The very usage of rights necessitates this: it imposes upon the individual the need to subjectify herself in order to make herself heard; it encloses her within certain logical, historical, cultural, institutional, administrative, and procedural limits that cannot but warp the individual's quest for a new form of life. By invoking the power of the law through the language of rights, the individual has immediately forsaken part of herself; in the theatre of law, becoming visible also means becoming invisible in the most dispossessing way: not only does the individual have to transform herself into the universal legal subject in order to speak, but also, her pleading, if victorious, is universalised into new law, the unrepeatable specificity of her situation always sclerotised into a static rendition which is alien to her. Second, the journey that Golder describes is not really an open-ended one; it necessarily ends up with the establishment of a new right which is, arguably, configured as the most classical of liberal rights. To take Golder's example: would not a Foucauldian right to die simply be an additional space of freedom that protects the individual from external interferences, liberating a life-space where the person can create and explore her own subjectivity? And would not such space be open to subjectifying impositions in line with the normalising dynamics we have explored so far? The attempt to make of one's own death a creative and aesthetic act is a 'post-legal' performance that necessitates a space of legal freedom for it to be exercised. The fact that the liberal *amicus curiae* brief constructed a narrow argument – a fine-tuned balance between individual autonomy and the state's interest in protecting its citizens from irrational, ill-informed, pressured, or unstable decisions concerning their own demise – couched in legalistic reasoning should not distract us from the fact that its authors' goal was to assert the capacity of individuals 'to make the "most intimate and personal choices central to personal dignity and autonomy"',[74] a goal perfectly in line with Golder's Foucauldian aims. Third, Golder's intimation of a tactical use of rights leaves completely untouched the legal structure, implicitly legitimising its operations. The performative use of rights cannot change what is the basic syntax of the modern legal discourse and therefore does not raise a challenge against its normalising effects. Borrowing from Golder's own observations, one must remark that such an approach would only dent or scratch the 'red and black tip' of the legal discourse by playing by its own rules: speaking the language of normalising rights cannot but replicate those rights, cannot but acquiesce in the underlying biopolitical dynamics on which they are based.

While the positive tactical use is too much steeped within the liberal discourse to challenge it in a meaningful way, the tactical retreat from rights might sound like a viable alternative. It is not clear, however, how far, in Golder's eyes, this problematisation should go. This manoeuvre could represent a kind of instrumental and momentary retreat which, coupled with a concurrent broader discursive critical engagement with the legal apparatus, can contribute to create, in the near or distant future, the conditions for a positive re-engagement. Hence, a tactical legal retreat is operated in order for a larger problematisation that would 'soften up' the selected target so that a rights-based approach could be efficiently and effectively deployed. But, if the negative approach is so interpreted, after all is said and done we are back to square one, because what is the endgame of such a scheme if not the eventual recognition of yet another right that is once again constructed according to the fundamental normalising syntax we have identified? To what extent is this a genuinely radical approach? As I have contended, any positive strategic deployment of rights cannot serve any truly subversive purpose because it is too parasitic on the liberal narrative and falls into the heterotopia fallacy I have mentioned earlier. Alternatively, we can imagine the tactical retreat from rights as a prelude to a radical rethinking of the legal field that would overhaul completely the discourse of law so as to avoid its normalising traps. It seems to me, however, that such an approach is exactly what is missing in Golder's work, as he does not problematise genealogically the modern legal discourse and therefore does not sufficiently question its working foundations.

At this juncture, it is important to make clear that I do not wish to accuse Golder of a misreading of Foucault's thought. As a matter of fact, I believe that Golder's interpretation of Foucault's later thinking on rights is compelling and very faithful to the spirit and methodology of Foucauldian theory, and develops a Foucauldian-inspired politics of rights to its very limits. My doubts are better framed as an attack on Foucault himself and on what I see as an underdeveloped analysis on his part of the legal field. My point is that Foucault was not sufficiently Foucauldian in his treatment of the modern legal discourse, because he did not attempt (for whatever reason) a genealogy of law of the kind that I have here proposed. If it is true that, following Foucault, we should historicise everything,[75] then Foucault failed in his engagement with law by his own standards, since he failed to historicise its evolution. As a consequence, I agree with all those scholars who have accused Foucault of inconsistency in his appeal to rights, but for altogether different reasons. However, while the liberal critique sees Foucault's move towards rights as a recantation of his totalising critical stance, I would argue that such a move went in the right direction but missed a fundamental preliminary step: that of a genealogical study of law as a *sui generis* apparatus that would tease out the contours of its discursive structure. Without an analysis that would take into consideration the normalising logic within which the modern legal discourse is rooted, Foucauldian theory is doomed to return meekly into the liberal fold.

An opening towards new avenues

Of course, the above remarks do not entirely do justice to the complex and sophisticated philosophical positions mentioned, both with regard to the liberal and the critical camps. Nonetheless, in the light of the above analysis, I believe I have more fully substantiated the proposition set forth at the beginning of the present conclusions, which is that contemporary legal and political thinking is facing a blockage as it is fails to address squarely the problem of the structural discursive limits of modern law. This prevents contemporary scholars from properly examining the functionality of law's syntax in the context of changing biopolitical dynamics. I would argue that this very issue, on the contrary, needs close attention if we wish to effectively address the most crucial lines of crisis of our contemporary legal landscape and to proceed to its truly radical rethinking. Is there a way out of this blockage? I must disappoint the reader and confess that, at this stage, I cannot propose a convincing line of flight. However, I would like to make two (very Foucauldian) observations.

First, the main goal of the present work is not to offer a solution but to elicit a problematisation or an eventalisation of the legal discourse, building on Foucault's insights on power, knowledge, truth, and subjectivity. In the previous pages, I have tried to build the initial stages of a critique of the structural limits of modern law. To this end, I have argued that the discourse of modern law has developed historically as a *sui generis* apparatus which formed a normalising complex together with disciplinary and governmental practices. Modern law has thus operated as an apparatus of normalisation, probably the foremost one, by recodifying the individual into the universal form of the legal subject upon which disciplinary and governmental practices could easily exercise their influence and effectively normalise the social body in its entirety. Exploring this concatenation, I have suggested that its formation was made possible by, among other things, the restructuring of the discourse of law itself along the lines of a new generative principle or syntax delimited by the features of generality and abstraction, and the principles of equality and freedom. Contemporary biopolitical dynamics, with the shift from normalisation to control and beyond, are increasingly dismantling this normalising complex, making law's modern syntax progressively obsolete. With all its limitations and shortcomings, it is hoped that the present work may be capable of prising open the black box that modern law represents in modern theory and providing a problematic point for redefining the contours of our legal landscape. Following, very modestly, in Foucault's steps, my purpose has not been to offer a complete set of solutions to certain specific issues but simply to outline a new theoretical approach to addressing certain problems which, to start with, could not even be properly framed, still less evaluated, without it.

Secondly, I would like to gesture towards a potentially viable way forward. In *The Order of Things*, Foucault famously argued that human knowledge is historically situated and can be framed within a given *episteme*.[76] He further suggested that the pre-classical period – broadly understood – was characterised by an episteme of similitude which eventually gave way, in the classical period, to an *episteme* of representation. Crucially, the emergence of the human as a historical object of study in the nineteenth century (the human as an object that is located within a contingent natural and social evolution) led to a paradoxical dilemma: the human is seen both as the active and the passive subject of knowledge, the foundation and end-point of a self-reflective Möbius strip. This opened up what Foucault called an analytics of finitude: the impossibility of being at the same time an empirical and transcendental subject, a conundrum of thought that we have yet to resolve.[77]

Is not such a pattern the same one that emerged in the preceding genealogical analysis? We have seen how law in sovereignty societies was dominated by a scheme of similitude: the worldly order must replicate the heavenly one. The modern legal discourse, which developed within a normalising order, follows, on the other hand, a scheme of representation:

law is an apparatus that can accurately reflect the truth of the subject to the extent that the subject itself is a representable one, an entity that stands for another one, a subject that can speak for and about herself only if and when she speaks another language with another voice, only insofar as she is the universal instantiation of humankind. But what happens when the episteme shifts again and we realise that the particular, virtual subject fundamentally escapes any universalising representation and its static mapping?

This is precisely the Gordian knot that we are facing in legal theory at the present time. We need to imagine a way forward that breaks with our normalising/representative legal discourse and addresses in a fresh and truly original way the problem of regulating a liquid society of virtual subjects. How can we restructure the syntax of law? How can we find ways out of the normalising system in which modern law has been articulated? How can law become an instrument capable of coping with the fluid demands of new biopolitical dynamics? Certainly this is a titanic task, no smaller than the task which people such as Hobbes, Kant, Hegel, the Founding Fathers, and the French revolutionaries had to face. The enormity of such an endeavour, however, should not reduce us to a daunting submission. As Deleuze said: 'It's not a question of worrying or of hoping for the best, but of finding new weapons'.[78]

Notes

Notes to Chapter 1

1. Baudrillard, 2007. Foucault's work has been used to analyse diverse areas of sociality ranging from medicine to social work and international relations. The articles and publications inspired by a Foucauldian framework are almost impossible to count (see *ex multis* Morton and Bygrave, 2008; Dillon and Neal, 2008; Oksala, 2005; Trigo, 2002; Strozier, 2002; Garland, 2001; Carrette, 2000; Chambon, Irving and Epstein, 1999; Petersen and Bunton, 1997; Barry, Osborne and Rose, 1996; Simons, 1995; Simon, 1993). As of 2007, Foucault was the most cited author in the field of humanities according to the database ISI Web of Science. See 'The most cited authors of books in the humanities', 26 March 2009, <https://www.timeshighereducation.co.uk> (last accessed 4 August 2016).
2. See Lemke, 2010.
3. For a survey of the criticisms levelled against Foucault's seeming disregard of law's role in modern society see Golder and Fitzpatrick, 2009.
4. Bobbio, 1996.
5. See, among others, Foucault, 1978, 144.
6. Koopman, 2013.
7. Foucault, 2000a, 279–98. For Foucault's own description of the concept of genealogy see Foucault, 2000b, 369–92; 1980a, 83ff.
8. O'Farrell, 2005, 72.
9. Foucault, 1972.
10. Gutting, 2010.
11. O'Farrell, 2005, 64.
12. Koopman, 2013, 95.
13. Koopman, 2013, 29.

14. Foucault, 1978, 141–3.
15. Foucault, 2002a, 137.
16. Foucault, 1978.
17. Foucault, 2008, 2007, 2003.
18. Foucault, 1978, 143.
19. Foucault explicitly argued that 'sovereignty and disciplinary mechanism are two absolutely integral constituents of the general mechanism of power in our society' (Foucault, 1980a, 108).
20. Foucault, 2003a, 242.
21. Foucault, 1977.
22. Foucault, 1977.
23. Foucault, 1977, 137–8.
24. Foucault, 2003a, 242.
25. Foucault, 2003a, 245.
26. Foucault, 1991. Foucault first mentioned 'governmentality' in the 1 February 1978 lecture at the Collège de France, which was subsequently published in the Italian journal *Aut-Aut*, no. 167–8, Sept.–Dec. 1978. One of the most comprehensive studies on governmentality is offered by Dean, 2010. See also Lemke, 2010.
27. Gordon, 1991, 2–3.
28. Gordon, 1991, 8ff.
29. Foucault, 1991, 93, 95.
30. Foucault, 1991, 102.
31. Foucault, 1991, 104.
32. Gordon, 1991, 3; Foucault, 2002b, 333–5.
33. Foucault, 2002b, 333.
34. Foucault, 2002c, 298ff.
35. Foucault, 2002b, 334.
36. For a critique of Foucault's work along these lines from a radical perspective see, among others, Kennedy, 1993; Hirst, 1986; Poulantzas, 1980.
37. Foucault, 1978, 135 *passim*.
38. Foucault, 2003a, 253.
39. On the relationship between norms and normalisation see Taylor, 2009.
40. Foucault, 1977, 183.
41. Foucault, 2003a, 253.
42. Canguilhem, 1991.
43. Foucault, 1977, 183.
44. Foucault, 1996, 196–9; 1978, 144.

45. Ewald, 1990, 140.
46. Ewald, 1990, 154 (emphasis added).
47. Habermas, 1999; Bobbio, 1996; Dahrendorf, 1988.
48. Foucault, 2008, 77.
49. *Ex multis* Foucault, 2002d, 437–8.
50. Habermas, 1994, 100.
51. Habermas, 1994, 100.
52. Habermas, 1994, 100–1.
53. Habermas, 1994, 101.
54. Habermas, 1994, 101.
55. Habermas, 1994, 102.
56. Hunt and Wickham, 1994.
57. Hunt and Wickham, 1994, 55–6.
58. Hunt and Wickham, 1994, viii.
59. Hunt and Wickham, 1994, 59–60.
60. Hunt and Wickham, 1994, 56–8.
61. Hunt and Wickham, 1994, 62–3.
62. Hunt and Wickham's thesis has encountered some strong criticism. See Golder and Fitzpatrick, 2009; Ivison, 1998; Beck, 1996; Goldstein, 1993.
63. Golder, 2008, 749. Foucauldian approaches have thus been used to formulate feminist critiques of law (Drakopoulou, 2007), and to analyse various legal fields such as human rights (Sokhi-Bulley, 2011; Evans, 2005), international law (Hammer, 2007), or criminal law (Garland, 2001), among others.
64. Rose and Valverde, 1998.
65. Rose and Valverde, 1998, 548.
66. Rose and Valverde, 1998, 549.
67. 'This is neither a matter of the constitution of subjects in legal form nor of the disciplining of subjects whose natural form is otherwise; but of the encouragement, support and shaping of self-projects in such ways that in specific practices, these come into alignment with the diverse objectives of regulation' (Rose and Valverde, 1998, 548).
68. Rose and Valverde, 1998, 545.
69. Rose and Valverde, 1998, 549.
70. 'Foucault does not mean to suggest ... that the development of bio-power is accompanied by a decline of law ... In fact, normalisation tends to be accompanied by an astonishing proliferation of legislation ... The norm, then, is opposed not to law itself but to what Foucault would call "the juridical": the institution of law as

the expression of a sovereign's power ... In the age of bio-power, the *juridical*, which characterised monarchical law, can readily be opposed to the normative, which comes to the fore most typically in constitutions, legal codes, and the constant and clamorous activity of the legislature' (Ewald, 1990, 138).
71. 'The normative allows us to understand how communication remains possible even within a historical moment characterised by the end of universal values. The norm is a means of producing social law, a law constituted with reference to the particular society it claims to regulate and not with respect to a set of universal principles. More precisely, when the normative order comes to constitute the modernity of societies, law can be nothing other than social' (Ewald, 1990, 154–5).
72. Ewald, 1986a.
73. 'If we understand as "juridical system" a normative order with its sources, its techniques, its organisation, the juridical experience refers to the manner in which, within certain "political economies", the juridical system – the law (*"le droit"*) – is, at the same time, programmed, problematised, and contested ... The way of opposing law and morality, of distinguishing law and non-law, of finalising it, all that refers to certain juridical experiences' (Ewald, 1986a, 30).
74. 'To describe the element of reflexivity of law, I propose to speak of a rule of judgement. Legislation, doctrine and case law are all practices of legal judgement. Their articulation, distribution and mutual competence depend on the type of rationality that this legal judgement obeys. This type of rationality defines, for a particular legal order, the economy of its 'juris-diction'. The rule of judgement is not a rule laid down by a body, but is what regulates the judgement of all bodies; accordingly, not something that one applies, but something whereby one judges' (Ewald, 1987, 38). See also Ewald, 1986a, 436.
75. Ewald, 1986a, 16-22.
76. Ewald, 1986a, 437–9.
77. Ewald, 1986a, 441–50. Error and balance make reference to statistical occurrences. The error is an event that is inherent to human activity and cannot be avoided (statistically), no matter the level of care exercised in a certain conduct. Balance, on the other hand, is the social equilibrium to be preserved between competing interests on the basis of the likely occurrence of a conflictual event; the concept of balance therefore contextualises the notion of fault within a

specific social environment and indexes compensation to the statistical recurrence of a damaging event. On the notion of balance see Ewald, 1986b, 61–71.
78. The emergence of a new 'law of accidents' therefore represents a new stage in the social history of causation. It is the moment in which society realises that it cannot master the rules of *subjective* causation (who caused what?), but can indeed establish a positive normative order of imputation based on *objective* criteria of causation (what is the statistical risk that something will occur?). See Ewald, 1986a, 438–40.
79. '[S]ocial law should be conceived of in relation to the notion of norm. Of course, this term designates, not certain legal expressions, but a system for formulating certain expressions, and a specific way of judging. In classical law, the Law – we give it a capital to distinguish it from the individual laws promulgated by the legislator – designated such a system for formulating expressions. In order to belong to the legal order, these had to take the form of (or derive from) the Law, a general expression intended to have perpetuity. For social law, the norm corresponds to what the Law could be for classical law' (Ewald, 1986b, 71).
80. Ewald, 1986a, 481.
81. Ewald, 1986a, 471–4.
82. Ewald, 1986a, 476–82.
83. Ewald, 1987, 36.
84. Ewald, 1986a, 34–5.
85. Ewald (1986b, 57) is quite explicit in calling law a 'formal garb' that 'social law' must adopt, and claiming that law 'serves to camouflage the machinations of power' (Ewald, 1990, 159). He also repeats the well-trodden expulsion thesis trope, according to which, in modern times, the rule of judges slides into the background in favour of the rule of technical experts (Ewald, 1986a, 490).
86. Tadros, 1998, 82.
87. '[A]n assemblage is first and foremost what keeps very heterogeneous elements together: e.g. a sound, a gesture, a position, etc., both natural and artificial elements. The problem is one of "consistency" or "coherence", and is prior to the problem of behaviour. How do things take on consistency? How do they cohere?' (Deleuze, 2006, 179).
88. Tadros, 1998, 87.
89. Tadros, 1998, 93.

90. Tadros, 1998, 99, combines and expands two ideas already present in Foucault. On the one hand, Foucault suggested that law works as a relay in his treatment of the penal system; on the other, he claimed that discipline and governmentality were connected through forms of concrete arrangements (such as the *dispositif* of sexuality).
91. 'Law's symbolic representation as a monopoly of the right to violence, primarily exercised by a Sovereign . . . The symbolic representation of law as the sovereign right to violence was a condition for the law's acceptance as well as a method for co-ordinating the form which the legal structure took' (Tadros, 1998, 87).
92. 'The power relations through which this [disciplinary] hierarchy was constructed were already more or less in place' (Tadros, 1998, 86–7).
93. Golder and Fitzpatrick, 2009, 12–25.
94. Golder and Fitzpatrick, 2009, 61.
95. Golder and Fitzpatrick, 2009, 63–4.
96. 'The scientificity of the disciplines hands to the law the power of . . . truth, although . . . it is law which guarantees for discipline its "unitary field of objects"' (Golder and Fitzpatrick, 2009, 66).
97. Golder and Fitzpatrick, 2009, 79.
98. Ibid.
99. Golder and Fitzpatrick, 2009, 77.
100. Golder and Fitzpatrick, 2009, 63–4.
101. When Golder and Fitzpatrick provide empirical evidence for their proposition (Golder and Fitzpatrick, 2009, 64–6), they analyse a judicial case that, eventually, appears to run contrary to their own Foucauldian ideas of law. The case they analyse is *R v. Board of Visitors of HM Prison, The Maze ex parte Hone* (1988 AC 379). Unfortunately – if I understand their argument correctly – it must be noted that the case itself, showing judicial deference in the face of a carcerial disciplinary regime, provides little support for their legal thesis. The case concerned the right of prisoners charged with carcerial disciplinary offences to be represented before a reviewing panel. Considering the discretionary administrative nature of the power exercised by the prison's authorities, the House of Lords declared that no such right existed. It is hard to see how, in this case, law positively legitimised in any way the disciplinary carcerial institution. Rather, it seems that the House of Lords simply showed deference to the authority of disciplines without properly questioning their limits. One might go so far as to say that the simple fact

that the procedures adopted in Her Majesty's prison could be legally challenged shows that law does work as a potential limit to disciplinary powers. Such an interpretation (which is not spelled out explicitly by Golder and Fitzpatrick), however, would simply beg the question: is law, *in fact*, legitimating disciplines by regulating their mechanisms or is it rubber-stamping their normalising claims and processes?

102. While I am sceptical about some aspects of Golder and Fitzpatrick's argument, it will become clear in the subsequent development of the present work that I agree with and build on their idea that the legal discourse is in a relationship of co-production with disciplinary and governmental regimes.
103. Foucault, 2007, 237–48.
104. Foucault, 1978.
105. Foucault, 2008, 282.
106. Foucault, 2008, 276.
107. Foucault, 2008, 275.
108. Foucault, 2008, 274.
109. Foucault, 2008, 280.
110. Foucault, 2008, 282.
111. Foucault, 2003a, 38.
112. Foucault (2008, 295–313) offers an argument to that effect while discussing the emergence of the original notion of civil society in the seventeenth and eighteenth centuries as an analytics of government and its incompatibility with classical depictions of the political community as a juridical one.
113. Foucault, 2002e.
114. Foucault, 2014b.
115. Gordon, 2002.
116. Foucault, 1978, 82.
117. For a summary of the various set of propositions that Foucault advanced see Kelly, 2009, 35–9.
118. Foucault, 1978, 93.
119. Foucault, 2002f, 225.
120. Foucault defines this ensemble as a *dispositif*, that is 'a structure of flexible and contingent but nonetheless relatively stable relationships between practices' (Barron, 2002, 960).
121. Foucault, 1978, 93. As Jessop summarises: 'Foucault stressed three themes in his "nominalist" analytics of power: it is immanent in all social relations, articulated with discourses as well as institutions,

and necessarily polyvalent because its impact and significance vary with how social relations, discourses and institutions are integrated into different strategies' (Jessop, 2007, 35).
122. Foucault, 1978, 94.
123. Kelly, 2009, 44.
124. 'Discourse transmits and produces power; it reinforces it, but also undermines and exposes it, renders it fragile and it makes it possible to thwart it. In like manner, silence and secrecy are shelter for power, anchoring its prohibition; but they also loosen its hold and provide for a relatively obscure areas of tolerance' (Foucault, 1978, 101).
125. 'Foucault is not a relativist or a solipsist, but he does not believe that knowledge confers ultimate acquaintance with reality, or that means of verification used to determine truth are available to us in forms which we know to be definitive' (Gordon, 2002, xvii–xviii).
126. Foucault, 1980b, 131.
127. Foucault, 1980b, 132–3.
128. Foucault, 1980a, 98.
129. Foucault, 2003a, 29–30.
130. Oksala, 2005, 95.
131. Kelly, 2009, 89.
132. Foucault, 2002b, 342.
133. Rose, 1999, 84.
134. Rose, 1999, 88.
135. Dean, 2010; Foucault, 2008; Rose, 1999; Barry, Rose and Osborne, 1996.
136. Miller and Rose, 2008, 216.
137. For an interesting analysis of the problem of translating the word *dispositif* into English see Kelly, 2013, 132–4.
138. Foucault, 1980c, 194–6.
139. Deleuze, 1992, 160–1.
140. Agamben, 2009, 14.
141. Agamben (ibid.) maintains that basically anything can function as an apparatus: '[P]risons, mad houses, the panopticon, schools, confession, factories, disciplines, juridical measures, and so forth (whose connection with power is in a certain sense evident), but also the pen, writing, literature, philosophy, agriculture, cigarettes, navigation, computers, cellular telephones and – why not – language itself, which is perhaps the most ancient of apparatuses – one in which

thousands and thousands of years ago a primate inadvertently let himself be captured, probably without realising the consequences that he was about to face'.
142. Chignola, 2016.
143. Foucault, 2002e.
144. Foucault, 2014b.
145. Foucault, 2002e, 16.
146. Foucault, 2002e, 4.
147. Hence, for example, the Germanic test is reflective of a society that settles disputes in a formalised continuation of warlike dynamics, the inquiry is the expression of a society where the production of truth is made possible only by the investigation performed by a centralised political power which peers into the private affairs of its citizens, and the examination is the primary mechanism used by emerging bourgeois societies to establish a system of surveillance that would protect its economic interests.
148. Foucault, 2002e, 15.
149. Foucault, 2014b, 15.
150. Foucault, 2014b, 17.
151. 'In the case of a critical philosophy of veridictions, the problem is not that of knowing how a subject in general may understand an object in general. The problem is that of knowing how subjects are effectively tied within and by the forms of their veridiction in which they engage. In this case, the problem is not that of determining historical accidents, external circumstances, mechanisms of illusions or ideologies, or even the internal economy or errors or failures in the logic that could have produced the falsehood. The problem is to determine how a mode of veridiction, a *Wahrsagen* could appear in history and under what conditions ... In a word, in this critical philosophy is not a question of the general economy of the true, but rather about historical politics, or a political history of veridictions' (Foucault, 2014b, 20).
152. Moving from slightly different premises, Ewald (1986a, 32) also urges study of the major Western juridical experiences as different modes of subjectivation proposed to individuals.
153. Foucault, 2008, 273–6.
154. Foucault, 2002f, 226–7.
155. H. L. A. Hart's *The Concept of Law* (1994), where modern law is unquestionably taken as the absolute horizon of the legal discourse, is but one example of this kind of approach.

156. See above, n. 63.
157. I am here using the term 'syntax' in the formal logic sense. Carnap defined the concept of syntax in the following way: 'By the logical syntax of a language, we mean the formal theory of the linguistic forms of that language – the systematic statement of the formal rules which govern it together with the development of the consequences which follow from these rules . . . Thus we are justified in designating as "logical syntax" the system which comprises the rules of formation and transformation' (Carnap, 1937, 1–2). In this perspective, with 'syntax' I will refer to the internal structural logic of the legal system regulating the latter's formation and production and change. I am not, however, referring to the purely formal dimension of the legal language which links the legitimation of legal rules to their abidance by certain elementary expressive rules (e.g. laws must be formulated in general and abstract terms to be properly called laws – see Jürgen Habermas, who understands this dimension as the 'grammatical form' of law, 1996, 189). More broadly, with the term 'syntax' I will define the most basic logical structure of modern law through the discursive interrelation of its constitutive elements as they appeared historically.
158. Ewald, 1986a is the one that has come closer to such a genealogy. However, as I have pointed out earlier, Ewald, in overlapping norms and law, is unable to offer a compelling picture of how law genealogically transformed as a *sui generis* apparatus with a distinctive discursive dimension. The result is that legal statements are thus deprived of a force of their own and law itself is effectively expelled from the locus of power.
159. I am therefore not including in my subsequent analysis authors such as Agamben (2003, 1998), Esposito (2008), and Hardt and Negri (2004, 2000), as they do not address the legal field proper, but take into consideration law only in an oblique fashion in order to address higher political and philosophical issues of sovereignty, immunity, and capitalist exploitation.
160. On this point, Foucault remarked that law's normativity is not to be confounded with 'procedures, processes, and techniques of normalization' (Foucault, 2007, 56). While modern law certainly deploys very complex and significant 'procedures, processes, and techniques' vis-à-vis other biopolitical apparatuses, I will argue that it nonetheless shares with them the same baseline logic of normalisation.
161. Koopman, 2013, 30.

162. Latour, 1999, 304, uses this term in relation to the scientific discourse: 'The way scientific and technical work is made invisible by its own success. When a machine runs efficiently, when a matter of fact is settled, one need focus only on its inputs and outputs and not on its internal complexity. Thus, paradoxically, the more science and technology succeeded the more opaque and obscure they become.'
163. Foucault, 1991, 103.
164. 'It is certain that, in contemporary societies, the state is not simply one of the forms of specific situations of the exercise of power – even if it is the most important – but that, in a certain way, all other forms of power relation must refer to it. But this is not because they are derived from it; rather, it is because power relations have become more and more under state control ... Using here the restricted meaning of the word "government", one could say that power relations have been progressively governmentalised, that is to say, elaborated, rationalised, and centralised in the form of, or under the auspices of, state institutions' (Foucault, 2002b, 345).
165. The following account of the changing meaning of the word state summarises the historical reconstruction offered by Skinner, 1989.
166. Skinner, 1989, 112.
167. Skinner, 1989, 112.
168. The exercise of political power is generally defined in relation to the possession of facilities by means of which physical violence may be exerted (Bobbio, Matteucci and Pasquino, 2004; Weber, 2004, 33; Poggi, 1990, 4) and its primary focus can be understood as 'the activity of attending to the general arrangements of a set of peoples whom chance or choice has brought together' (Laslett, 1956, 2).
169. Skinner, 1989, 102.
170. Skinner, 1989, 123.
171. Runciman, 2003.
172. It should be stressed that the term 'modern state' is somewhat pleonastic, for the characteristics of the state are not to be found 'in any large-scale political entities other than those which began to develop in the early modern phase of European history' (Poggi, 1990, 25).
173. See, for example, Oppenheimer, 2007; Tilly 1990; Poggi 1978; Anderson 1974b.
174. Strath and Torstendahl, 1992; Mann, 1984; Habermas, 1975.
175. Marxist analyses have traditionally emphasised the subservient role of the state vis-à-vis capitalistic bourgeois interests. More recent

leftist approaches, however, have recognised a more autonomous role of the state (see Jessop, 2008; Poulantzas, 1980). For a review that presents a more favourable interpretation of the autonomous nature of the state see also Skocpol (1979).
176. Poggi, 1990, 18, borrows this concept from the German sociologist Heinrich Popitz.
177. Vincent, 1987, 21.
178. Poggi, 1990, 33.
179. Poggi, 1990, 33.
180. Poggi, 1990, 29.
181. Weber, 1968, 37.
182. Weber, 1968, 56. Similarly, see Vincent, 1987, 19–21; Skinner, 1978, 353; Tilly, 1975, 88–90.
183. Held, 1991, 44.
184. For a general overview see Held, 2006, and Sartori, 1987, 257ff.
185. 'From the outset, consent has for democrats been the undisputed principle of legitimate rule' (Held, 1991, 203).
186. Held, 1991, 198.
187. Neumann and Kirchheimer, 1996, 101–42; Hart, 1994, 21; Weber, 1968, 655–8; Kelsen, 1945, 135, 287.
188. Hayek, 1960, 11.
189. Hayek, 1960, 11, 85.
190. Hayek, 1960, 149–50.
191. Hayek, 1960, 153.
192. Hayek, in his argument, aimed at defending an ideal form of the *Rechtsstaat* against the advance of the Welfare State. Within the latter model, Hayek saw an undue expansion of governmental discretion which was dangerous for the very idea of the rule of law, and thus for individual freedom. It should be made clear that an inquiry into the possible causal relationships between these four elements goes beyond the purpose of this work.
193. It is at this juncture that I will depart more markedly from the Foucauldian canon and the presence of Foucault's own voice will be (quite paradoxically) less felt. As I have already mentioned, Foucault was sceptical about the role of law in the formation of the general environment of power in modernity, and his few thoughts on the development of legal thinking through history are not particularly useful to my endeavour.
194. Foucault, 2007, 57.
195. Foucault, 2007, 63.

196. I use this term as developed by Deleuze (2004), and, more recently, by Lévy (1998), and Massumi (2002), that is, an entity whose potentiality is always in becoming and cannot be fixed in preconceived categories and schemes.

Notes to Chapter 2

1. As a consequence, certain notable thinkers such as Machiavelli and Montesquieu will be avoided because, greatly important though they were for the development of political thinking, they focused mainly on the craftsmanship or on a taxonomy of the political form of their times.
2. Foucault, 1977.
3. Foucault, 1967.
4. Foucault, 2002i.
5. Barron, 2002, 982.
6. Foucault, 1977, 47.
7. Foucault, 1977, 53.
8. Foucault, 1977, 50.
9. Foucault, 2003a, 34. As will be manifest in the following pages, I do not share Foucault's equation of the regime of sovereignty with Hobbesian political philosophy.
10. McGrade (1982, 746) suggests that 'Much later medieval philosophy of law can be understood only in relation to factors usually excluded from modern legal discussions: cosmic religious values and moral leadership'.
11. Blumenthal, 1988.
12. Jordan, 1999, 306–13; Strayer, 1980, 251–79; Wood, 1967.
13. The Golden Bull of 1356 was a document promulgated by the Holy Roman Emperor Charles IV to regulate the imperial election and was meant to prevent the possibility that the papacy could influence the election as the secular princes outnumbered the archbishops. See Hlavacek, 2000, 555–6; Zophy, 1980, 183–6; Heer, 1968, 116–17.
14. For a broad overview on Aquinas see Kretzmann and Stump, 1993, in particular 217–32.
15. Aquinas in the *Summa Theologica* refers to Aristotle as 'the Philosopher'. The most thorough edition of the *Summa Theologica* is Aquinas, 1911–25.
16. ST II, I, qu 90, see also ibid. qu 20 and 17. This is entirely compatible with the basic tenets of Aquinas's philosophy, which considered metaphysics as significantly cognitive (Lisska, 1996, 84–9).

17. ST II, I, qu 71.
18. ST II, I, qu 91.
19. ST II, I, qu 71. See also McInerny and O'Callaghan, 2010, section 11.1.
20. ST II, I, qu 95 art. 2 in combination with qu. 91, art. 2.
21. ST II, I, qu 18; Lisska, 1996, 104–6; Welzel, 1965; 89–90.
22. Sabine, 1973, 239.
23. Sabine, 1973, 239.
24. Foucault, 2007, 232–4.
25. Patterson, 1991, 376–82.
26. Aquinas, on some occasions, discussed the importance of the rule of law, constitutional forms of government and political consent (see Finnis, 2008; 1998). It is undeniable, however, that Aquinas's thinking is fundamentally bound to a metaphysical framework that subordinates reason to religion, by integrating the former within Catholic doctrines. This subordination, if taken in its historical context, implies that religious thinking always has the upper hand over any kind of secular claim, thus emasculating any 'democratic' flavour in Saint Thomas's thought. Not surprisingly, while asserting a separation between secular and religious authority, Aquinas recognised that the Pope had the power to dismiss civil rulers whenever they infringed a natural law or they were guilty of heresy (ST. II, II, qu. 10 art. 10; qu. 12 art. 2), thus granting the Catholic Church the ultimate supremacy in political matters and negating any true possibility of self-determination by society.
27. See above, n. 12. On the Avignon Papacy see Zutshi, 2000, 653–73.
28. Jean de Paris was a French philosopher, theologian, and Dominican monk. He taught at the University of Paris and wrote during the controversy between Philip the Fair and Boniface VIII.
29. See Coleman, 2000, 118–33, esp.124–6.
30. See Coleman, 2000, 124; Dunning, 1927, 226.
31. Kilcullen, 2010, sec. 1,1.
32. Sabine, 1973, 265.
33. The Empire was the conception of universal power, deriving its authority from the Roman Empire and, in the Middle Ages, stood roughly as a synonym for secular power. For the theory of an idealised universal Empire, especially in the writings of Dante (*De Monarchia*, c.1312), see Sabine, 1973, 243–6.
34. Dunning, 1927, 226.
35. Sabine, 1973, 251–2.

36. Marsilius of Padua, 1956.
37. As Sabine (1973, 276) observes, 'Whatever reverence faith may deserve as a means of eternal salvation, it has become from a secular point of view simply irrelevant'.
38. *Defensor Pacis*, I, 6.8.
39. On the 'silent opposition' of Marsilius against Aquinas see Strauss and Cropsey, 1963, 227.
40. Strauss and Cropsey, 1963, 235. This automatically excludes any concept of rational natural law as universal consensus is a faulty instrument with which to understand the divine laws of nature (ibid., 243).
41. Sabine, 1973, 277.
42. Sabine, 1973, 279.
43. Sabine, 1973, 274.
44. It must be stressed, however, that scholastic thought was not entirely dominated by Aquinas, but was, in fact, composed by many, sometimes conflicting, strands. See Sabine, 1973, 286ff.; Mayer, 1939, 102ff.
45. On the many strands and trends in political philosophy of the Renaissance see Skinner, 1978, vol. I; 1988, 389–452, and Mayer, 1939, 108–44.
46. It is impossible to provide here a detailed account of the epistemological shift that occurred in the Renaissance. However, I am following the famous thesis of Burckhardt (1990, 98), who observed that, during the Renaissance, for the first time after many centuries '[A]n *objective* treatment and consideration of the state and of all things of this world became possible. The *subjective* side at the same time asserted itself with corresponding emphasis.' Along these lines see also Mayer, 1939, 111–22.
47. Turchetti, 2010.
48. Sabine,1973, 377; King, 1974, 74, 84.
49. In his *Methodus ad facilem historiarum cognitionem* (Bodin, 1945), Bodin asserted that to construct a truly universal legal science is to compare '[A]ll the laws of all, or the most famous, states and select the best variety' (see Franklin, 1991, 301). The most important result of his effort was his analysis of the concept of sovereignty which, famously, led him to the conclusion that the unity of a legal system necessitated the concentration of the whole power under a single entity (be it individualistic, like a monarch, or collegial); see Franklin, 1973, 23ff. This idea, notwithstanding the limitations that

Bodin invoked against monarchical power (in Bodin's thinking the King is *legibus solutus* only in relation to positive law, as he is still subject to natural and divine law and also, to some extent, to customs; see Skinner, 1978, Vol. II, 298–301; King, 1974, 136; Franklin, 1973, 79ff.), has traditionally been identified as the theoretical basis for the absolutist rule.
50. Foucault, 2014a, 9–11.
51. Sabine, 1973, 386–7.
52. Sabine, 1973, 390. On the foundational and path-breaking value of Grotius in moral and political philosophy see Tuck, 1991.
53. One of the most telling examples is the hierarchy that Grotius recognises between the natural law and civil power. The latter, in a way not dissimilar from Aquinas, is subject to the limitation of the former, which coincides with the command of God (see Strauss and Cropsey, 1963, 349). Another example would be Grotius's conviction that certain acts are intrinsically good or evil.
54. Prolegomena, *De Jure Belli Ac Pacis*, §11. For the English translation see Tuck, 2005.
55. Prolegomena, §6–9.
56. See above, n. 54. The passage proposed this idea in hypothetical terms suggesting that the conclusions reached in relation to natural law would be true even if God did not exist. This statement was not original as it had already been proposed by Gregorio da Rimini in the tradition of scholastic rationalism (see Tuck, 1979, 68). Grotius, however, considered this thesis only as intellectual possibility, without refuting the role of God's will in establishing natural law, following, in this sense, the more moderate positions of Francisco Suarez. For a more detailed account of the '*etiamsi daremus*' hypothesis and the philosophical scholastic genealogy of Grotius see Crowe, 1999.
57. In modern times, the classical work on the subject is Gierke, 1934. Following Gierke, see Haakonssen, 1985.
58. Strauss and Cropsey, 1963, 346–7.
59. See Prolegomena, §9–10.
60. Sabine, 1973, 394.
61. Grotius had a remarkable humanist background, and most of his sources and textual authority came from antiquity; see Bederman, 1996, 3.
62. *DJBP*, I cap 1, 12.
63. Strauss and Cropsey, 1963, 347. On the empirical method used by Grotius see Haakonssen, 1985, 250–1.

64. In this particular historical approach lies the modernity of Grotius, and we can appreciate a distance from earlier thinkers. Along these lines see Sabine, 1973, 394.
65. Strauss and Cropsey, 1963, 346.
66. See Miller, 2011, sec. 4.
67. Tuck, 1999, 84; Haakonssen, 1996, 28; Haakonssen, 1985, 240.
68. See Jesseph, 1996, 87ff.; Kavka, 1986, 4–8; Sabine, 1973, 423–7; Watkins, 1965, 43; Strauss and Cropsey, 1963, 354–5. The interest of Hobbes in constructing his political philosophy, moving from the demonstrable principles of geometry, is deeply rooted. It was dictated by his desire to find a solid and 'demonstrable' basis for social living and to avoid civic disagreement (see Bobbio, 1993, 32–5).
69. Sabine (1973, 423–5, 423) points out that 'Hobbes was . . . the first of the great modern philosophers who attempted to bring political theory into intimate relation with a thorough modern system of thought, and he strove to make this system broad enough to account, on scientific principles, for all the facts of nature, including human behaviour both in its individual and social aspects'.
70. *De Cive*, ch. 2, 1 (Hobbes, 1998); *Leviathan*, ch. 14 (Hobbes, 1962).
71. On the state of nature in Hobbes see Ryan, 1996, 216–25.
72. *Leviathan*, ch. 13.
73. This right to everything is described by Bobbio (1993, 39) in the following terms: 'This is the right to all things which nature gives to anyone living outside civil society. To have a right to all things means that, where civil laws have not yet introduced a criterion to distinguish between mine and thine, every human being has the right to appropriate all that falls into his power.'
74. *Leviathan* ch. 13; *De Cive* preface sec. 14.
75. *Leviathan* ch. 17.
76. As a consequence, the state is wholly instrumental to the survival of the individual and is not intended for his moral perfection: 'For Hobbes, the state is one of those machines produced by human beings in order to compensate for the shortcomings of nature, and to replace the deficient products of nature with a product of human ingenuity, that is, an *artificium*' (Bobbio, 1993, 36).
77. Ryan, 1996, 226; Haakonssen, 1985, 240–1.
78. Sabine, 1973, 432.
79. Sabine, 1973, 426.
80. As Strauss and Cropsey (1963, 360) suggest, '[T]he laws of nature, as distinguished from the rights of nature, are precepts of reason

which instruct men as to what they ought to do to avoid the perils to their own self-preservation that follow equally from their natural rights and from their irrational desires'. Similarly see Gauthier (2001). Strauss (1952, 136–7, 155–7) emphasises that the modernity of Hobbes is to be found in the fact that for the first time the basis of the state was not in the law of nature, but in the rights of nature. As we have seen, in the state of nature the individual has a right to everything and this leads inevitably to the war of all against all. To avoid this outcome laws of nature are set up to limit the destructive freedom of all. In this sense, laws are a mere consequence of right.

81. Strauss and Cropsey, 1963, 358. In this perspective it could be said that Hobbes had a tendency towards nominalism, as he refused to attach any predetermined value to human actions, which achieved moral status only within the system of society, *De Cive*, ch. 12, 1. See Sabine, 1973, 435; Welzel, 1965 117–79.
82. *Leviathan* ch. 17. The fact that the Sovereign is considered as an 'earthly God', however, is simply an instrumental device for the organisation of society and does not impinge on the ontological nature of the sovereign, who is a social individual without any divine right.
83. *Contra*, see Dyzenhaus (2001), who, within Hobbes's theory, argues for a concept of constitutional sovereignty essentially limited by the rule of law.
84. Hobbes explicitly argues that the violation of positive law cannot be excused (*Leviathan* ch. 47; *De Cive* ch. 7 sec. 14). The political philosophy of Hobbes is particularly baffling when it comes to the right to resistance, which cannot be properly found in Hobbes's ideas. As a matter of fact, '[t]he point of the whole political philosophy of Hobbes was to discredit any theory of resistance' (Ryan, 1996, 237–41). On the right of resistance in Hobbes see Sabine, 1973, 435–6 and Strauss and Cropsey, 1963, 365–6.
85. Bobbio, 1993, 57 suggests that 'Hobbes's moral theory [is] one of the most daring, though not always consistent, expressions of ethical legalism. This is the theory which holds that the sovereign (and thus God as well) does not command what is just, but what is right is what the sovereign commands.'
86. Welzel, 1965, 184.
87. *Leviathan*, ch. 26; *De Cive*, ch. 14. Famous proponents of this conception of law are Bentham (1970) and Austin (1995).
88. Foucault, 2008, 34.

89. Locke, 1988.
90. Tully, 1993, 10–14. Locke describes political power in the following terms: '*Political power*, then, I take to be a *right* of making laws with penalties of death, and consequently all less penalties, for the regulating and preserving of property, and of employing the force of the community, in the execution of such laws, and in the defence of the common-wealth from foreign injury; and all this only for the public good' (§3). With regard to the exact period and contingent political motivation that led to the writing of the *Two Treatises* see Ashcraft, 1986.
91. A general overview of the interpretations of the meaning of (tacit or explicit) consent in Locke's theory is provided in Milton, 1999, part V.
92. Traditionally, Locke's and Hobbes's states of nature are considered opposite to each other; however, some authors have highlighted some similarities, especially in relation to self-preservation (Sabine, 1973, 487–8; Strauss and Cropsey, 1963, 442). In any case Dunn (1969, 79–83) argues that the influence Hobbes might have had on Locke is 'irrelevant' to the historical comprehension of the *Two Treatises* as the two philosophers had different premises and goals in mind.
93. *Two Treatises* §4.
94. The state of nature is hence not a perfect original situation, but a basic condition menaced by things like the lack of respect for basic rights on the part of other human fellows, conflicting interpretations of the meaning of natural law, and vulnerability to external aggression (see *Two Treatises*, §13).
95. Strauss and Cropsey, 1963, 441.
96. Laslett, 1988, 127–8.
97. It is not clear whether these fundamental rights (which Locke gathers under the 'general name' of property, *Two Treatises*, §123) are an exhaustive list of natural rights.
98. For Locke '[T]he state exists to safeguard the rights and liberties of citizens who are ultimately the best judges of their own interests; . . . accordingly the state must be restricted in scope and constrained in practice in order to ensure the maximum possible freedom of every citizen' (Held, 1985, 13). It is interesting to note that, unlike Hobbes, for Locke the state's power is entirely derivative from natural law and public authorities have no more right than each single citizen (Sabine, 1973, 490; Strauss and Cropsey, 1963, 454). To this

end, the separation of powers assumes for Locke a paramount importance (see *Two Treatises* §143).

99. Held argues for the modernity of Locke and stresses his role in the development of liberal democratic ideas (Held, 1985, 14). This claim, however, should not be overemphasised; see Dunn, 1980, 53–77.

100. Sabine, 1973, 488 observes that Locke's natural law showed little innovation over older versions, retaining their 'emotional connotations and almost religious compulsions'. In this perspective Locke's individualism seems watered down by the assumption that in the harmony of nature the good of the community and the good of all individuals necessarily coincide. *Contra*, Strauss (1953) argues that the theological references in Locke have a merely rhetorical function.

101. Although Locke was very vague about the actual content of natural law; see Tuckness, 2011, sec. 1; Sabine, 1973, 486; Dunn, 1969, 187.

102. Sabine aptly notes that natural, positive, and moral law perfectly coincide (1973, 494). In this perspective, the question of whether natural law is focused on rights (as Strauss, 1953, 202–51, suggests) or duties (this position is taken by Tully, 1993; Ashcraft, 1986; Dunn, 1969) does not seem entirely relevant.

103. Not surprisingly, Locke's theory works well as a justification of rebellion (Tully, 1993, 21–3; Strauss and Cropsey, 1973, 461–4), but is rather vague on how government and citizens are linked by trust.

104. 'Human political arrangements derive their sole legitimacy from their embodiment of the purposes of God' (Dunn, 1969, 93, 124–7; similarly Uzgalis, 2010, sec. 3.2; Jolley, 1999, 195). Consequently the adoption of a majority rule has no proper moral value as it does not necessarily involve any process of mutual recognition and can lead to a dictatorship of majority (see Sabine, 1973, 491–2; Kendall, 1941).

105. Pitkin, 1965. Similarly Strauss and Cropsey, 1973, 460.

106. Dunn, 1980, 34–5. As a matter of fact, people exercise their supreme power actively only in society without government, but where a government is in place the power of the people is entirely latent (*Two Treatises* §149). Other authors, however, understand 'consent' in Locke's theory as active political participation (see Tully, 1993, 33–7 and Palmenatz, 1963, 228, who link consent with a relationship of trust between government and citizens).

107. A stronger understanding of consent would lead to anarchic consequences; see Simmons, 1993.
108. Held, 1985, 13.
109. It does not come as a surprise that the theories of Hobbes and Locke are mainly centred, though with different outcomes, on the issue of rebellion and civil war.
110. Foucault, 1980b, 121.
111. Habermas, 1992; Blumenberg, 1985.
112. Habermas, 1989.
113. Foucault, 2007, 106–8.
114. 'The problem is to find a form of association which will defend and protect with the whole common force the person and goods of each associate, and in which each, while uniting himself with all, may still obey himself alone, and remain as free as before' (*The Social Contract*, I, 6). Quotations are taken from Rousseau, 1995.
115. *Social Contract* II, 3.
116. Sabine, 1973, 539–44; Strauss and Cropsey, 1963; Dunning, 1927, 23.
117. Lemos, 1977, 148–52. This interpretation could easily lead us to consider Rousseau's theory as one supporting the dictatorship of majority; see Talmon, 1960, 40–8.
118. Shklar, 1969, 184–97.
119. Riley, 1995, 2: 'In Rousseau, the general will is non-natural: it is artificially produced (over time) through the "denaturing", counter-egoistic educative ministrations of Lycurgus or Moses.'
120. For an analysis of the difference see Allen, 1961. For the use of the term 'general will' prior to Rousseau see Riley, 1986.
121. Rawls, 2007, 224.
122. Rawls, 2007, 227.
123. *Social Contract*, II, 6; Strauss and Cropsey, 1963, 523.
124. 'When I say that the object of laws is always general, I mean that law considers subjects en masse and actions in the abstract, and never a particular person or action' (*Social Contract* II, 6).
125. I am not sure whether this position is entirely original or not. The author who seems most proximate to this interpretation is Masters, 1968, 327–34. As he suggests: 'The general will, which is to say an "act of sovereignty" or any "law", must fulfil two formal or definitional requirements: it must be willed by all members of the society, and it must apply to all members of the society' (ibid., 328).
126. Viroli (1988, 148–87) emphasises the role of law in upholding

liberty within Rousseau's theory. It seems to me that this interpretation solves some of the fallacies that might otherwise be seen in Rousseau's thought. For example, such a reading places in a different light the problem of the infallibility of the general will and the danger of a dictatorship of the majority that would otherwise arise (see above, n. 117).
127. *Social Contract* II, 4.
128. It must be noted, however, that Rousseau was at best ambiguous in relation to the democratic rule; see Viroli, 1987.
129. *Social Contract*, III, 15. His ideal state would be a city-state or a very small and rural country like Corsica where people could make direct use of their sovereignty without the need for any government or magistrate, and where there would be no party politics (Sabine, 1973, 539; Shklar, 1969, 174; Strauss and Cropsey, 1963, 516, 526; Dunning, 1927, 34–8). On the problem of the relationship between the acts of sovereignty as declarations of principle and the role of magistrates in the actualisation of those principles see Shklar, 1969, 188–90; Masters, 1968, 335–40.
130. Notably, Kant's political philosophy is unsystematic and scattered among different texts (on the difficulty of conceiving a unitary political theory in Kant see Arendt, 1982, 7–10). The main work dealing with the problem of legality is *Rechstlehren* (1790) (Kant, 2002), which forms the first part of *The Metaphysics of Morals* (1797). Traditionally, Kant's theory of law is conceived as a complement to his moral theory (Kersting, 1992a, 347) and was considered a lesser achievement by the philosopher.
131. Kant, 2002, 56.
132. Welzel, 1965, 257. It must be noted that although Kant firmly believed in the power of human morality, he was conscious freedom was a matter of personal choice: 'Theoretical philosophy can prove the possibility of freedom of the will . . . but not its actuality; this can follow only from our firm consciousness . . . of being bound by the moral law itself' (Guyer, 1993, 19).
133. Kant, 2002, Introduction B, 45.
134. On the relationship between Kant's and Rousseau's political theory see Welzel, 1965, 239–40.
135. Kant, 2002, §6, 72.
136. The categorical imperative is Kant's fundamental moral principle that '[C]ommands us to exercise our *wills* in a particular way, not to perform some action or other. It is *categorical* in virtue of applying

to us unconditionally, or simply because we possess rational wills, without reference to any ends that we might or might not have' (Johnson, 2010, sec. 4). On the role of the categorical imperative in Kant's political theory see O'Neill, 1992, 50–80. It is not a surprise, then, that Kant, while employing the concept of the social contract, empties it of any voluntaristic content (distancing himself from Rousseau) and depicts it as a practically necessary principle of reason: 'The norm of the contract is obviously the counterpart to the categorical imperative of political action. Just as the categorical imperative as a moral principle allows for the evaluation of the lawfulness of maxims, so does the original contract as the principle of public justice serve to measure the justice of positive law' (Kersting, 1992a, 355).
137. Habermas, 1996, 28–9.
138. Kersting (1992b, 144–7) suggests in this regard that Kant's state is a '*Rechtsstaat* and nothing else: its ground, its form and its purpose is right'.
139. Kersting (1992a, 344–5) further argues that '[I]n the philosophy of right and in the political philosophy that is grounded upon it, exactly as was already done in moral philosophy, the way is thereby barred to every application of natural purposes, human needs and interests, and substantive ethical considerations ... Only the properties of reason itself are available to make determinate the nonempirical concept of right: lawfulness, universality, formality, and necessity.'
140. Kersting (1992a, 342) opines that Kant provided an entirely new theoretical foundation for justification in practical philosophy, identifying it in the laws of human reason alone.
141. Kant, 2002, §46, 166–9.
142. Kersting, 1992b, 158–63.
143. Kersting, 1992b, 152.
144. Kersting, 1992a, 345.
145. Kersting, 1992a, 354–5.
146. For example, Kant identifies economic independence as the basis for active citizenship and seems to deny to women any political rights (Kant, 2002, §46, 168).
147. Weinrib emphasises the significance of the practical reality of an idea of reason in Kant's thinking, identifying in the freedom of will the focal point that unites the various aspects of the practical idea of reason into a network of conceptual independencies: '[F]ree will can ... be identified as the point on which everything practical (in

Kant's sense), including law, converges' (Weinrib, 1992, 21). As a consequence the principle of right has to be seen as the external aspect of practical reason, or practical reason as it pertains to interaction among free wills. (ibid. 27). 'As a philosophy of compromise and reform, Kant's political philosophy forms a pragmatic synthesis of Hobbes's sense of political reality and Rousseau's ideal of justice' (Kersting, 1992a, 359).

148. Dunning (1927, 130–6) has little consideration for Kant's political doctrine, resenting its 'inconsistency and incoherence'. On these 'philosophical misdemeanours' that contradict Kant's own premises see Kersting, 1992a, 153–4.

149. Kersting, 1992b, 345. Kant's proceduralism of democratic will is hence very different from the discourse ethics of Apel or Habermas, precisely because '[the] procedure of a genesis through a democratic plebiscite can be simulated and replaced by the thought-experiment of universalisability' (Kersting, 1992b, 355).

150. It can rightly be said that Kant's concept of the state of right completely dispenses with a social component (Kersting, 1992a, 356) and that the state in Kant is akin to a simulation or a 'thought experiment' (Kersting, 1992b, 157–8). Various scholars, however, defend Kant's perspective. Weinrib, while recognising that Kant's conception of the self might run the risk of 'denying our experience as socially and historically situated beings constituted in some crucial sense by the communities in which we live and by the forms of life in which we participate', suggests that the construction of an abstract free will requires interaction with others (1992, 40–2, 40). Arendt (1982) suggests that Kant's philosophy relies on an idea of communication that is based on the community sense that everyone has in relation to her social world. Consequently, 'One judges always as a member of a community, guided by one's community sense, one's *sensus communis*. But in the last analysis, on is a member of a world community by the fact of being human; this is one's "cosmopolitan existence"' (ibid., 75). O'Neill (1992, 75–9), following this line of thinking, stresses that in the *Critique of Judgement* Kant relies, in the formation of the categorical imperative, on the *sensus communis*, which is 'a critical faculty which in its reflective act takes account of the mode of representation of everyone else in order, as it were, to weight its judgement with the collective reason of mankind' (ibid., 76). As a result Kant does not deify reason, but shows that 'the only route by which we can vindicate certain ways of thinking and acting,

and claim that those ways have authority, is by considering how we must discipline our thinking' (ibid. 78). The process that allows us to move from the general to the specific and vice versa is made possible, according to Arendt, by the use of the *example* (as described in the *Critique of Judgement*: Kant, 1952), which, in contrast to the epistemic *schema* (as described in the *Critique of Pure Reason*: Kant, 1933), is 'the particular that contains in itself, or is supposed to contain, a concept or a general rule' (Arendt, 1982, 84). This interesting reading might conclusively resolve some doubts regarding the supposed capacity of reason to imagine the Other, however, it seems somehow to neglect the dry abstractness of Kant's moral and political philosophy (that shies away from direct practical action and places a messianic faith in the purposive future of mankind).

151. Similar critiques have been put forward by Sandel (1998) against John Rawls's Kantian-based constructivist political doctrine contained in *A Theory of Justice* (1972).
152. Taylor (1979, 69) suggests that Hegel's political philosophy was an attempt to define two trends in the Romantic generation: '[T]he aspiration to radical autonomy on one hand, and the expressive unity with nature and within society on the other'.
153. *Philosophy of Right*, §258 Addition; §260 (quotations are taken from Hegel, 1967). On this point see Strauss and Cropsey, 1963, 628.
154. The dialectical method is a specific mode of reasoning developed by Hegel that accounts for all dynamics of reality and changes in the world. The term 'dialectics' goes as far back as Plato. In Hegel, however, it assumes a new meaning. Inwood sketches it out as follows: '[The dialectical method] . . . involves three steps: (1) One or more concepts or categories are taken as fixed, sharply defined and distinct from each other. This is the stage of UNDERSTANDING. (2) When we reflect on such categories, one or more contradictions emerge in them. This is the stage of dialectic proper, or of dialectical or negative REASON. (3) The result of this dialectic is a new, higher category, which embraces the earlier categories and resolves the contradiction involved in them. This is the stage of SPECULATION of positive reason' (1992, 81–2). See Hegel's *Encyclopaedia*, §79–82 (Hegel, 1975).
155. This is not an ontological starting point (the individual is not the fundamental 'atom' of society), but simply an 'immediate' starting point to demonstrate that what is simple is determinate only if part of a complex structure or process; see Redding, 2010, sec. 3.3.

156. As Taylor (1979, 83) puts it, 'Sittlichkeit refers to the moral obligations I have to an on-going community of which I am part ... The crucial characteristic of Sittlichkeit is that it enjoins us to bring about what already is. This is a paradoxical way of putting it, but in fact the common life which is the basis of my sittlich obligation is already there in existence ... Hence in Sittlichkeit there is no gap between what ought to be and what is, between Sollen and Sein.' Man, in other words, is not able by himself alone to constitute a moral world, but needs an embeddedness in and a confrontation with the 'concrete on-going life of the community' (Plant, 1973, 160).
157. For example, in the Addition to PR §252–5 the corporations are clearly understood in these terms. They are described as fictional second families for their members, thus replicating, while incorporating, the lower system of the private family.
158. Avineri, 1972, viii, suggests that 'Hegel's theory of the state is also a theory of social relations on a much wider sense'.
159. For a discussion of the political structure as a system of mediation through representation see Sabine 1973, 599, and Avineri, 1972, 161–6. At the highest level, these systems are embodied in corporations in the first instance and in the parliamentary system secondly (Taylor, 1979, 108).
160. Hegel (PR §302 Addition) describes the constitution, which informs all social formations, as a system of mediation that is able to integrate within the state the multitude of a population as one of its organs. Plant (1973, 89) rightly observes that for Hegel 'political experience is not a construction of the Ego, nor a mere addendum to human life, a necessary convenience', but a true development of the self-consciousness of the individual in relation to her community.
161. PR §217 Addition. Sabine rightly identifies Hegel's state with a Rechtsstaat (1973, 600). On the rule of law in Hegel's Philosophy of Right see Avineri, 1972, 190–3.
162. Plant, 1973, 153. Hegel, in §258, defines subjective freedom and objective freedom respectively as 'freedom of everyone in his knowing and in his volition of particular ends' and 'freedom of the universal or substantial will' (that is, the general freedom of society).
163. PR, §147.
164. Avineri, 1972, 179.
165. Strauss and Cropsey, 1963, 629, 632.
166. The reading of some passages from the Philosophy of Right could help to clarify Hegel's vision of rights and their relation to the

law. In the remark to §211 Hegel argues: 'In becoming law, what is right acquires for the first time not only the form proper to its universality, but also its determinacy. Hence making a law is not to be represented as merely the expression of a rule of behaviour valid for everyone, though that is one moment in legislation; the more important moment, the inner essence of the matter, is knowledge of the content of the law in its determinate universality.' He then continues (§212), to suggest: 'It is only because of this identity between its implicit and its posited character that positive law has obligatory force in virtue of its rightness. In being posited in positive law, the right acquires determinate existence.' See also §217 and Addition.
167. PR §258. That posited law is therefore the central mover of the political dynamic of society seems also confirmed by §230, where the Police and the Corporations are understood as mere means of actualisation of law.
168. See the critiques by Russell, 2005, and Popper, 1995.
169. Hegel is generally depicted as a conservative if not a reactionary (Sabine, 1973, 571), and it must be recognised that the Hegelian theory of the state and law recognises freedom and equality only within the limits of law (Strauss and Cropsey, 1963, 646–7). The dynamics of the formation of law, however, are precisely intended to give an ethical meaning to those limits. See *ex multis* Taylor, 1979; Plant, 1973; Avineri, 1972.
170. PR §265 Addition.
171. *Encyclopaedia* §539 (Hegel, 1971): 'That the citizens are equal before the law contains a great truth, but which so expressed is a tautology: it only states that the legal status in general exists, that the laws rule. But, as regards the concrete, the citizens – besides their personality – are equal before the law only in these points when they are otherwise equal outside the law. Only that equality which (in whatever way it be) they, as it happens, otherwise have in property, age, physical strength, talent, skill, etc. – or even in crime, can and ought to make them deserve equal treatment before the law: only it can make them – as regards taxation, military service, eligibility to office, etc.– punishment, etc. – equal in the concrete.'
172. PR §260 and Addition. Sabine (1973, 592–3) suggests that Hegel's philosophy of law dealt with two principal subjects: an ethical theory of freedom and its relation to authority, and a theory of the state, its constitutional structure and its relation to the institutions of civil society. In this regard, the *Philosophy of Right* for Hegel is a

philosophical science that investigates the authority of the state through the process of formation of its laws.
173. This line of reasoning is entirely congruent with the dialectic method as understood by Hegel, which famously unifies the opposites. The substantive argument of coextensiveness is strikingly similar to the legal and political theory Habermas proposes in *Between Facts and Norms* (1996).
174. Taylor, 1979, 93.
175. Along these lines (although with some reservations about the practicability of such theory) see Wolff, 2004, 291–322. Hegel's attempt was in fact to combine the abstract notion of a right bearer individual (which could hardly withstand historical of psychological scrutiny) with the ethical dimension of a political community (Sabine, 1973, 592–8). In his theory, therefore, the state and the individual are not put into a hierarchical position; rather, they are in a mutually informing and constituting relationship evoking the image of a living being. In this regard see Pelczynski, 1984, 56–7; Taylor, 1979, 87; Plant, 1973, 91.
176. According to Sabine (1973, 604), with Hegel 'Politics was enriched and made vastly more realistic when legalism and individualism were supplemented by the historical study of institutions and by a concrete understanding of social and economic factors in government and in human psychology'. Along the same lines Avineri, 1972, x, states: '[W]hile political philosophy before Hegel was preoccupied with legitimacy, Hegel introduced the dimension of change and historicity which has since become central to modern political thought.'
177. Taylor, 1979, 116, credits Hegel with identifying one of the major problems of modern democracy, which 'put at its simplest, is this: the modern ideology of equality and of total participation leads to a homogenisation of society. This shakes men loose from their traditional communities, but cannot replace them as a focus of identity.'
178. PR §276–7.
179. The danger of alienation is hence always a possible threat lurking in the dynamics of the state, and arises 'when goals, norms or ends which define the common practices or institutions begin to seem irrelevant or even monstrous, or when the norms are redefined so that the practices appear a travesty of them' (Taylor, 1979, 90).
180. Pelczynski (1984, 63) defines the Hegelian state as 'an institutional public forum in which matters concerning the community as a

whole are debated and decided upon, and the decisions carried out by the government', and where 'the needs of civil society and of the national community are appraised and evaluated, and the unity of private interests and community values is realized in a conscious and organized manner'. Similarly Plant, 1979, 171–2.

181. Graus (1976) identifies in the Great Peasant War of 1525 one of the greatest political calls for equality and freedom in the Middle Ages and a firm rejection of static social structures resulting from the divine will.
182. Wilks, 1963, iii.
183. Locke, *Two Treatises* §4–5. Dahl (1989, 85) refers to this as the 'idea of intrinsic equality'. This idea does not immediately imply a democratic discourse which is connected with the more complex 'strong principle of equality' – i.e. 'all the members of the association are adequately qualified to participate on an equal footing with the other in the process of governing the association' (ibid., 31). As Dahl points out, however, democracy is not automatically an inclusive practice (1989, 32–3). For it to be really inclusive, the 'strong principle of equality' must be supported, what Dahl calls the 'principle of equal consideration of interests' and the 'presumption of personal autonomy' (1989, 97–105; on the problem of inclusion see ch. 9).
184. Sartori (1987, 278–97) stresses the substantive difference that exists between ante-liberal democracy (which he identifies with the ideal-type of ancient Greek democracy where the individual did not enjoy a legitimate private space conceived as the moral as well as the juridical protection of the single human person) and liberal democracy (which Sartori identifies with modern Western democracies based on a 'theory and practice of the juridical defence, through the constitutional state, of individual political freedom, of individual liberty', ibid. 380). Similarly, and for a broader account of the differences between ancient and liberal democracy, see Held, 2006, chs 1 and 3.

Notes to Chapter 3

1. Here 'constitution' is understood in the modern sense as the ensemble of all those formalised rules that make possible and regulate the constitution of society as a legal entity. In this sense, the term 'constitution' is intrinsically linked with the idea of 'constitutionalism' (see Vile, 1967; Waluchow, 2014).

2. This is no place for a comprehensive account of the historical development of political, institutional and legal arrangements from medieval times onwards. For an overview of feudal society and its socio-political structure see Lupoi, 2000; Poggi, 1978; Anderson, 1974a; LeGoff, 1968; Ganshof, 1964; Bloch; 1961; Strayer, 1959; Gierke, 1938. On absolutism see Wiesner-Hanks, 2006; Merriman 2004; Doyle 1992; Henshall, 1992; Tilly, 1990; Koenigsberger, 1987; Shennan 1986; Kamen, 1984; Weber, 1981; Tigar, 1977; Rabb, 1975; Anderson, 1974b; Shennan, 1974.
3. Hayek (1960, 150) suggests a theoretical distinction between commands and abstract laws: 'The important difference between the two concepts lies in the fact that, as we move from commands to laws, the source of the decision on what particular action is to be taken shifts progressively from the issue of the command of law to the acting person. The ideal type of command determines uniquely the action to be performed and leaves those to whom it is addressed no chance to use their own knowledge or follow their own predilections. The action performed according to such commands exclusively serves the purposes of him who has issued it. The ideal type of law, on the other hand, provides merely additional information to be taken into account in the decision of the actor.' In abstract laws, therefore, rules merely provide the framework within which the individual must move but within which the decisions are his' (ibid., 152). As Hayek himself recognises (ibid. 159–61), within more structured and complex societies abstract laws provide a more efficient means of social co-ordination while commands are typical of simpler communities. By contrast, the social structure of feudalism was more apt to the concrete command of local powerful authorities (Bloch, 1961, 442ff.).
4. Simmonds, 1984, 42.
5. Patterson, 1991, 376–401.
6. It might be argued that my analysis has been specific in relation to the UK and USA but over-generalised in relation to the civil law constitutional discourse in taking the French Declaration as paradigmatic of the whole continental European experience. In this regard I should emphasise the importance of the French regime in two ways. First, France was the country that expressed the clearest instance of an absolutist regime, and also the clearest example of an early European republican and liberal democracy. France, having swung from one extreme to the other on the spectrum of political

forms (from perfect absolutism to democratic republic and back to Restoration and Imperial rule), seems to represent an ideal example for the study of the emergence of a legal discourse of equality and freedom in Europe (where absolutist rule dominated and then faded into obscurity thereafter). Secondly, it should be recalled that the basic tenets of the French legal revolutionary discourse were exported across Europe by the Napoleonic Code, thus having a profound impact on the legal systems of many European countries (see Lyons, 1994, 102–3; Bergeron, 1981, 5–14; Lefebvre, 1969, 152–3).

7. Bailyn, 1967.
8. Palmer, 1959.
9. By the fifteenth century the feudal mode of production had reached its intrinsic limits. The economic and societal crisis of the time was the evidence of the structural deficiencies of that system. The basic dynamic that gave way to the formation of absolutist states in Europe can be said to be the product of the conflicting relationship among feudal lords, a burgeoning bourgeoisie concentrated in towns and the peasantry (Anderson, 1974b). From the beginning of the fifteenth century onwards, these three groups entered into a harsh confrontation that reshaped the institutional, legal and political structures of feudalism (Shennan, 1986; Rabb, 1975). Conflict was caused, on the one hand, by the fundamental event represented by the transformation of dues into money rents, which disrupted the mechanism of political and economic oppression of the peasantry that constituted the backbone of feudalism (Anderson, 1974b, 19). On the other hand, the rise of towns as centres of political and economic power began to challenge also the rule of local lords, establishing themselves as 'centres of solidarity action by single powerless individuals . . . [claiming] rights that were corporate in nature, i.e. that attached to individuals only by virtue of their membership in a constituted collectivity capable of operating as a collective entity' (Poggi, 1978, 37). The answer of the system to these threats was a 'displacement of politico-legal coercion upwards towards a centralised, militarised summit – the absolutist state' (Anderson, 1974b, 19). The absolutist state can therefore be read as the arrangement that feudal nobility organised to maintain its positions of power: '[A]bsolutism was essentially just this: a redeployed and recharged apparatus of feudal domination . . . the new political carapace of a threatened nobility' (Anderson, 1974b, 18).

10. The Revolution was dubbed 'glorious' only at the beginning of the eighteenth century, and the steady use of such a definition is traceable to the 1850s (Hertzler, 1987).
11. Burke, 1923, §51.
12. Anderson, 1974b, 113–42.
13. Already identifiable in some ways in the clause 61 of the Magna Carta and first established in a very basic form through the Provisions of Oxford of 1258 during the reign of Henry III, the Parliament developed as an institution from Edward I onwards until it adopted its modern form to a large extent under the Tudor dynasty. The attempts made by James I and after by his son Charles II at the beginning of the seventeenth century to restrain parliamentary power and to introduce an absolutist regime in England failed, generating the English Civil War. For a good overview of the topic see Davies and Denton, 1981.
14. Marongiu, 1968.
15. For the origins and evolution of the medieval Parliaments, see Holmes, 1962, 83–8; Sayles, 1952, 448–57.
16. The creation of the House of Commons dates back to Edward III and is linked with the need to levy taxes; see Harriss, 1975, 509–17.
17. For the role of parliament in England see Sayles, 1975. On this issue, however, Patterson (1991, 370) suggests that the English parliament evolved into a territorial system of representation only because of a series of 'lucky' convergences. According to Holt (1981, 24), the parliament in the Middle Ages was just a means of good administration by which the King could be aware of 'how a liberty or privilege, once conceded, was working'.
18. The so-called Whig interpretation of history and the constitution is described by Pocock (1957, 46) in the following terms: 'Put very briefly, what occurred was that belief in the antiquity of the common law encouraged belief in the existence of an ancient Constitution, reference to which was constantly made, precedents, maxims and principles from which were constantly alleged, in which was constantly asserted to be in some way immune from the King's prerogative action; and discussion in these terms formed one of the century's chief modes of political argument.'
19. The classic modern work on the Glorious Revolution is Macaulay, 1906. Obviously the topic has been heavily researched since. For further reference see Pincus, 2009; Miller, 1997; Ashley, 1966;

Trevelyan, 1938. On the very immediate events that preceded the Revolution see Jones, 1990.
20. Pincus, 2009.
21. Pincus, 2009, 159–62, 216–17, 480–6.
22. This thesis is perfectly compatible with the argument proposed by Anderson, 1974b, 136–43, about the late development of an absolutist drive in England and the impossibility of its success.
23. Lovell (1962, 408–14) emphasises the growth in statutory legislation after the 1688 Revolution.
24. This evolution towards a Parliament that was going to consider itself unbound by law was completely at odds with the theory of 'artificial reason' advanced by Coke (Pocock, 1957, 35ff.).
25. The first document explicitly mentioning 'fundamental law' in England dates back to 1596 in the *Epistle Dedicatory to Bacon's Maxims of the Law*, but the concept had an older history (Gough, 1955, 51).
26. It must be noted that the term 'constitution' acquired the contemporary meaning of 'fundamental legal text' only during the American Revolution. Originally, it referred to the political-institutional arrangement which 'constituted' a given polity. As such, the term 'constitution' in late medieval times had a natural and not a positivistic legal meaning (McIlwain, 1947, 23–41).
27. There was a widespread consensus over the position proposed by Sir John Fortescue (1394–1479) in *De Laudibus Legum Angliae* (1468–71) that England was characterised by a *dominium politicum et regale* whereby the King ruled with the consent and advice of the Parliament. Not only was this idea widely shared during the Restoration, implying that neither the King nor the Parliament were supreme in their decisions, but even after the Glorious Revolution the notion of 'mixed monarchy' was never abandoned. As a matter of fact, Robert Ferguson (*A Brief Justification of the Prince of Orange's Descent into England*, 1689) and William Atwood (*The Fundamental Constitution of the English Government, proving King William and Queen Mary our Lawful and Rightful King and Queen*, 1690) echoed earlier works of Charles Herle (*A Fuller Answer to a Treatise written by Dr Ferne*, 1642) and Philip Hunton (*A Treatise on monarchy*, 1643) about mixed monarchy.
28. This idea has been established at least since the 'Age of Bracton' in the thirteenth century (Pollock and Maitland, 1952).
29. Disputes such as Bate's Case or Case of Impositions (1606) and the

Ship Money Case (1637), revolved precisely around the question of the presence of a situation of emergency that would empower the King to act without seeking the consent of the Parliament (see Lobban, 2007, 47–51, 59–61).
30. James I affirmed the divine rights of kings in *The True Law of Free Monarchies* (1598) and *Basilikon Doron* (1599).
31. The Parliamentarian position was epitomised by Sir Edward Coke (1552–1664), who, referring to Bracton's formula that kings were subject to God and the law, claimed that the English monarch was bound by the law (see Lobban, 2007, 41).
32. The struggle over sovereignty was a later historical by-product of the seventeenth-century confrontation between the King and the Parliament. The idea of absolute parliamentary sovereignty over a balanced constitution had historically hardly any supporters; James I's reckless attempts to affirm absolutism led to a radicalisation of constitutional positions and, eventually, to a clash that saw supporters of parliamentary sovereignty victorious (Gough, 1955, 55–6).
33. Dicey, 1959, 3.
34. Bellamy (2007, 80) frames this point in the following terms: '[T]he only alternative to the domination of personal rule is for the people to be citizens and rule themselves. Paradoxically, therefore, the rule of law depends on the democratic self-rule of persons. It can be secured only if all citizens, usually through their elected representatives, can command equal consideration in the making of collective rules, and everyone in the body politic – including those authorised to rule – is equally subject to whatever laws they impose upon themselves.'
35. Hart, 1994.
36. Austin, 1995.
37. See above, n. 27.
38. See above, n. 31.
39. As is known, in England, Coke's legal judgments were cherry-picked by later legal scholars to the effect that only his considerations on the supremacy of the Parliament over the King were accepted, while his ideas about a Parliament similarly bound by the fundamental law of the land were rejected as a lapse of judgement.
40. Burgess, 1996, 180. For the idea that the English Parliament operated as a court see Gough, 1955; McIlwain, 1910, 1947.
41. Dr Bonham's case, where Coke declared (English Report 77: 652) that 'the common law will control Acts of parliament, and some-

times adjudge them to be utterly void', is the most famous and studied example.
42. See *ex multis* Lobban, 2007; Tubbs, 2000; Stoner, 199; Berger 19692; Plucknett 1926.
43. Lobban, 2007, 33–5.
44. Lobban, 2007, 66.
45. Hooker (1977, VIII.2.11) did not have a vision of the constitution as something static and unchangeable.
46. Hooker 1977, Preface, 6.6.
47. Lobban, 2007, 68.
48. Hale (1713) 1971, 3.
49. Selden explicitly declared (echoing Hunton; see above, n. 27) that, in the event of open conflict between the monarch and Parliament, law could not settle the dispute, and the final decision of who is supreme 'is by arms' (Selden, 1927, 137).
50. Parker. *Some Few Observations upon his Majesties late answer to the Declaration, or remonstrance of the Lords and Commons of the 19 of May 1642*, cited by Lobban, 2007, 75.
51. 'The theory of equal access to the law was often hard to translate into practice. So, if the law was meant to be universal, not only symbolically but also in reality, it was often remote' (Hoppit, 2000, 461). However, the same author highlights the fact that among elites there was an extensive debate with regard to the inadequacies of the rule of law. Plumb (1967, 66–97) observes that the beginning of parliamentary rule was characterised by the progressive establishment of a political aristocratic oligarchy and the emergence of office venality; similarly Trevelyan, 1944, 509–12.
52. Hoppit, 2000.
53. Holt, 1992, 1985. However, against the 'myth' of Magna Carta see Radin, 1947 and Jenks, 1902.
54. It can be said, to a certain extent, that such a journey is still under way, considering the orthodox view on absolute parliamentary sovereignty in the UK.
55. The Bill of Rights is actually framed within the context of the theory of the original contract between the monarch and his subjects. For an overview on this subject, and to explore the problem of whether Charles II abdicated (which would make the foundation of the Bill on the original contract shaky) or was deposed (which would prove the breaking of the contract by the King), see Miller, 1982; Slaughter, 1981; Kenyon, 1977, 7–11; Kenyon, 1974.

56. Dicey, 1959, Part II, Ch. XIII.
57. In other words, when a collective body self-regulates it necessarily follows the logic of the norm.
58. The amount of scholarly work on this subject is massive. For a general reference see Middlekauff, 2005.
59. Kelly, Harbison and Belz, 1991, 59; Wood 1972, 10–18. This interpretation in a certain way downplays the role of natural law theories (especially Locke's) in the political debate between England and the Colonies (a classical thesis based on Jefferson's own declaration and supported by Becker, 1958) but it reflects accurately the terms of the dispute. See also Reid, 1991, 5.
60. Reid, 1993, 66–7. The English society was increasingly seen in America as a corruption of the ideals of the Glorious Revolution; see Wood, 1972, 28–36; Bailyn, 1967, 46–7.
61. Reid, 1993, 63–79.
62. There was indeed a sense of impending conspiracy against American liberties among colonists: see Wood, 1972, 36–43; Bailyn, 1967, 144–60. On the concept of liberty in the age of the American Revolution see Reid, 1988.
63. On the theory of contract and its non-fictitious nature in the context of the American Revolution see Reid, 1991, 116.
64. Reid, 1991, 52; Mayer, 1994, 37.
65. 'For American Whigs, Parliament was now Charles I and James II. Parliament was king' (Reid, 1991, 54).
66. The bafflement of British Tories in front of a revolution that had so 'little real cause' is telling of the different views across the Atlantic about the American revolt (Wood, 1972, 3–4).
67. Self-government was a concept strictly related to liberty (that is, the protection against arbitrary power – see Reid, 1991, 142–51) and to consent (that is, that only laws that were consented to were actually binding, see ibid., 111–26).
68. On the issue of virtual vs actual representation in the Anglo-American debate see Reid, 1993, 83–96.
69. Representation can thus be understood as the institutional mechanism that guaranteed Consent and as a consequence Liberty (Reid, 1993, 90).
70. What made this conception of virtual representation intelligible, and lent it its force in English thought, was the assumption that the English, despite great inequalities among their ranks, were essentially a unitary homogeneous people with a fundamental interest

in common (Wood, 1972, 174). On the issue of virtual vs actual representation see Reid, 1993, 83–96; Bailyn, 1967, 162–74. On representation more generally see Reid, 1989.

71. It must also be noted that the thirteen colonies did not opt later for a universal suffrage that would go beyond the virtual representation, thus demonstrating that the issue of representation did not have the overriding importance it was claimed to have. See Middlekauff, 2005.
72. Pole, 1983, 65–86.
73. This doctrine supposed 'that representatives represented the interests, conditions and circumstances of the constituency sending them to the House of Commons' (Reid, 1993, 86).
74. According to this doctrine 'there was always some member who shared the interests of every nonelector and, therefore, represented the interests of that nonelector' (Reid, 1993, 86).
75. Reid, 1993, 87.
76. Middlekauff, 2005.
77. See Reid, 1993, 76–82.
78. It should be noted that the Declaration was more a political document than a legal one. It was, in other words, an attempt to justify rebellion against the motherland and to establish the rightness of Colonies' actions: 'The Declaration of Independence is a short document aimed at justifying legally and morally an action already undertaken' (Howard, 1990, 63). For an overview of the significance of the Declaration see the classical study by Becker, 1958.
79. It must be stressed that I am referring here to the characteristics that modern law has (generality of application and abstraction of its provisions) and not to the constitutional mechanisms that regulate its production.
80. Lobban, 2007, 123.
81. Wood, 1972, 132.
82. Hamilton, Madison and Jay (1788) 1961, 80.
83. Hamilton, Madison and Jay (1788) 1961, 289.
84. Hamilton, Madison and Jay (1788) 1961, 83.
85. Hamilton, Madison and Jay (1788) 1961, 83.
86. Hamilton, Madison and Jay (1788) 1961, 323; see also Wood, 1992.
87. Hamilton, Madison and Jay (1788) 1961, 322–3.
88. E.g. his endorsement of limited suffrage (Madison (1821) 1981, 395; Graber, 2014, 337), as well as his instrumental stance on the

so-called 'three-fifth' clause (Hamilton, Madison and Jay (1788) 1961, 332).
89. Madison favoured the expansion of government because it would 'refine and enlarge the public views, by passing them through the medium of a chosen body of citizens, whose wisdom may best discern the true interest of their country, and whose patriotism and love of justice will be least likely to sacrifice it to temporary or partial considerations' (Hamilton, Madison and Jay (1788) 1961, 82). He also believed that constitutional arrangements should aim at preventing ambitious individuals from taking power (Hamilton, Madison and Jay (1788) 1961, 80) and at 'skimming officials so as to elevate to office virtuous ones' (Hamilton, Madison and Jay (1788) 1961, 350). It is almost superfluous to point out how such ideas are redolent of a normalising logic.
90. See above, n. 77.
91. Reid, 1988.
92. So far as I know, the only relevant text from the time of the founding of the American constitution that explicitly mentions equality before the law is Thomas Paine's *The Rights of Man*, written in 1791 during the French Revolution.
93. Moving from autocratic government to self-government necessarily implies a shift from the paradigm of the command to that of the norm. This can be seen by looking at the perception of the British Parliament during the American Revolution. The British Parliament was, at the same time, an entity operating through commands and through norms depending on the perspective of the peoples it ruled. For the British people – whose politically active citizens were actually quite well represented in the Parliament – the Parliament ruled through norms; for the colonists – not really represented in the Parliament at any social level, objects of rules that did not apply to British people in the motherland, subjugated to a Parliament in which they did not participate – the British Parliament was speaking in the language of commands. The colonists therefore revolted against the Parliament when it ceased to be an instrument of their own self-ruling through norms and was seen as an alien sovereign.
94. Racial discrimination is only the most macroscopic and glaring infringement of the right to equality in the USA (other gross discriminations being related, for example, to women's rights, other minorities' rights or workers' rights) and is addressed here as paradig-

matic of the difference between the theory and practice of political declarations and documents.
95. See Anderson, 1974b, 15–43.
96. This thesis was famously suggested by Tocqueville's work *The Old Regime and the Revolution* (1955), which argues that the Revolution's political and legal effects were the continuation of the dynamic of centralisation arising from feudal structures. In line with this interpretation, particularly regarding the paradoxical continuities of the Old Regime with Revolutionary politics, see Furet, 1981.
97. Bossenga, 2012, and the classical study by Duby, 1997, where Duby identifies as the main theorists of the orders ideology Adalberon of Laon (977–c.1035) and Gerard I de Cambrai (1012–51).
98. Bien, 1994, 24–7; Sewell, 1980, 25–32.
99. See the analysis of status advanced by Maine, 1917.
100. Bien (1994, 59–60) rightly identifies in the laws that applied equally to the members of corps the feudal ancestor of the concept of equality as established through the French Revolution: 'The institutions associated persons alike socially and identical in occupation, who shared not only a general culture but memberships, rights, privileges, kinds of property.'
101. Doyle, 1988, 53–65.
102. Poggi, 1978, 71–4.
103. Baker, 1990, 115–17.
104. Hobsbawm, 1962.
105. 'What gives to the French Declaration an historical importance of first rank, even greater than that of the American "bill of rights", is that is offered to all European people still under the yoke of absolutist regimes, a theoretical model of liberty, which inspired them – more than anything else – in their political demands, associating since then the idea of a free government to that of the fundamental determination of the rights of citizens' (Del Vecchio, 1979, 49).
106. The bibliography on this topic is massive and diverse. A classical work on the French Revolution, its history and its interpretation is represented by Tocqueville, 1955. Lefebvre, 1967 and Soboul, 1964 represent the orthodox Marxist reading of the French Revolution as a class struggle between nobility and bourgeoisie, finally won by the latter. Against this thesis, Furet, 1981, Taylor, 1967, and Cobban, 1964 are the most representative scholars of 'revisionism', arguing for political causes in the making of the Revolution stressing the absence of a bourgeois capitalistic class in eighteenth-century

France. On a different note, Baker, 1990, and Doyle, 1988 take a deeper interest in the ideological discourses that preceded and followed the Revolution. For a complete overview of the different positions see Davies, 2006.
107. As in England, this was not the initial goal of the Third Estate, which was more favourable to a moderate reform that would ensure a limited monarchy, and was pushed to radical solutions only by the insipience of the King and his court (Lefebvre, 1962).
108. Duclos-Grécourt, 2014, represents an invaluable survey on the subject for its wealth of references to original texts.
109. See above.
110. Duclos-Grécourt, 2014, 350–4.
111. Duclos-Grécourt, 2014, 344.
112. Duclos-Grécourt, 2014, 345–6.
113. Duclos-Grécourt, 2014, 348–9.
114. Duclos-Grécourt, 2014, 353–4.
115. Verge, 2006, 144–5.
116. Duclos-Grécourt, 2014, 354–7.
117. Habermas, 1974, 82–120.
118. Habermas, 1974, 105.
119. The issue of whether the French Declaration outlined a system of supremacy of fundamental human rights against the command of society or vice versa is of no direct relevance for the present inquiry. For an analysis of this implicit tension in the text of the Declaration and in revolutionary political thought see Baker, 1994.
120. This obviously is not meant to imply that the American experience was not radical in its effect and that it did not transform American society, but only to stress the different logics operating in the background of these two revolutions. For an account of the social and political impact of the American Revolution on the USA see Wood, 1992.
121. 'The declaration of rights has therefore a double meaning: negation of the past and preparation for the future' (Del Vecchio, 1979, 31). The dismantling of privileges by the National Assembly with the decrees of 11 August destroyed in one spectacular blow the backbone of the feudal regime in France, paving the way for a society based on classes, see Baker, 1990, 267 and Doyle 1988, 207–8. As Sewell (1980, 136) emphatically suggests, 'The National Assembly, by abolishing privileges, changed the French nation from a hierarchical community composed of corporate bodies united by a common rev-

erence for and subjection to the will of the king into an association of free individual citizens living together under the law common to all Frenchmen . . . the abolition of privilege created free and equal citizens; the transformation of property empowered them to act as genuinely independent individuals.'

122. The deputies of the National Assembly gathered to draft the Declaration were perfectly aware of the social and historical differences between France and the Anglo-Saxon experiences; see Baker, 1990, 264–7.
123. See above, pp. 75–6.
124. Pierre-Louis de Lecretelle, in 'De la convocation de la prochaine tenue des États généraux', 1788, affirms that the general interest is the 'supreme law' of political associations. His opinion is shared by Emmanuel-Joseph Sieyès ('Qu'est-ce que le tiers-état?', 1789) and Pierre-Paul Le Mercier de a Rivière (Essais sur les maximes et lois fondamentales de la monarchie françoise, 1789).
125. Le Mercier de la Rivière claims that the interests of the minority should never be sacrificed to those of the majority (1789) and that all individual interests should be subordinated to the general interest, with which they should overlap. See also Guy-Jean-Baptise Target, Les États-Généraux convoqués par Louis XVI (1789), Jacques-Guillaume Thouret, Avis des bons Normands à leur freres tous les bons François de toutes les provinces et de tous les orders, Sur l'envoi des Lettres de Convocation aus États-généraux (1789) and Sieyès (1789).
126. Slimani, 2004, 37–58.
127. Duclos-Grécourt, 2014, 492–3, 524.
128. See Chapter 2.
129. Guillaume-Joseph Saige (Catéchisme du citoyen, 1775), following Rousseau, declares that sovereign power and legislative power are synonyms.
130. Gabriel Bonnot de Mably, Des droits et des devoirs du citoyen, 1789; Saige, 1775.
131. Furet, 1989. Conac (1993, 24) remarks that this abolition was necessary for the 'regeneration of French society'.
132. Conac, 1993, 37–9.
133. Both the Marquis of De LaFayette and Barnave explicitly defined the declaration as a 'catechisme' (Conac, 1993, 9, 16). La Fayette, during the debate, defined the objectives of the declaration as follows: '[D]efine the principles of action for the constituent and legislator;

give them a guide that would lead them to the source of natural and social rights; contribute to the political and civic formation of the members of the nation by declaring incontestable truths' (cited by Conac, 1993, 16). See also Fitzsimmons, 1994, 62–3; Aulard, 1965, 146.
134. Roubi and Romi, 1993, 61–2.
135. The remark made by Muguet de Nanthou during the Assembly makes explicit this difference: 'Somehow, by declaring [the fundamental rights of man and citizen], the Assembly has made them explicit, it has not posited them. When it declares, it says the law droit], when it adopts the constitution, it makes the law [droit]' (Conac, 1993, 35).
136. Koubi and Romi, 1993, 58–60.
137. 'The Declaration of rights marks precisely this moment: in other words, it represents the passage in the positive order of the juridical a-priori, of the absolute exigencies of reason' (Del Vecchio, 1979, 55).
138. Ewald, 1990.
139. 'The antinomic structure of the language of the preamble is an illusion that is resolved by juridical complexity . . . The knowledge of human rights is modulated in the juridical field and the adjective "natural" disappears from the vocabulary in so far as (and because) human rights are the object of an insertion in positive law (droit positif). It is for the legislative power to define the limits on the exercise of those rights' (Koubi and Romi, 1993, 62).
140. Rials, 1988, 398.
141. 'The founding character of the principles established by article 1 of the declaration appears in its full scope: in conferring to liberty and equality in rights . . . a fundamental, consubstantial value, maybe pre-existing the social order, it makes clear while at the same time founds the principles that support, in its goals and in its modes of functioning, the social and political organisation' (Pretot, 1993, 68). In this respect it is important to highlight that the article states that 'men are born and *remain* free and equal in rights'. Rials (1988, 393) notes that the word 'remain' signifies that not even society can deprive individuals of those fundamental entitlements.
142. Article Four reads: 'Liberty consists in the freedom to do everything which injures no one else; hence the exercise of the natural rights of each man has no limits except those which assure to the other members of the society the enjoyment of the same rights. These

limits can only be determined by law.' Article Six reads: 'Law is the expression of the general will. Every citizen has a right to participate personally, or through his representative, in its foundation. It must be the same for all, whether it protects or punishes. All citizens, being equal in the eyes of the law, are equally eligible to all dignities and to all public positions and occupations, according to their abilities, and without distinction except that of their virtues and talents.' For a historical analysis of these two articles see Costa, 1993 and Teboul, 1993.
143. While Rousseau is generally credited as one of the main sources of inspiration for the Declaration, especially with regard to the idea of 'general will', it must be noted that his name was never mentioned in the Assembly Debates (Rials, 1988).
144. See Baker, 1994, 194–6; Doyle, 1988, 208–9.

Notes to Chapter 4

1. Foucault, 1980b, 132–3.
2. Possibly, Dworkin's magniloquent statement errs on the side of legalism (Dworkin, 1986, 1).
3. Holmes, *Southern Pacific Company v. Jensen*, 244 U.S. 205, 222 (1917).
4. See above, ch. 1.
5. See above, ch. 3, n. 3.
6. Let us consider a general guiding his army on the battlefield. The command is inextricably devised in relation to the contingent spatial–temporal characteristic of the battle and not as an abstract rule of conduct that is to be applied all the time (left-flanking the enemy might be useful on a very specific occasion, but hardly on any occasion).
7. Hayek, 1960, 11.
8. Patterson, 1991; Hayek, 1960.
9. It must be noted that the French Declaration attempted a definition of what liberty is in Article Four. See ch. 3, n. 142.
10. Obviously this space is never completely secure or knowable in advance: the problem of legal interpretation is exactly the problem of freedom, of the relationship between law and command.
11. The typical example being Austin, 1995.
12. By 'ideological level' here I am not referring to ideology as 'false consciousness' in Marx, but to a set of ideas that delimit the production of sense in a given society, following Žižek, 1989 and Jameson, 1977.

Foucault was notoriously wary of the Marxist notion of ideology see Foucault, 1980b, 118.
13. The creation of the legal normal subject is, in my opinion, a striking feature of modern law which, surprisingly, has been largely overlooked by those authors who have attempted a Foucauldian analysis of the legal field. The shortcomings in their attempts at clarifying how modern law and normalising apparatuses acted together without the former being simply swallowed by the latter can be partly explained by their neglect of the problem of a new legal conception of the subject ushered in by the logic of the norm.
14. Gellner, 2006; Anderson, 1983.
15. Marx and Engels, 1998.
16. Tadros, 1998, 93.
17. Boyd White, 2008.
18. Jasanoff, 2006, 2–3.
19. 'Scientific discourses do not only *seek* truth, they also *claim* truth. The extent to which a scientific discourse can establish its claims to truth, can command acceptance of the veracity of its explanations of certain phenomena, is crucial for the relations which can obtain between that discourse and the various social practices within which it circulates. Firstly, within the field of scientific practice itself. But furthermore within the various other practices – technical, judicial, pedagogic, governmental and so forth – within which that discourse or the explanations which it produces may be deployed' (Rose, 1985, 8).
20. In the first sense, we could say the law performs an institutionalising function by according to a certain discourse a role of veridiction, thus sanctioning its authority over certain aspects of life. In the second sense, law, through rights and procedures, establishes juridical mechanisms that arbitrate between different discourses as well as between the discourses and subjects. These instances are, in fact, two sides of the same coin. In one case law operates directly by legislatively drawing the contours of the field. In the other case the delimitation of a field is not imposed through direct legislation but indirectly and locally through judicial procedures initiated by legal subjects.
21. This phenomenon can be appreciated through what Ezrahi (1990, 1996) has mapped as the expansion of technical and scientific idioms, areas formerly regulated by the legal (but also religious and moral) language.

22. Jasanoff, 2012, 264; see also Hacking, 1983; Latour, 1983, 1988.
23. Jasanoff, 2012, 245–73. It must be noted that the impact that scientific discourses have on the legal system can vary greatly in its scope and depth. Arguably, science affects the legal discourse only in a local fashion, requiring the adaptation of legal rules within a specific field (e.g. in the field of criminal evidence with the advancement of DNA fingerprinting, Koehler and Saks, 1991). However, it has been suggested that the scale of current scientific discoveries is shifting the epistemological foundations of our societies to such an extent that they are playing 'a constitutive role in determining how power will be exercised – and, equally important, constrained – in the emerging global order' (Jasanoff, 2012, 247). It is therefore possible to imagine a future moment when the claims advanced by scientific discourses will reach such a critical mass (transforming our ideas of the self, identity, community, power relations and so forth) that they will warp from the inside the whole of the modern legal discourse and its basic syntax. After all, was not the modern legal discourse rooted in a new conception of the individual that was as much philosophical and political as scientific and technical?
24. 'Each institution shores up the other's status. Neither legal nor scientific practitioners seem inclined to probe too deeply each other's claims concerning the authority of their respective epistemic and normative practices' (Jasanoff, 2007, 768).
25. This is not to say that the subject is a passive recipient of exogenous discourses. Quite the contrary: the subject maintains her agency and actively makes use of the legal discourse as well as all the other discourses she has access to. She constantly reshapes the environment that in turn moulds her subjectivity, thus participating herself in the dynamic of co-production.
26. 'As agents of power, law and science also collaborate in sustaining wider understandings of how society works, including ideas of the human self and agency, the market, and the collective good' (Jasanoff, 2007, 772).
27. Hobsbawm, 1975.
28. Habermas, 2001.
29. Anderson, 1983.
30. Hobsbawm, 1992.
31. Bauman, 2000, 2.
32. Bauman, 2000, 25.
33. As Bauman argues, the phrase 'melting the solids' was present in the

Communist Manifesto. But the first wave of modernity 'melted' old solids only 'to clear the site for *new and improved solids*; to replace the inherited set of deficient and defective solids with another set, which was much improved and preferably perfect, and for that reason no longer alterable' (2000, 3). As icons of solid modernity Bauman cites the Fordist factory, bureaucracy, the Panopticon, the Big Brother, and the *Konzlager* (ibid. 25–6).
34. Bauman, 2000, 29.
35. Beck, 1992, 137, as cited by Bauman, 2000, 34.
36. In this regard Bauman (2000, 36), recalling Tocqueville, argues that individualisation is intrinsically at odds with a communal political project centred on citizenship.
37. Bauman, 2000, 34.
38. Bauman, 2000, 62.
39. The problem of self-made identities – as opposed to externally imposed identities of solid modernity – is central in Bauman's considerations about the 'fate of individualisation' of liquid times: 'Consider, for instance, the contradiction of self-made identities which must be solid enough to be acknowledged as such and yet flexible enough not to bar freedom of future movements in the constantly changing, volatile circumstances' (2000, 50).
40. Bauman, 2000, 90.
41. The icons of solid modernity that Bauman uses are all disciplinary apparatuses (the Fordist factory, the Panopticon, etc.).
42. Deleuze, 1990, 179. It must be noted that he refers to disciplinary societies when, in fact, what he has in mind are, more precisely, normalising societies.
43. Deleuze, 1990, 180.
44. Deleuze, 1990, 179.
45. I am referring, of course in very general terms, to certain life situations that were considered socially 'normal' and acceptable and are now increasingly questioned. See Beck, 1992, 103–26.
46. Benhabib, 1992.
47. Lévy, 1998.
48. Massumi, 2002.
49. Deleuze, 2004, 208.
50. Braun, 2007, 17.
51. Deleuze, 2004, 209.
52. Lévy, 1998, 24.
53. Lévy, 1998, 25.

54. Lévy, 1998, 27.
55. See e.g. Foucault, 2002b.
56. Ewald, 1990.
57. Foucault, 2003b, 109ff.
58. Foucault, 2003b, 113.
59. Foucault, 1977.
60. Foucault, 2003b, 114.
61. See the account of the trial by Forbes, Tweedie and Conolly, 1833–5, Vol. IV, 52–3.
62. The concept of the Other goes back to Hegel and his dialectic of subjective recognition in *The Phenomenology of Spirit* (1807) (Hegel, 1977). The concept has enjoyed ever since a central role in modern thinking, especially within the context of continental philosophy, with scholars like Husserl, Sartre, Lacan and Levinas, among others.
63. Patterson, 1991; LeGoff, 1988; Burton Russell, 1968; Bloch, 1961.
64. See for example Warner, 1999; Canguilhem, 1991; Said, 1978; Beauvoir, 1953.
65. Ewald, 1990, 154.
66. I previously mentioned nationalism as one pertinent example.
67. Mahoney, 2007.
68. See, for example, Habermas's analysis of the success of feminist struggles in contemporary democratic societies (Habermas, 1999).
69. See *ex multis* Foucault, 2008, 267–86.
70. Habermas, 1999.
71. Notably, the resurgence of nationalistic movements or the recent political debate about the failure of the multicultural model can be interpreted as the resisting response of the order of normality against the xenomorphic shift towards control. Such a phenomenon can also be seen, for example, in the current legislation about immigrating Third Country Nationals in the EU: the European model, while in principle inclusive and open to non-EU member state nationals, in fact presents complex national systems that tend to reject outsiders or to accord them recognition insofar as they have shown themselves to have acquired some cultural traits belonging to the nation of destination (for a legal and political analysis of the issue see Acosta, 2009, and Acosta and Martire, 2014). In the face of the virtual subject the conservative reaction is to regress to some general ideological identities based on shared ethnic or cultural traits.
72. See, for example, Foucault's analysis on the use of state racism as a rhetorical device in the struggle between bourgeoisie and aristocracy

in seventeenth- and eighteenth-century France and the UK (Foucault, 2003a).
73. Hart, 1994; Raz, 1979; Weber, 1968; Kelsen; 1945.
74. Hart, 1994.
75. Vogel, 2007.

Notes to Conclusions

1. Latour, 1999, 304.
2. Habermas, 1996, 38–41, 447.
3. Habermas, 1996, 28–32.
4. Habermas, 1992.
5. Habermas, 1984–7.
6. 'If law is essentially constituted by a tension between facticity and validity – between its factual generation, administration, and enforcement in social institutions on the one hand and its claim to deserve general recognition on the other – then a theory that situates the idealising character of validity claims in concrete social contexts recommends itself for the analysis of law. This is just what the theory of communicative action allows, without the metaphysical pretensions and moralistic oversimplification we find in Kant' (Rehg, 1996, xii).
7. Habermas, 1996, 107.
8. Habermas, 1996, 110.
9. Habermas, 1996, 119.
10. Habermas, 1996, 121–36.
11. Habermas, 1996, 460.
12. Rehg, 1996, xxviii.
13. Habermas, 1996, 448–9.
14. Habermas, 1996, 122–3.
15. Habermas, 1999, 261.
16. Habermas, 2001, 779.
17. Gellner, 2006; Smith, 2001; Miller, 2000.
18. Often construed along lines of pure fiction; see Hobsbawm, 1992; Anderson, 1983.
19. Bauman, 2004, 20.
20. Foucault, 2003a, 29–30.
21. Habermas, 2001, 67. Habermas sees the national state is caught in a double envelopment, both internally and externally: 'Globalisation forces the nation-state to open itself up internally to the multiplicity of foreign or new, forms of cultural life. At the same time, globalisa-

tion shrinks the scope of action for national governments, insofar as the sovereign state must also open itself externally, in relation to international regimes' (Habermas, 2001, 84).
22. Habermas, 2001, 63–5.
23. 'We will be able to meet the challenges of globalisation in a reasonable manner if the postnational constellation can successfully develop new forms for the democratic self-steering of society' (Habermas, 2001, 88).
24. Habermas, 2001, 99.
25. On the 'no-demos' thesis see Grimm, 1995; for a reply, see Habermas, 1995. See also Weiler, 1995.
26. Habermas, 2001, 102 attacks the fictitious nature of national identity: '[P]recisely the artificial conditions in which national consciousness arose argue against a defeatist assumption that a form of civic solidarity among strangers can only be generated within the confines of the nation. If this form of collective identity was due to a highly abstractive leap from the local and dynastic to national and then to democratic consciousness, why shouldn't this learning process be able to continue?'
27. Habermas, 2001, 74.
28. After acknowledging the bloody and tragic history of Europe, Habermas depicts the Old Continent and the process of European integration in these rosy tones: 'These experiences of successful forms of social integration have shaped the normative self-understanding of European modernity into an egalitarian universalism that can ease the transition to postnational democracy's demanding contexts of mutual recognition for all of us – we, the sons, daughters, and grandchildren of a barbaric nationalism' (Habermas, 2001, 103). Looking back at recent European history, however, we cannot be so cheerful. Indeed, we are experiencing in Europe a period of relative peace and prosperity, but we must not forget the violent tensions that have shaken and still shake Europe. The political revolt of '68, the Italian and German terrorism of the '70s and '80s, the Yugoslavian civil war and the Kosovo war, the more recent French (2005) and English (2011) riots, and, finally, the current rise of Islamic terrorist attacks perpetrated by European nationals point towards a worrying lack of harmony.
29. Antonisch, 2009; Kaldor, 2004; Delanty and O'Mahony, 2002.
30. Strange, 1996.
31. Habermas himself is fully aware of Europe's shortcomings in terms of actual integration. Habermas, 2009, 2007.

32. The rise of xenophobic movements across the globe and especially in advanced liberal democracies is just one of the many examples of such a worrying tendency (Roemer, Lee and Straeten, 2007). Separatism is also a relevant (and growing) concern, see Laible, 2008.
33. Tilly (1996, 7) defines identity in the following terms: 'an actor's experience of a category, its role, network, group or organisation, coupled with a public representation of that experience; the public representation often takes the form of a shared story, a narrative'.
34. See Patterson, 1991.
35. Bloch, 1961.
36. Habermas, 1989.
37. Held, 2002a.
38. Held, 2002b, 24.
39. Rawls, 1972, 1999.
40. Norris, 2003.
41. Held and al., 1999.
42. Held and McGrew, 2002.
43. Held and McGrew, 2002, 310.
44. Held and McGrew, 2002, 311.
45. Held and McGrew, 2002, 311.
46. Held and McGrew, 2002, 311.
47. Foucault, 1986. The same article, with some minor omissions and a different title ('Different spaces'), appears also in Foucault, 2000c, 175–87.
48. Foucault, 1986, 24.
49. It is quite interesting that the legal field reflects all of the six heterotopic principles individuated by Foucault:
    - Law as heterotopia of crisis/deviation: law works at the same time as a space where a crisis between two parties is brought to the fore and resolved, and also as a space where deviation is examined, assessed and disciplined.
    - Law as heterotopia of difference: law is a social phenomenon whose meaning and function might dramatically shift in relation to the cultural and historical context.
    - Law as heterotopia of juxtaposition: Law is not only a system where domination is imposed from above, but is also a place where different claims coexist and develop in a dialectical fashion.
    - Law as heterotopia of time: law is a space that has a complex relationship with time. On the one hand, the meaning of law changes over time and is shaped by its dimension (e.g. precedents); but, on

the other, law rejects the workings of time by imposing itself as an immutable force (e.g. natural rights).
- Law as heterotopia of inclusion/exclusion: law can be a place of recognition but also a place of misrecognition and rejection.
- Law as heterotopia of illusion/compensation: law can be seen both as a space of illusion that exposes every real space as still more illusory, and as a space that incessantly attempts to counterbalance the messiness and confusion of the real world.

50. This is basically the idea of agonistic democracy proposed by Laclau and Mouffe, 1985, an idea that does not fall too far from the liberal tree. In fact, Habermas can be read – with some caveats – as a proponent of agonistic politics. For a critical analysis of Habermas's (and Rawls's) democratic theories from the point of view of agonistic pluralism see Mouffe, 2001.
51. Foucault, 1980d. The two Maoists were Bernard Henri-Lévy and André Glucksmann.
52. Other figures include Ernesto Laclau, Slavoj Žižek, Duncan Kennedy, and Costas Douzinas. Of course, I am offering here a very superficial and sketchy account of a diverse, profound, and multi-faceted theoretical field.
53. Golder, 2015.
54. Butler, 1990.
55. Butler, 2005.
56. Butler, 1997.
57. Butler, 2004b, 33.
58. Zivi, 2008, 167.
59. Butler, 2004a, 55.
60. Butler, 2004a, 68.
61. Butler, 2004a, 77.
62. Butler, 2004a, 98.
63. Loizidou, 2007, 90.
64. Butler, 1990.
65. Dworkin et al., 1997, 'Assisted suicide: the philosophers' brief', *New York Review of Books*, <http://www.nybooks.com/articles/archives/1997/mar/27/assisted-suicide-the-philosophers-brief/> (last accessed 31 January 2017).
66. *Washington v. Glucksberg* 521 US 702 (1997).
67. Golder, 2015, 132.
68. The two fundamental texts in which Foucault addressed the right to die are Foucault, 2002g, and 1996.

69. 'Foucault uses the right to die in order to play a different game: the imaginative game of attempting to generate changes in subjectivities and attitudes toward life and death that disrupt or work against the dictates of medicalised, biopolitical self-management. Rights are hence tactically instrumentalised to this wider, more diffuse, yet at the same time highly individualised purpose . . . In other words, rights are the tactic called in aid of the strategy of an aesthetics of existence' (Golder, 2015, 137–8).
70. Golder, 2015, 138–9.
71. Foucault, 2002h.
72. Golder (2015, 143) observes: 'In short, Foucault worries that a tactical deployment of rights will lead not to the overcoming of the death penalty but either to its possible refinement or an abolition that stops short of critically engaging the penal apparatus that nourishes it.'
73. 'For Foucault, one simply could not, through a rights strategy that would serve to focus and narrow the inquiry on the legitimacy of the state's right to put to death, abstract from the quotidian violence of disciplinary conditions' (Golder, 2015, 146).
74. Dworkin et al., 1997, 43.
75. Brown, 2001, 102.
76. An episteme could be defined as 'The total set of relations that unite, at a given period, the discursive practices that give rise to epistemological figures, sciences, and possibly formalised systems' (Foucault, 1972, 191).
77. Foucault, 2002i, 340ff.
78. Deleuze, 1990, 178.

Bibliography

Please note that all translations from original French texts are mine.

Acosta Arcarazo, D. (2009). 'The good, the bad and the ugly in EU migration law: is the European parliament becoming bad and ugly?' (The adoption of Directive 2008/15: the returns directive) *European Journal of Migration and Law*, 11, 19–39.

Acosta Arcarazo, D. and Martire, J. (2014). 'Trapped in the lobby: Europe's revolving doors and the Other as Xenos'. *European Law Review*, 39(3), 362–79.

Agamben, G. (1998). *Homo Sacer. Sovereign Power and Bare Life*. (D. Heller-Roazen, trans.) Stanford, CA: Stanford University Press.

Agamben, G. (2005). *State of Exception*. (K. Attell, trans.) Chicago: University of Chicago Press.

Agamben, G. (2009). *What Is an Apparatus?* (D. Kishik and S. Pedatella, trans.) Stanford, CA: Stanford University Press.

Allen, G. O. (1961). 'Le volonté de tous and le volonté générale: a distinction and its significance'. *Ethics*, 71(4), 263–75.

Anderson, B. (1983). *Imagined Communities*. London; New York: Verso.

Anderson, P. (1974a). *Passages from Antiquity to Feudalism*. London: NLB.

Anderson, P. (1974b). *Lineages of the Absolutist State*. London: NLB.

Antonisch, M. (2009). 'National identities in the age of globalisation: the case of Western Europe'. *National Identities*, 11(3), 281–99.

Aquinas, T. (1911–25). *Summa Theologica*. (Fathers of the English Dominican Province, trans.) London; New York: Burns, Oates & Washbourne; Benziger.

Arendt, H. (1982). *Lectures on Kant's Political Philosophy*. (R. Beiner, ed.) Brighton: Harvester.

Ashcraft, R. (1986). *Revolutionary Politics & Locke's Two Treatises of Government*. Princeton, NJ: Princeton University Press.

Ashley, M. P. (1966). *The Glorious Revolution of 1688*. London: Hodder & Stoughton.

Aulard, F. V. (1965). *The French Revolution: A Political History 1789–1804*. New York: Russell & Russell.

Austin, J. (1995). *The Province of Jurisprudence Determined*. (W. Rumble, ed.) Cambridge: Cambridge University Press.

Avineri, S. (1972). *Hegel's Theory of the Modern State*. London: Cambridge University Press.

Bailyn, B. (1967). *The Ideological Origins of the American Revolution*. Cambridge, MA: Belknap Press of Harvard University Press.

Baker, K. M. (1990). *Inventing the French Revolution: Essays on French Political Culture in the Eighteenth Century*. Cambridge: Cambridge University Press.

Baker, K. M. (1994). 'The idea of a Declaration of Rights'. In D. V. Kley (ed.), *The French Idea of Freedom* (pp. 154–97). Stanford, CA: Stanford University Press.

Barron, A. (2002). 'Foucault and law'. In J. E. Penner, D. Schiff and R. Nobles (eds), *Introduction to Jurisprudence and Legal Theory: Commentary and Materials* (pp. 1,035–121). Oxford: Oxford University Press.

Barry, A., Osborne, T. and Rose, N. (eds). (1996). *Foucault and Political Reason: Liberalism, Neo-Liberalism and Rationalities of Government*. London: UCL Press.

Baudrillard, J. (2007). *Forget Foucault*. Cambridge, MA; London: Semiotext(e).

Bauman, Z. (2000). *Liquid Modernity*. Cambridge: Polity Press.

Bauman, Z. (2004). *Identity*. Cambridge; Malden, MA: Polity Press.

Beauvoir, S. de (1953). *The Second Sex*. (H. Parshley, trans.) London: Cape.

Beck, A. (1996). 'Foucault and law: the collapse of law's empire'. *Oxford Journal of Legal Studies*, 16, 489.

Beck, U. (1992). *Risk Society: Towards a New Modernity*. London: Sage.

Becker, C. L. (1958). *The Declaration of Independence: A Study in the History of Political Ideas*. New York: Vintage.

Bederman, D. J. (1996). 'Reception of the classical tradition in international law: Grotius' De Iure Belli Ac Pacis'. *Emory International Law Review*, 10, 1ff.

Bellamy, R. (2007). *Political Constitutionalism: A Republican Defence of the Constitutionality of Democracy*. Cambridge: Cambridge University Press.

Benhabib, S. (1992). *Situating the Self: Gender, Community and Postmodernism in Contemporary Ethics*. Oxford: Polity Press.

Bentham, J. (1970). *An Introduction to the Principles of Morals and Legislation*. (J. H. Burns and H. L. Hart, eds) London: Athlone Press.

Berger, R. (1969). 'Doctor Bonham's case: statutory construction or constitutional theory.' *University of Pennsylvania Law Review*, 117, 521–45.

Bergeron, L. (1981). *France Under Napoleon*. (R. R. Palmer, trans.) Princeton, NJ: Princeton University Press.

Bien, D. D. (1994). 'Old regime origins of democratic liberty'. In D. V. Kley (ed.), *The French idea of freedom* (pp. 23–72). Stanford, CA: Stanford University Press.

Bloch, M. (1961). *Feudal Society*. (L. A. Manyon, trans.) London: Routledge & Kegan Paul.

Blumenberg, H. (1985). *The Legitimacy of the Modern Age*. Cambridge, MA: MIT Press.

Blumenthal, U.-R. (1988). *The Investiture Controversy: Church and Monarchy from the Ninth to the Twelfth Century*. Philadelphia: University of Pennsylvania Press.

Bobbio, N. (1993). *Thomas Hobbes and the Natural Law Tradition*. (D. Gobetti, trans.) Chicago: University of Chicago Press.

Bobbio, N. (1996). *The Age of Rights*. (A. Cameron, trans.) Oxford: Polity Press.

Bobbio, N., Matteucci, N. and Pasquino, G. (2004). *Dizionario di Politica*. Turin: UTET.

Bodin, J. (1945). *Method for the Easy Comprehension of History*. (B. Reynolds, trans.) New York: Columbia University Press.

Bossenga, G. (2012). 'Estates, orders, and corps'. In W. Doyle (ed.), *The Oxford Handbook of the Ancien Régime* (pp. 141–66). Oxford: Oxford University Press.

Boyd White, J. (2008) 'Establishing relations between law and other forms of thought and language.' *Erasmus Law Review*, 1(3), 3–22.

Braun, B. (2007). 'Biopolitics and the molecularization of life'. *Cultural Geographies*, 14, 6–28.

Brown, W. (2001). *Politics Out of History*. Princeton, NJ: Princeton University Press.

Burckhardt, J. (1990). *The Culture of the Renaissance in Italy*. (S. G. Middlemore, trans.) London; New York: Penguin.

Burgess, G. (1996). *Absolute Monarchy and the Stuart Constitution*. New Haven, CT: Yale University Press.

Burke, E. (1923). *Reflections on the French Revolution*. London: Methuen.
Burton Russell, J. (1968). *Medieval Civilization*. New York; London: Wiley.
Butler, J. (1990). *Gender Trouble*. New York, London: Routledge.
Butler, J. (1997). *Excitable Speech*. New York; London: Routledge.
Butler, J. (2004a). *Precarious Life*. London: Verso.
Butler, J. (2004b). *Undoing Gender*. New York; London: Routledge.
Butler, J. (2005). *Giving an Account of Oneself*. New York: Fordham University Press.
Canguilhem, G. (1991). *The Normal and the Pathological*. (C. R. Fawcett, trans.) New York: Zone Books.
Carnap, R. (1937). *The Logical Syntax of Language*. (A. Smeaton, trans.) London: Kegan Paul, Trench, Trubner.
Carrette, J. R. (2000). *Foucault and Religion: Spiritual Corporality and Political Spirituality*. London; New York: Routledge.
Chambon, A. S., Irving, A. and Epstein, L. (eds). (1999). *Reading Foucault for Social Work*. New York: Columbia University Press.
Chignola, S. (2016). Sobre el dispositivo. Foucault, Agamben, Deleuze. In R. Castro Orellana and A. Salinas Araya (eds), *Le actualidad de Michel Foucault* (pp. 169–84). Madrid: Escolar y Mayo Editores.
Coleman, J. (2000). *A History of Political Thought. Vol. 2, From the Middle Ages to the Renaissance*. Oxford; Malden, MA: Blackwell.
Conac, G. (1993). 'L'elaboration de la déclaration des droits de l'homme et du citoyen'. In G. Conac, M. Debene and G. Teobul (eds), *La déclaration des droits de l'homme et du citoyen de 1789. Histoire, analyse et commentaires*. (pp. 7–52). Paris: Economica.
Costa, J.-P. (1993). 'Article 4'. In G. Conac, M. Debene and G. Teboul (eds), *La déclaration des droits de l'homme et du citoyen de 1789. Histoire, analyse et commentaires*. (pp. 101–14). Paris: Economica.
Crowe, M. B. (1999). 'The impious hypothesis: a paradox in Hugo Grotius?' In K. Haakonssen (ed.), *Grotius, Pufendorf and Natural Law*. Aldershot: Ashgate.
Dahl, R. A. (1989). *Democracy and Its Critics*. New Haven, CT; London: Yale University Press.
Dahrendorf, R. (1988). *The Modern Social Conflict: An Essay on the Politics of Liberty*. London: Weidenfeld & Nicolson.
Davies, P. (2006). *The Debate on the French Revolution*. Manchester: Manchester University Press.
Davies, R. G. and Denton, J. H. (eds). (1981). *The English Parliament in the Middle Ages*. Manchester: Manchester University Press.

Dean, M. (2010). *Governmentality: Power and Rule in Modern Society*. London; Thousand Oaks, CA: Sage.
Delanty, G. and O'Mahony, P. (2002). *Nationalism and Social Theory: Modernity and the Recalcitrance of the Nation*. London: Sage.
Deleuze, G. (1990). 'Postscript on control societies'. In *Negotiations* (M. Joughin, trans., pp. 177–82). New York: Columbia University Press.
Deleuze, G. (1992). 'What is a dispositif?' In *Michel Foucault, Philosopher: Essays* (T. J. Armstrong, trans., pp. 159–68). New York: Routledge.
Deleuze, G. (2004). *Difference and Repetition*. (P. Patton, trans.) London: Continuum.
Deleuze, G. (2006). 'Eight years later: 1980 interview'. D. Lapoujade (ed.), *Two Regimes of Madness: Texts and Interviews 1975–1995* (A. Hodges and M. Taormina, trans., pp. 175–80). New York: Semiotext(e).
Dicey, A. V. (1959). *Introduction to the Study of the Law of the Constitution*. London; New York: Macmillan; St Martin's Press.
Dillon, M. and Neal, A. W. (eds). (2008). *Foucault on Politics, Security and War*. Basingstoke; New York: Palgrave Macmillan.
Doyle, W. (1988). *Origins of the French Revolution*. Oxford: Oxford University Press.
Doyle, W. (1992). *The Old European Order, 1660–1800*. Oxford: Oxford University Press.
Drakopoulou, M. (2007). 'Feminism and the siren call of law'. *Law and Critique*, 18(3), 331–60.
Duby, G. (1997). *The Three Orders: Feudal Society Imagined*. Chicago: University of Chicago Press.
Duclos-Grécourt, M.-L. (2014). *L'idée de loi au XVIIIe siècle dans la pensée des juristes français (1715–1789)*. Poitiers: Presses universitaires juridiques Université de Poitiers.
Dunn, J. (1969). *The Political Thought of John Locke: An Historical Account of the Argument of the 'Two Treatises of Government'*. London: Cambridge University Press.
Dunn, J. (1980). *Political Obligation in Its Historical Context: Essays in Political Theory*. Cambridge: Cambridge University Press.
Dunning, W. A. (1927). *A History of Political Theories: Ancient and Mediaeval*. New York: Macmillan.
Dworkin, R. (1986). *Law's Empire*. London: Fontana Press.
Dworkin, R. et al. (1997, March 27). 'Assisted suicide: the philosophers' brief'. *New York Review of Books*, pp. 41–7, <http://www.nybooks.com/articles/1997/03/27/assisted-suicide-the-philosophers-brief/>

Dyzenhaus, D. (2001). 'Hobbes and the legitimacy of law'. *Law and Philosophy*, 20, 461–98.

Esposito, R. (2008). *Bíos: Biopolitics and Philosophy*. (T. Campbell, trans.) Minneapolis, MN: University of Minnesota Press.

Evans, T. (2005). 'International human rights law as power/knowledge'. *Human Rights Quarterly*, 27(3), 1,046–68.

Ewald, F. (1986a). *L'État providence*. Paris: B. Gasset.

Ewald, F. (1986b). 'A concept of social law'. In G. Teubner (ed.), *Dilemmas of Law in the Welfare State*. (pp. 40–75). Berlin: de Gruyter.

Ewald, F. (1987). 'The law of law'. In G. Teubner (ed.), *Autopoietic Law: A New Approach to Law and Society* (pp. 36–50). Berlin; New York: de Gruyter.

Ewald, F. (1990). 'Norms, discipline and the law'. *Representations*, 30, 138–61.

Ezrahi, Y. (1990). *The Descent of Icarus, Science and the Transformation of Contemporary Democracy*. Cambridge, MA: Harvard University Press.

Ezrahi, Y. (1996). 'Modes of reasoning and the politics of authority in the modern state'. In D. R. Olson and N. Torrance (eds), *Modes of Thought, Explorations in Culture and Cognition* (pp. 72–89). New York: Cambridge University Press.

Finnis, J. (2008, Fall Edition). 'Aquinas' moral, political, and legal philosophy'. (E. N. Zalta, ed.) *The Stanford Encyclopedia of Philosophy*, <http://plato.stanford.edu/archives/fall2008/entries/aquinas-moral-political/>

Fitzsimmons, M. P. (1994). *Remaking of France: The National Assembly and the Constitution of 1791*. Cambridge: Cambridge University Press.

Forbes, J., Tweedie, A. and Conolly, J. (eds) (1833–5). *The Cyclopaedia of Practical Medicine: Comprising Treatises on The Nature and Treatment of Diseases, Materia Medica and Therapeutics, Medical Jurisprudence, etc. etc.* London: Sherwood, Gilbert & Piper.

Foucault, M. (1967). *Madness and Civilization*. (R. Howard, trans.) London: Tavistock.

Foucault, M. (1972). *The Archaeology of Knowledge*. (A. M. Sheridan Smith, trans.) London: Tavistock.

Foucault, M. (1977). *Discipline and Punish*. (A. Sheridan, trans.) London: Allen Lane.

Foucault, M. (1978). *The History of Sexuality. Vol. I An Introduction*. (R. Hurley, trans.) New York: Pantheon.

Foucault, M. (1980a). 'Two lectures'. In C. Gordon (ed.), *Power/ Knowledge. Selected Interviews and Other Writings 1972–1977* (C. Gordon, L. Marshall, J. Mepham and K. Soper, trans., pp. 78–108). New York: Pantheon.
Foucault, M. (1980b). 'Truth and power'. In C. Gordon (ed.), *Power/ Knowledge. Selected Interviews and Other Writings 1972–1977* (C. Gordon, L. Marshall, J. Mepham and K. Soper, trans., pp. 109–33). New York: Pantheon.
Foucault, M. (1980c). 'The confession of the flesh'. In C. Gordon (ed.), *Power/Knowledge. Selected Interviews and Other Writings 1972–1977* (C. Gordon, L. Marshall, J. Mepham and K. Soper, trans., pp. 194–228). New York: Pantheon.
Foucault, M. (1980d). 'On popular justice: a discussion with Maoists'. In C. Gordon (ed.), *Power/Knowledge. Selected Interviews and Other Writings 1972–1977* (C. Gordon, L. Marshall, J. Mepham and K. Soper, trans., pp. 1–36). New York: Pantheon.
Foucault, M. (1986). 'Of other spaces'. *Diacritics*, 16, 22–7.
Foucault, M. (1991). 'Governmentality'. In G. Burchell, C. Gordon and P. Miller (eds), *The Foucault Effect: Studies in Governmentality: With Two Lectures by and an Interview with Michel Foucault* (pp. 87–104). Chicago: University of Chicago Press.
Foucault, M. (1996). 'The simplest of pleasures'. In S. Lotringer (ed.), *Foucault Live: Collected Interviews, 1961–1984* (L. Hochroth and J. Johnston, trans., pp. 295–7). New York: Semiotext(e).
Foucault, M. (2000a). 'On the ways of writing history'. In J. D. Faubion (ed.), *Aesthetics: Method, and Epistemology. The Essential Works of Michel Foucault, 1954–1984* (R. Hurley et al., trans., Vol. 2, pp. 279–98). London: Penguin.
Foucault, M. (2000b). 'Nitezsche, genealogy, history'. In J. D. Faubion (ed.), *Aesthetics: Method, and Epistemology. The Essential Works of Michel Foucault, 1954–1984* (R. Hurely et al., trans., Vol. 2, pp. 369–392). London: Penguin.
Foucault, M. (2000c). 'Different spaces'. In J. D. Faubion (ed.), *Aesthetics: Method, and Epistemology. The Essential Works of Michel Foucault, 1954–1984* (R. Hurley et al., trans., Vol. 2, pp. 175–86). London: Penguin.
Foucault, M. (2002a). 'The birth of social medicine'. In J. D. Faubion (ed.), *Power. The Essential Works of Michel Foucault, 1954–1984* (R. Hurley et al., trans., Vol. 3, pp. 134–56). London: Penguin.
Foucault, M. (2002b). 'The subject and power'. In J. D. Faubion (ed.),

Power. The Essential Works of Michel Foucault 1954–84 (R. Hurley et al., trans., Vol. 3, pp. 328–48). London: Penguin.

Foucault, M. (2002c). '"Omnes et singulatim", toward a critique of political reason'. In J. D. Faubion (ed.), *Power. The Essential Works of Michel Foucault 1954–84*. (R. Hurley et al., trans., Vol. 3, pp. 298–327). London: Penguin.

Foucault, M. (2002d). 'Lemon and milk'. In J. D. Faubion (ed.), *Power. The Essential Works of Michel Foucault 1954–84* (R. Hurley et al., trans., Vol. 3, pp. 435–8). London: Penguin.

Foucault, M. (2002e). 'Truth and juridical forms'. In J. D. Faubion (ed.), *Power. The Essential Works of Michel Foucault 1954–84* (R. Hurley et al., trans., Vol. 3, pp. 1–89). London: Penguin.

Foucault, M. (2002f). 'Questions of method'. In J. D. Faubion (ed.), *Power. The Essential Works of Michel Foucault 1954–84* (R. Hurley et al., trans., Vol. 3, pp. 223–38). London: Penguin.

Foucault, M. (2002g). 'The risks of security'. In J. D. Faubion (ed.), *Power. The Essential Works of Michel Foucault 1954–1984* (R. Hurley et al., trans., Vol. 3, pp. 365–81). London: Penguin.

Foucault, M. (2002h). 'Pompidou's two deaths'. In J. D. Faubion (ed.), *Power. The Essential Works of Michel Foucault 1954–1984* (R. Hurley et al., trans., Vol. 3, pp. 418–22). London: Penguin.

Foucault, M. (2002i). *The Order of Things*. London: Routledge.

Foucault, M. (2003a). *Society Must Be Defended: Lectures at the Collège de France, 1975–1976*. (M. Bertrani, A. Fontana, eds and D. Macey, trans.) New York: Picador.

Foucault, M. (2003b). *Abnormal: Lectures at the Collège de France 1974–1975*. (V. Marchetti, A. Salomoni, eds and G. Burchell, trans.) New York: Picador.

Foucault, M. (2007). *Security, Territory, Population: Lectures at the Collège de France, 1976–1977*. (M. Senellart, ed. and G. Burchell, trans.) New York: Palgrave Macmillan.

Foucault, M. (2008). *The Birth of Biopolitics: Lectures at the Collège de France 1978–1979*. (M. Senellart, ed. and G. Burchell, trans.) New York: Palgrave Macmillan.

Foucault, M. (2014a). *On the Government of the Living: Lectures at the Collège de France, 1979–1980*. (M. Senellart, ed. and G. Burchell, trans.) New York: Palgrave Macmillan.

Foucault, M. (2014b). *Wrong-doing, Truth-telling: The Function of Avowal in Justice*. (F. Brion and B. E. Harcourt, eds and S. W. Sawyer, trans.) Chicago: University of Chicago Press.

Franklin, J. H. (1973). *Jean Bodin and the Rise of Absolutism*. Cambridge: Cambridge University Press.
Franklin, J. H. (1991). 'Sovereignty and the mixed constitution: Bodin and his critics'. In J. H. Burns (ed.), *The Cambridge History of Political Thought, 1450–1700* (pp. 299–308). Cambridge: Cambridge University Press.
Furet, F. (1989). 'Night of August 4'. In F. Furet and M. Ozouf (eds), *A Critical Dictionary of the French Revolution* (A. Goldhammer, trans., pp. 107–14). Cambridge, MA: Harvard University Press.
Furet, F. (1981). *Interpreting the French Revolution*. (E. Forster, trans.) Cambridge: Cambridge University Press.
Ganshof, F. L. (1964). *Feudalism* (3rd English edn). (P. Gierson, trans.) London: Longman.
Garland, D. (2001). *The Culture of Control: Crime and Social Order in Late Modernity*. Chicago: University of Chicago Press.
Gauthier, D. (2001). 'Hobbes: the laws of nature'. *Pacific Philosophical Quarterly*, 82, 258–84.
Gellner, E. (2006). *Nations and Nationalism*. Malden, MA: Blackwell.
Gierke, O. (1934). *Natural Law and the Theory of Society*. (E. Baker, ed.) Cambridge: Cambridge University Press.
Gierke, O. (1938). *Political Theories of the Middle Ages*. (F. W. Maitland, trans.) Cambridge: Cambridge University Press.
Golder, B. (2008). 'Foucault and the incompletion of law'. *Leiden Journal of International Law*, 21, 747–63.
Golder, B. (2015). *Foucault and the Politics of Rights*. Stanford, CA: Stanford University Press.
Golder, B. and Fitzpatrick, P. (2009). *Foucault's Law*. London: Routledge-Cavendish.
Goldstein, J. (1993). 'Framing discipline with law: problems and promises of the liberal state'. *American Historical review*, 98, 364.
Gordon, C. (1991). 'Governmental rationality: an introduction'. In G. Burchell, C. Gordon and P. Miller (eds), *The Foucault Effect: Studies in Governmentality: With Two Lectures by and an Interview with Michel Foucault* (pp. 1–51). London: Harvester Wheatsheaf.
Gordon, C. (2002). 'Introduction'. In J. D. Faubion (ed.), *Power. The Essential Works of Michel Foucault 1954–84* (R. Hurley et al., trans., Vol. 3, pp. xi–xli). London: Penguin.
Gough, J. (1955). *Fundamental Law in English Constitutional History*. Oxford: Clarendon Press.
Graber, M. A. (2014). 'James Madison's Republican constitutionalism'. In D. Galligan (ed.), *Constitutions and the Classics: Patterns of*

Constitutional Thought from Fortescue to Bentham (pp. 327–53). Oxford: Oxford University Press.

Graus, F. (1976). 'From resistance to revolt: the later medieval peasant wars in the context of social crisis'. In J. Bak (ed.), *The German Peasant War of 1525* (pp. 1–9). London: Cass.

Grimm, D. (1995). 'Does Europe need a constitution?' *European Law Journal*, 1(3), 282–302.

Gutting, G. (2010, Spring Edition). 'Michel Foucault'. (E. N. Zalta, ed.), *The Stanford Encyclopedia of Philosophy*, <http://plato.stanford.edu/archives/spr2010/entries/foucault/>

Guyer, P. (1993). 'Introduction: the starry heavens and the moral law'. In P. Guyer (ed.), *The Cambridge Companion to Kant* (pp. 1–25). Cambridge: Cambridge University Press.

Haakonssen, K. (1985). 'Hugo Grotius and the history of political thought'. *Political Theory* (13), 247–53.

Haakonssen, K. (1996). *Natural Law and Moral Philosophy: from Grotius to Scottish Enlightenment*. New York: Cambridge University Press.

Habermas, J. (1974). *Theory and Practice*. (J. Viertal, trans.) Cambridge: Polity Press.

Habermas, J. (1975). *Legitimation Crisis*. (T. McCarthy, trans.) Cambridge: Polity Press.

Habermas, J. (1984–7). *The Theory of Communicative Action*. (T. McCarthy, trans.) Boston: Beacon.

Habermas, J. (1989). *The Structural Transformation of the Public Sphere*. (T. Burger, trans.) Cambridge: Polity Press.

Habermas, J. (1992). *Post-metaphysical Thinking*. (W. M. Hohengarten, trans.) Oxford: Polity Press.

Habermas, J. (1994). 'Some questions concerning the theory of power: Foucault again'. In M. Kelly (ed.), *Critique and Power: Recasting the Foucault/Habermas Debate* (pp. 79–108). Cambridge, MA; London: MIT Press.

Habermas, J. (1995). 'Remarks on Dieter Grimm's "Does Europe need a constitution?"'. *European Law Journal*, 1(3), 303–7.

Habermas, J. (1996). *Between Facts and Norms: Contributions to a Discourse Theory of Law and Democracy*. (W. Rehg, trans.) Cambridge, MA: MIT Press.

Habermas, J. (1999). *The Inclusion of the Other: Studies in Political Theory*. (C. Cronin and P. D. Greif, eds) Cambridge: Polity Press.

Habermas, J. (2001). *The Postnational Constellation: Political Essays*. (M. Pensky, trans.) Cambridge, MA: MIT Press.

Habermas, J. (2007). *The Divided West*. (C. Cronin, trans.) Cambridge: Polity Press.

Habermas, J. (2009). *Europe: The Faltering Project*. (C. Cronin, trans.) Cambridge; Malden, MA: Polity Press.

Hacking, I. (1983). *Representing and Intervening: Introductory Topics in the Philosophy of Natural Science*. Cambridge: Cambridge University Press.

Hale, M. ([1713] 1971). *The History of the Common Law of England*. (C. M. Gray, ed.) Chicago: University of Chicago Press.

Hamilton, A., Madison, J. and Jay, A. J. ([1788] 1961). *The Federalist Papers*. New York: New American Press.

Hammer, L. M. (2007). *A Foucauldian Approach to International Law: Descriptive Thoughts for Normative Issues*. Aldershot: Ashgate.

Hardt, M. and Negri, A. (2000). *Empire*. Cambridge, MA; London: Harvard University Press.

Hardt, M. and Negri, A. (2004). *Multitude: War and Democracy in the Age of Empire*. London: Penguin.

Harriss, G. L. (1975). *King, Parliament and Public Finance in Medieval England to 1369*. Oxford: Clarendon Press.

Hart, H. L. (1994). *The Concept of Law*. Oxford: Clarendon Press.

Hayek, F. A. (1960). *The Constitution of Liberty*. London: Routledge & Kegan Paul.

Heer, F. (1968). *The Holy Roman Empire*. (J. Sondheimer, trans.) London: Weidenfeld & Nicolson.

Hegel, G. W. (1967). *The Philosophy of Right*. (T. M. Knox, trans.) London; New York: Oxford University Press.

Hegel, G. W. (1971). *Hegel's Philosophy of Mind: Being Part Three of the 'Encyclopaedia of the Physical Sciences'* (1830). (W. Wallace and A. Miller, trans.) Oxford: Clarendon Press.

Hegel, G. W. (1975). *Hegel's Logic: Being Part One of 'Encyclopaedia of the Philosophical Sciences'*. (W. Wallace, trans.) Oxford: Clarendon Press.

Hegel, G. W. (1977). *The Phenomenology of Spirit*. (A. V. Miller, trans.) Oxford: Clarendon Press.

Held, D. (1985). *States and Societies*. Oxford: Blackwell/Open University.

Held, D. (1991). *Political Theory Today*. Cambridge: Polity Press.

Held, D. (2002a). 'Cosmopolitanism: ideas, realities and deficits'. In *Governing Globalization: Power, Authority and Global Governance* (pp. 305–24). Cambridge; Malden, MA: Polity Press; Blackwell.

Held, D. (2002b). 'Law of states, law of peoples'. *Legal Theory*, 8(1), 1–44.

Held, D. (2006). *Models of Democracy*. Cambridge; Malden, MA: Polity Press.
Held, D. et al. (1999). *Global Transformations: Politics, Economics and Culture*. Stanford, CA: Stanford University Press.
Held, D. and McGrew, A. (eds). (2002). *Governing Globalization: Power, Authority and Global Governance*. Cambridge: Polity Press.
Henshall, N. (1992). *The Myth of Absolutism: Change and Continuity in Early Modern European Monarchy*. London; New York: Longman.
Hertzler, J. R. (1987). 'Who dubbed it "The Glorious Revolution"?' *Albion: A Quarterly Journal Concerned with British Studies*, 4, 579–85.
Hirst, P. (1986). *Law, Socialism and Democracy*. London: Allen & Unwin.
Hlavacek, I. (2000). 'The Luxemburgs and Rupert of the Palatinate'. In M. Jones (ed.), *The New Cambridge Medieval History* (Vols. 6, c.1300–c.1415, pp. 551–69). Cambridge: Cambridge University Press.
Hobbes, T. (1962). *Leviathan*. (M. Oakeshott, ed.) New York; London: Collier; Collier Macmillan.
Hobbes, T. (1998). *On the Citizen*. (R. Tuck and M. Silverthorne, trans.) Cambridge: Cambridge University Press.
Hobsbawm, E. J. (1962). *The Age of Revolution 1789–1848*. London: Weidenfeld & Nicolson.
Hobsbawm, E. J. (1975). *The Age of Capital, 1848–1875*. London: Weidenfeld & Nicolson.
Hobsbawm, E. J. (1992). *Nations and Nationalism Since 1780: Programme, Myth and Reality*. Cambridge: Cambridge University Press.
Holmes, G. (1974). *The Latter Middle Ages, 1272–1485*. London: Sphere.
Holt, J. C. (1981). 'The prehistory of Parliament'. In R. G. Davies and J. H. Denton (eds), *The English Parliament in the Middle Ages* (pp. 1–28). Manchester: Manchester University Press.
Holt, J. C. (1985). *Magna Carta and Medieval Government*. London: Hambledon.
Holt, J. C. (1992). *Magna Carta*. Cambridge: Cambridge University Press.
Hooker, R. (1977). *Of the Laws of Ecclesiastical Polity*. (G. Edelen, W. S. Hill and P. G. Stanwood, eds) Cambridge, MA: Belknap Press of Harvard University Press.
Hoppit, J. (2000). *A Land of Liberty? England, 1689–1727*. Oxford: Oxford University Press.
Howard, D. (1990). *The Birth of American Political Thought*. (D. A. Curtis, trans.) Basingstoke: Macmillan.
Hunt, A. and Wickham, G. (1994). *Foucault and the Law: Towards a Sociology of Law as Governance*. London; Boulder, CO: Pluto Press.

Inwood, M. (1992). *A Hegel Dictionary*. Oxford: Blackwell.
Ivison, D. (1998). 'The disciplinary moment: Foucault, law and the reinscription of rights'. In J. Moss (ed.), *The Later Foucault: Politics and Philosophy* (pp. 129–48). London: Sage.
James, B. W. (2008). Establishing relations between law and other forms of thought and language. *Erasmus Law Review*, 1(3), 3–22.
Jameson, F. (1977). 'Imaginary and symbolic in Lacan: Marxism, psychoanalytic criticism, and the problem of the subject'. *Yale French Studies*, 55–6, 338–95.
Jasanoff, S. (2006). 'The idiom of co-production'. In *States of Knowledge* (pp. 1–12). London: Routledge.
Jasanoff, S. (2007). 'Making order: law and science in action'. In E. J. Hackett, O. Amsterdamska and M. E. Lynch (eds), *The Handbook of Science and Technology Studies* (pp. 761–86). Cambridge, MA: MIT Press.
Jasanoff, S. (2012). *Science and Public Reason*. London: Routledge.
Jenks, E. (1902). 'The myth of the Magna Carta'. *Independent Review*, 4, 260–73.
Jesseph, D. (1996). 'Hobbes and the method of natural science'. In T. Sorell (ed.), *The Cambridge Companion to Hobbes* (pp. 86–107). Cambridge: Cambridge University Press.
Jessop, B. (2007). 'From micro-powers to governmentality: Foucault's work on statehood, state formation, statecraft and state power'. *Political Geography*, 26, 34–40.
Jessop, B. (2008). *State Power: A Strategic-Relational Approach*. Cambridge: Polity Press.
Johnson, R. (2010, Summer Edition). 'Kant's moral philosophy'. (E. N. Zalta, ed.), *The Stanford Encyclopedia of Philosophy*, <http://plato.stanford.edu/archives/sum2010/entries/kant-moral/>
Jolley, N. (1999). *Locke: His Philosophical Thought*. Oxford: Oxford University Press.
Jones, G. H. (1990). *Convergent Forces: Immediate Causes of the Revolution of 1688 in England*. Ames: Iowa State University Press.
Jordan, W. C. (1999). 'The Capetians from the death of Philip II to Philip IV'. In D. Abulafia (ed.), *The New Cambridge Medieval History* (Vols. 5, c.1198–c.1300, pp. 279–313). Cambridge: Cambridge University Press.
Kaldor, M. (2004). 'Nationalism and globalisation'. *Nations and Nationalism*, 10(1/2), 161–77.
Kamen, H. (1984). *European Society, 1500–1700*. London: Hutchinson.

Kant, I. (1933). *Critique of Pure Reason*. (N. K. Smith, trans.) London: Macmillan.

Kant, I. (1952). *The Critique of Judgement*. (J. C. Meredith, trans.) Oxford: Clarendon Press.

Kant, I. (2002). *The Philosophy of Law*. (W. Hastie, trans.) Union, NJ: Lawbook Exchange.

Kavka, G. S. (1986). *Hobbesian Moral and Political Theory*. Princeton; NJ: Princeton Univeristy Press.

Kelly, A. H., Harbison, W. A. and Belz, H. (1991). *The American Constitution: Its Origins and Development* (7th edn). New York: Norton.

Kelly, M. G. (2009). *The Political Philosophy of Michel Foucault*. New York: Routledge.

Kelsen, H. (1945). *General Theory of Law and State*. (A. Wedberg, trans.) Cambridge, MA: Harvard University Press.

Kendall, W. (1941). *John Locke and the Doctrine of Majority-Rule*. Urbana: The University of Illinois Press.

Kennedy, D. (1993). *Sexy Dressing Etc*. Cambridge, MA: Harvard University Press.

Kenyon, J. P. (1974). 'The Revolution of 1688: resistance and contract'. In N. McKendrick (ed.), *Historical Perspectives: Studies in English Thought and Society in Honour of J. H. Plumb* (pp. 43–69). London: Europa.

Kenyon, J. P. (1977). *Revolution Principles: The Politics of Party, 1689–1720*. Cambridge: Cambridge University Press.

Kersting, W. (1992a). 'Kant's concept of the state'. In H. Williams (ed.), *Essays on Kant's Political Philosophy* (pp. 143–65). Cardiff: University of Wales Press.

Kersting, W. (1992b). 'Politics, freedom, and order'. In P. Guyer (ed.), *The Cambridge Companion to Kant* (pp. 342–66). Cambridge: Cambridge University Press.

Kilcullen, J. (2010, Fall Edition). 'Medieval political philosophy'. (E. N. Zalta, ed.), *The Stanford Encyclopedia of Philosophy*, <http://plato.stanford.edu/archives/fall2010/entries/medieval-political/>

King, P. (1974). *The Ideology of Order: A Comparative Analysis of Jean Bodin and Thomas Hobbes*. London: Allen & Unwin.

Koehler, J. J. and Saks, M. J. (1991). 'What DNA "fingerprinting" can teach the law about the rest of forensic science'. *Cardozo Law Review*, 13, 361–72.

Koenigsberger, H. G. (1987). *Early Modern Europe, 1500–1789*. London: Longman.

Koopman, C. (2013). *Genealogy as Critique. Foucault and the Problems of Modernity.* Bloomington, IN: Indiana University Press,

Koubi, G. and Romi, R. (1993). 'Préambule'. In G. Conac, M. Debene and G. Teobul (eds), *La déclaration des droits de l'homme et du citoyen de 1789. Histoire, analyse et commentaires.* (pp. 55–64). Paris: Economica.

Kretzmann, N. and Stump, E. (eds). (1993). *The Cambridge Companion to Aquinas.* Cambridge: Cambridge University Press.

Laclau, E. and Mouffe, C. *Hegemony and Socialist Strategy: Towards a Radical Democratic Politics.* 1985: London: Verso.

Laible, J. (2008). *Separatism and Sovereignty in the New Europe.* New York; London: Palgrave Macmillan.

Laslett, P. (ed.). (1956). *Philosophy, Politics and Society: A Collection.* Oxford: Blackwell.

Laslett, P. (1988). 'Introduction'. In J. Locke and P. Laslett (ed.), *Two Treatises of Government* (pp. 3–15). Cambridge: Cambridge University Press.

Latour, B. (1983). 'Give me a laboratory and I will raise the world'. In K. Knorr-Cetina and M. Mulkay (eds), *Science Observed: Perspectives on the Social Studies of Science* (pp. 141–70). London: Sage.

Latour, B. (1988). *The Pasteurization of France.* Cambridge, MA: Harvard University Press.

Latour, B. (1999). *Pandora's Hope: Essays on the Reality of Science Studies.* Cambridge, MA; London: Harvard University Press.

Lefebvre, G. (1962). *The French Revolution from Its Origins to 1793.* London; New York: Routledge & Kegan Paul; Columbia University Press.

Lefebvre, G. (1967). *The Coming of the French Revolution, 1789.* Princeton, NJ: Princeton University Press.

Lefebvre, G. (1969). *Napoleon: from 18 Brumaire to Tilsit, 1799–1807.* (H. F. Stockhold, trans.) New York: Columbia University Press.

LeGoff, J. (1988). *Medieval Civilization 400–1500.* (J. Barrow, trans.) Oxford: Blackwell.

Lemke, T. (2010). 'Foucault's hypothesis: from the critique of the juridico-discursive concept of power to an analytics of government'. *Parreshia* (9), 31–43.

Lemos, R. (1977). *Rousseau's Political Philosophy: An Exposition and Interpretation.* Athens: University of Georgia Press.

Lévy, P. (1998). *Becoming Virtual: Reality in the Digital Age.* (R. Bononno, trans.) New York; London: Plenum.

Lisska, A. (1996). *Aquinas's Theory of Natural Law: An Analytic Reconstruction*. Oxford: Clarendon Press.
Lobban, M. (2007). *A History of the Philosophy of Law in the Common Law World, 1600–1900*. Dordrecht: Springer.
Locke, J. (1988). *Two Treatises of Government*. (P. Laslett, ed.) Cambridge: Cambridge University Press.
Loizidou, E. (2007). *Judith Butler: Ethics, Law, Politics*. New York: Routledge-Cavendish.
Lovell, C. R. (1962). *English Constitutional and Legal History: A Survey*. New York: Oxford University Press.
Lupoi, M. (2000). *The Origins of the European Legal Order*. (A. Belton, trans.) Cambridge: Cambridge University Press.
Lyons, M. (1994). *Napoleon Bonaparte and the Legacy of the French Revolution*. London: Macmillan.
Macaulay, T. B. (1906). *The History of England from the Accession of James II*. London; New York: Dent; Dutton.
Madison, J. ([1821] 1981). 'Property and suffrage: second thoughts on the constitutional convention'. In M. Meyers (ed.), *The Mind of the Founder: Sources of the Political Thought of James Madison* (pp. 394–400). Hanover: University Press of New England.
Mahoney, J. (2007). *The Challenge of Human Rights: Origin, Development, and Significance*. Malden, MA: Blackwell.
Maine, H. S. (1917). *Ancient Law*. London: Dent.
Mann, M. (1984). 'The autonomous power of the state: its origins, mechanisms and results'. *Archives européennes de sociologie*, 25, 185–213.
Marongiu, A. (1968). *Medieval Parliaments: A Comparative Study*. (S. J. Woolf, trans.) London: Eyre & Spottiswoode.
Marsilius of Padua. (1956). *The Defender of Peace, The Defensor Pacis*. (A. Gewirth, ed.) New York: Harper & Row.
Marx, K. and Engels, F. (1998). *The Communist Manifesto*. London; New York: Verso.
Massumi, B. (2002). *Parables for the Virtual: Movement, Affect, Sensation*. Durham, NC: Duke University Press.
Masters, R. D. (1968). *The Political Philosophy of Rousseau*. Princeton, NJ: Princeton University Press.
Mayer, J. et al. (1939). *Political Thought: The European Tradition*. London: Dent.
McGrade, A. S. (1982). 'Rights, natural rights, and philosophy of law'. In N. Kretzmann, A. Kenny and J. Pinborg (eds), *The Cambridge History of Later Medieval Philosophy: From the Rediscovery of Aristotle to the*

Disintegration of Scholasticism (pp. 738–56). Cambridge: Cambridge University Press.

McIlwain, C. H. (1910). *The High Court of Parliament and Its Supremacy: An Historical Essay on the Boundaries between Legislation and Adjudication in England*. New Haven, CT: Yale University Press.

McIlwain, C. H. (1947). *Constitutionalism Ancient and Modern*. Ithaca, NY: Cornell University Press.

McInerny, R. and O'Callaghan, J. (2010, Winter Edition). 'Saint Thomas Aquinas'. (E. N. Zalta, ed.), *The Stanford Encyclopedia of Philosophy*, <http://plato.stanford.edu/archives/win2010/entries/aquinas/>

Merriman, J. (2004). *A History of Modern Europe: From the Renaissance to the Present*. New York; London: Norton.

Middlekauff, R. (2005). *The Glorious Cause: The American Revolution, 1763–1789*. Oxford, New York: Oxford University Press.

Miller, D. (2000). *Citizenship and National Identity*. Cambridge: Polity Press.

Miller, J. (1982). 'The Glorious Revolution, "contract" and "abdication" reconsidered'. *Historical Journal*, 25(3), 541–55.

Miller, J. (1997). *The Glorious Revolution*. London; New York: Addison Wesley Longman.

Miller, J. (2011, Fall Edition). Hugo Grotius. (E. N. Zalta, ed.), *The Stanford Encyclopedia of Philosophy*, <http://plato.stanford.edu/archives/fall2011/entries/grotius/>

Miller, P. and Rose, N. (2008). *Governing the Present: Administering Economic, Social and Personal Life*. Cambridge: Polity Press.

Milton, J. R. (1999). *Locke's Moral, Political and Legal Philosophy*. Aldershot: Ashgate; Dartmouth.

Morton, S. and Bygrave, S. (eds). (2008). *Foucault in an Age of Terror: Essays on Biopolitics and the Defence of Society*. Basingstoke; New York: Palgrave Macmillan.

Mouffe, C. (2000). *The Democratic Paradox*. London: Verso.

Neumann, F. and Kirchheimer, O. (1996). *The Rule of Law Under Siege*. (W. E. Scheuerman, ed.) Berkeley; London: University of California Press.

Norris, P. (2003). 'Global governance and cosmopolitan citizens'. In D. Held and A. McGrew (eds), *The Global Transformations Reader: An Introduction to the Globalization Debate* (pp. 287–98). Cambridge; Malden, MA: Polity Press; Blackwell.

O'Farrell, C. (2005). *Foucault*. London; Thousands Oaks, CA: Sage.

Oksala, J. (2005). *Foucault on Freedom*. Cambridge; New York: Cambridge University Press.

O'Neill, O. (1992). 'Reason and politics in the Kantian enterprise'. In H. Williams (ed.), *Essays on Kant's Political Philosophy* (pp. 50–80). Cardiff: University of Wales Press.

Oppenheimer, F. (2007). *The State*. Montreal; New York: Black Rose.

Palmenatz, J. P. (1963). *Man and Society: A Critical Examination of Some Important Social and Political Theories from Machiavelli to Marx* (Vol. I). London: Longmans.

Palmer, R. R. (1959). *The Age of Democratic Revolution: A Political History of Europe and America, 1760–1800*. Princeton, NJ: Princeton University Press.

Patterson, O. (1991). *Freedom in the Making of Western Culture*. London: Tauris.

Peclzynski, Z. A. (1984). 'Political community and individual freedom in Hegel's philosophy of state'. In Z. A. Pelczynski (ed.), *The State and Civil Society: Studies in Hegel's Political Philosophy* (pp. 55–76). Cambridge: Cambridge University Press.

Petersen, A. and Bunton, R. (eds). (1997). *Foucault, Health and Medicine*. London: Routledge.

Pincus, S. (2009). *1688: The First Modern Revolution*. New Haven, CT; London: Yale University Press.

Pitkin, H. (1965). 'Obligation and consent I'. *American Political Science Review*, 59, 991–9.

Plant, R. (1973). *Hegel*. London: Allen & Unwin.

Plucknett, T. F. (1926). 'Bonham's case and judicial review'. *Harvard Law Review*, 40, 30–70.

Plumb, J. H. (1967). *The Growth of Political Stability in England, 1675–1725*. London: Macmillan.

Pocock, J. G. (1957). *The Ancient Constitution and the Feudal Law: A Study of English Historical Thought in the Seventeenth Century*. Cambridge: Cambridge University Press.

Poggi, G. (1978). *The Development of the Modern State: A Sociological Introduction*. Stanford, CA: Stanford University Press.

Poggi, G. (1990). *The State, its Nature, Development and Prospects*. Oxford: Polity Press.

Pole, J. R. (1983). *The Gift of Government: Political Responsibility from the English Restoration to American Independence*. Athens: University of Georgia Press.

Pollock, F. and Maitland, F. W. (1952). *The History of English Law Before*

the Time of Edward I. Vol.1. London: Cambridge University Press.
Popper, K. R. (1995). *The Open Society and its Enemies*. London: Routledge.
Poulantzas, N. (1980). *State, Power, Socialism*. London: Verso.
Prétot, X. (1993). 'Article 1'. In G. Conac, M. Debene and G. Teobul (eds), *La déclaration des droits de l'homme et du citoyen de 1789* (pp. 65–76). Paris: Economica.
Rabb, T. K. (1975). *The Struggle for Stability in Early Modern Europe*. New York: Oxford University Press.
Radin, M. (1947). 'The myth of the Magna Carta'. *Harvard Law Review*, 60, 1,060–91.
Rawls, J. (1972). *A Theory of Justice*. Oxford: Clarendon Press.
Rawls, J. (1999). *Law of Peoples*. Cambridge, MA: Harvard University Press.
Rawls, J. (2007). *Lectures on the History of Political Philosophy*. Cambridge, MA; London: Belknap Press of Harvard University Press.
Raz, J. (1979). *The Authority of Law: Essays on Law and Morality*. Oxford: Clarendon Press.
Redding, P. (2010, Fall Edition). 'Georg Wilhelm Friedrich Hegel'. (E. N. Zalta, ed.) *The Stanford Encyclopedia of Philosophy*, <http://plato.stanford.edu/archives/fall2010/entries/hegel/>
Rehg, W. (1996). 'Translator's introduction'. In J. Habermas, *Between Facts and Norms* (pp. ix–xxxvii). Cambridge: Polity Press.
Reid, J. P. (1988). *The Concept of Liberty in the Age of the American Revolution*. Chicago; London: University of Chicago Press.
Reid, J. P. (1989). *The Concept of Representation in the Age of the American Revolution*. Chicago; London: University of Chicago Press.
Reid, J. P. (1991). *Constitutional History of the American Revolution: The Authority to Legislate*. Madison: University of Wisconsin.
Reid, J. P. (1993). *Constitutional History of the American Revolution: The Authority of Law*. Madison; London: University of Wisconsin.
Rials, S. (1988). *La déclaration des droits de l'homme et du citoyen*. Paris: Hachette.
Riley, P. (1986). *The General Will before Rousseau*. Princeton, NJ: Princeton University Press.
Riley, P. (1995). 'Rousseau's general will: freedom of a particular kind'. In R. Wokler (ed.), *Rousseau and Liberty* (pp. 1–28). New York: Manchester University Press.
Roemer, J. E., Lee, W. and Straeten, K. V. (2007). *Racism, Xenophobia, and Distribution: Multi-Issue Politics in Advanced Democracies*. New

York; Cambridge, MA: Russell Sage Foundation; Harvard University Press.

Rose, N. (1985). *The Psychological Complex*. London: Routledge & Kegan Paul.

Rose, N. (1999). *Powers of Freedom: Reframing Political Thought*. Cambridge; New York: Cambridge University Press.

Rose, N. and Valverde, M. (1998). 'Governed by law?' *Social & Legal Studies*, 7(4), 541–51.

Rousseau, J. J. (1995). *The Social Contract and Discourses* (G. D. Cole, trans.) London: Dent.

Runciman, D. (2003). 'The concept of the state: the sovereignty of a fiction'. In *States and Citizens: History, Theory, Prospects* (pp. 28–38). Cambridge: Cambridge University Press.

Russell, B. (2005). *History of Western Philosophy*. London: Routledge.

Ryan, A. (1996). 'Hobbes's political philosophy'. In T. Sorell (ed.), *The Cambridge Companion to Hobbes* (pp. 208–44). Cambridge: Cambridge University Press.

Sabine, G. H. (1973). *A History of Political Theory*. Hillsdale, IL: Dryden Press.

Said, E. W. (1978). *Orientalism*. London: Routledge & Kegan Paul.

Sandel, M. (1998). *Liberalism and the Limits of Justice*. Cambridge: Cambridge University Press.

Sartori, G. (1987). *The Theory of Democracy Revisited*. Chatham, NJ: Chatham House.

Sayles, G. O. (1952). *The Medieval Foundations of England*. London: Methuen.

Selden, J. (1927). *Table Talk of John Selden*. (F. Pollock, ed.) London: Quaritch.

Sewell, W. H. (1980). *Work and Revolution in France: The Language of Labor from the Old Regime to 1848*. Cambridge: Cambridge University Press.

Shennan, J. H. (1974). *The Origins of the Modern European State*. London: Hutchinson.

Shennan, J. H. (1986). *Liberty and Order in Early Modern Europe: The Subject and the State, 1650–1800*. London: Longman.

Shklar, J. (1969). *Men and Citizens: A Study of Rousseau's Social Theory*. Cambridge: Cambridge University Press.

Simmonds, N. E. (1984). *The Decline of Juridical Reason*. Manchester: Manchester University Press.

Simmons, A. J. (1993). *On the Edge of Anarchy: Locke, Consent, and the*

Limits of Society. Princeton, NJ; Chichester: Princeton University Press.
Simon, J. (1993). *Poor Discipline: Parole and the Social Control of the Underclass, 1890–1990*. Chicago; London: University of Chicago Press.
Simons, J. (1995). *Foucault and the Political*. London; New York: Routledge.
Skinner, Q. (1978). *The Foundations of Modern Political Thought*. Cambridge: Cambridge University Press.
Skinner, Q. (1988). 'Political philosophy'. In C. Schmitt, Q. Skinner, E. Kessler and J. Kraye (eds), *The Cambridge History of Renaissance Philosophy* (pp. 387–452). Cambridge: Cambridge University Press.
Skinner, Q. (1989). 'The state'. In T. Ball, J. Farr and R. L. Hanson (eds), *Political Innovation and Conceptual Change* (pp. 90–131). Cambridge: Cambridge University Press.
Skocpol, T. (1979). *States and Social Revolutions: A Comparative Analysis of France, Russia and China*. Cambridge: Cambridge University Press.
Slaughter, T. P. (1981). '"Abdicate" and "contract" in the Glorious Revolution'. *Historical Journal*, 24(2), 323–37.
Slimani, A. (2004). *La modernité du concept de nation au XVIIIe siècle*. Marseille: Presse Universitaire d'Aix-Marseille.
Smith, A. D. (2001). *Nationalism: Theory, Ideology, History*. Cambridge: Polity Press.
Soboul, A. (1977). *A Short History of the French Revolution*. (G. Simcox, trans.) Berkeley; London: University of California Press.
Sokhi-Bulley, B. (2011). 'Government(ality) by experts: Human Rights as governance'. *Law and Critique*, 22(3), 1–21.
Stoner, J. R. (1992). *Common Law and Liberal Theory: Coke, Hobbes, and the Origins of American Constitutionalism*. Lawrence, KS: University Press of Kansas.
Strange, S. (1996). *The Retreat of the State: The Diffusion of Power in the World Economy*. New York: Cambridge University Press.
Strath, B. and Torstendahl, R. (1992). 'State theory and state development: states as network structures in change in modern European history'. In R. Torstendahl (ed.), *State Theory and State History* (pp. 12–37). London: Sage.
Strauss, L. (1952). *The Political Philosophy of Hobbes: Its Basis and Its Genesis*. (E. M. Sinclair, trans.) Chicago: University of Chicago Press.
Strauss, L. (1953). *Natural Right and History*. Chicago: University of Chicago Press.

Strauss, L. and Cropsey, J. (eds). (1963). *History of Political Philosophy*. Chicago: Rand McNally.

Strayer, J. R. (1959). *The Middle Ages 395–1500*. London: Bell.

Strayer, J. R. (1980). *The Reign of Philip the Fair*. Princeton; Guilford: Princeton University Press.

Strozier, R. M. (2002). *Foucault, Subjectivity, and Identity: Historical Constructions of Subject and Self*. Detroit, MI: Wayne State University Press.

Tadros, V. (1998). 'Between governance and discipline: the law and Michel Foucault'. *Oxford Journal of Legal Studies*, 18, 75–103.

Talmon, J. L. (1970). *The Origins of Totalitarian Democracy*. New York: Norton.

Taylor, C. (1979). *Hegel and Modern Society*. Cambridge: Cambridge University Press.

Taylor, D. (2009). 'Normativity and normalization'. *Foucault Studies*, 7, 45–63.

Taylor, G. V. (1967). 'Noncapitalist wealth and the origins of the French Revolution'. *The American Historical Review*, 72(2), 469–96.

Teboul, G. (1993). 'Article 6'. In G. Conac, M. Debene and G. Teboul (eds), *La déclaration des droits de l'homme et du citoyen de 1789. Histoire, analyse et commentaires*. (pp. 135–54). Paris: Economica.

Tigar, M. E. (1977). *Law and the Rise of Capitalism*. New York, London: Monthly Review Press.

Tilly, C. (1975). *The Formation of National States in Western Europe*. Princeton; London: Princeton University Press.

Tilly, C. (1990). *Coercion, Capital, and European States, A.D. 990–1990*. Oxford: Blackwell.

Tilly, C. (ed.). (1996). *Citizenship, Identity and Social History*. New York: Cambridge University Press.

Tocqueville, A. (1955). *The Old Régime and the French Revolution*. (S. Gilbert, trans.) Garden City, NY: Doubleday.

Trevelyan, G. M. (1938). *The English Revolution, 1688–1689*. London: Oxford University Press.

Trevelyan, G. M. (1944). *English Social History: A Survey of Six Centuries: Chaucer to Queen Victoria*. London: Longmans, Green.

Trigo, B. (ed.). (2002). *Foucault and Latin America: Appropriations and Deployments of Discoursive Analysis*. New York; London: Routledge.

Tubbs, J. W. (2000). *The Common Law Mind: Medieval and Early Modern Conceptions*. Baltimore, MD: Johns Hopkins University Press.

Tuck, R. (1979). *Natural Rights Theories*. Cambridge: Cambridge University Press.

Tuck, R. (1991). 'Grotius and Selden'. In J. H. Burns (ed.), *The Cambridge History of Political Thought, 1450–1700* (pp. 499–529). Cambridge: Cambridge University Press.

Tuck, R. (1999). *The Rights of War and Peace: Political Thought and the International Order from Grotius to Kant*. Oxford: Oxford University Press.

Tuckness, A. (2011, Fall Edition). 'Locke's political philosophy'. (E. N. Zalta, ed.), *The Stanford Encyclopedia of Philosophy*, <http://plato.stanford.edu/archives/fall2011/entries/locke-political/>.

Tully, J. (1993). *An Approach to Political Philosophy: Locke in Contexts*. Cambridge: New York: Cambridge University Press.

Turchetti, M. (2010, Summer Edition). 'Jean Bodin'. (E. N. Zalta, ed.), *The Stanford Encyclopedia of Philosophy*, <http://plato.stanford.edu/archives/sum2010/entries/bodin/>

Uzgalis, W. (2010, Winter Edition). 'John Locke'. (E. N. Zalta, ed.), *The Stanford Encyclopedia of Philosophy*, <http://plato.stanford.edu/archives/win2010/entries/locke/>

Vecchio, G. D. (1979). *La déclaration des droits de l'homme et du citoyen dans la Révolution française*. (P. G. Antoinette, trans.) Roma: Nagard.

Verge, A. (2006). *La notion de constitution d'après les cours et assemblées à la fin de l'Ancien Régime (1750–1789)*. Paris: De Boccard.

Vile, M. J. (1967). *Constitutionalism and the Separation of Powers*. Oxford: Clarendon Press.

Vincent, A. (1987). *Theories of the State*. Oxford: Blackwell.

Viroli, M. (1987). 'The concept of ordre and the language of classical republicanism in Jean-Jacques Rousseau'. In A. Pagden (ed.), *The Languages of Political Theory in Early-Modern Europe* (pp. 156–78). Cambridge: Cambridge University Press.

Viroli, M. (1988). *Jean-Jacques Rousseau and the 'Well-ordered Society'*. (D. Hanson, trans.) Cambridge: Cambridge University Press.

Vogel, M. E. (2007). *Coercion to Compromise: Plea Bargaining, The Courts, and the Making of Political Authority*. Oxford: Oxford University Press.

Waluchow, W. (2014, Spring). 'Constitutionalism'. (E. N. Zalta, ed.), *The Stanford Encyclopedia of Philosophy*, <http://plato.stanford.edu/archives/spr2014/entries/constitutionalism/>

Warner, M. (1999). *The Trouble with Normal: Sex, Politics, and the Ethics of Queer Life*. Cambridge, MA: Harvard University Press.

Watkins, J. (1989). *Hobbes's System of Ideas*. Aldershot: Gower, in association with the London School of Economics and Political Science.

Weber, M. (1968). *Economy and Society*. (G. Roth and C. Wittich, eds, E. Fishoff et al., trans.) New York: Bedminster Press.

Weber, M. (2004). *The Vocation Lectures*. (D. Owen and T. B. Strong, eds and R. Livingstone, trans.) Indianapolis, IN: Hackett.

Weiler, J. (1995). 'Does Europe need a Constitution? Demos, telos, ethos and the Maastricht Decision'. *European Law Journal*, 1(3), 219–58.

Weinrib, E. J. (1992). 'Law as idea of reason'. In H. Williams (ed.), *Essays on Kant's Political Philosophy* (pp. 15–49). Cardiff: Cardiff University Press.

Welzel, H. (1965). *Diritto naturale e giustizia materiale*. (G. De Stefano, trans.) Naples: Giuffé.

Wiesner-Hanks, M. E. (2006). *Early Modern Europe, 1450–1789*. Cambridge: Cambridge University Press.

Wilks, M. (1963). *The Problem of Sovereignty in the Later Middle Ages*. Cambridge: Cambridge University Press.

Wolff, M. (2004). 'Hegel's organicist theory of the state: on the concept and method of Hegel's "science of State"'. In R. B. Pippin and O. Hoffe (eds), *Hegel on Ethics and Politics* (N. Walker, trans., pp. 291–322). Cambridge: Cambridge University Press.

Wood, C. T. (ed.). (1967). *Philip the Fair and Boniface VIII: State vs. Papacy*. New York: Holt, Rinehart & Winston.

Wood, G. S. (1972). *The Creation of the American Republic, 1776–1787*. New York: Norton.

Wood, G. S. (1992). *The Radicalism of the American Revolution*. New York: Knopf.

Zivi, K. (2008). 'Rights and the politics of performativity'. In T. Carver and S. A. Chambers (eds), *Judith Butler's Precarious Politics* (pp. 157–69). New York: Routledge.

Žižek, S. (1989). *The Sublime Object of Ideology*. London: Verso.

Zophy, J. W. (ed.). (1980). *The Holy Roman Empire: A Dictionary Handbook*. Westport, CT: Greenwood Press.

Zutshi, P. N. (2000). 'The Avignon Papacy'. In M. Jones (ed.), *The New Cambridge Medieval History* (pp. 653–73). Cambridge: Cambridge University Press.

Index

abnormal, 7, 126–8, 130
absolutism, 32, 39, 45, 50–4, 56, 72, 76, 78–80, 83, 92–4, 102
abstraction, of law, 33, 41, 44, 56, 62–3, 67, 70, 72–3, 83, 86, 90, 92, 100, 107, 138–9, 144, 155, 161, 172n157
accident, 6
actual *see* virtual
Adalberon of Laon, 201n97
Agamben, G., 25, 27, 154
American Constitution, 84, 88–9, 91
American Declaration of Independence, 75, 86, 90, 95, 98, 100
American Revolution, 73, 84–5, 87, 89–90
ancien régime, 73, 76, 95, 102
Anderson, P., 193n9
apparatus
  concept of, 25, 27, 29, 170n141, 171n142
  normalising, 113, 115, 118–19, 123, 126, 129, 131, 136, 154
  see also law as apparatus
Aquinas, 40–3, 46–7
archaeology, 3, 28
Aristotle, 4, 40, 43, 47
assemblage, 15, 35, 118, 167n87
Augustine, 40–1
Austin, J., 80
autonomy, personal, 1–2, 23, 54, 60–1, 73, 106, 111–12, 117, 121, 132, 134, 143, 148–50, 158
Avignonese captivity, 42

Baudrillard, J., 1
Bauman, Z., 3, 35, 105, 120–1, 123, 144

Beck, U., 120
behaviour *see* conduct
Bill of Rights, English, 75, 78, 84, 87, 98, 100
biopolitics, 2–4, 8, 11–12, 16–19, 28, 35, 45, 69, 105, 113–14, 118–23, 125, 129, 131, 133–4, 136–9, 141, 150, 159–62
Bodin, J., 31, 45–6
body, human, 4–5, 7, 39, 157
body politic, 45, 55, 59, 81, 91, 94–5
Boniface VIII, 12, 40
Botero, G., 19
bourgeoisie, 152, 171n147, 173n175
Braun, B., 124
Brown, W., 156
bureaucracy, 31, 65
Burke, E., 77–8
Butler, J., 152–6

Canguilhem, G., 7
capital punishment, 127, 157
capitalism, 5
carcerial system, 135
Carnap, R., 172n157
categorical imperative, 184n136, 186n150
Charles I, 79–80
Charles II, 75
checks and balances, 88–91, 102
Christodoulidis, E., 156
Church, 42–3
citizen, 29, 32–3, 50–6, 58–61, 63–6, 75, 86–7, 118, 142, 144–6, 158
coercion, 18, 33–4, 43, 60–1, 67, 107, 122, 143
Colonies, American *see* USA

command
  concept of, 34, 106–7, 109–10
  theory of law, 10, 12, 26–8, 35, 40, 43–8, 80, 112
common good, 58–9, 82–3, 88–91, 96–8, 102
common interest *see* common good
conduct, 6–7, 11, 22–4, 32, 35, 46, 50, 52–3, 55–6, 62, 67, 72, 105, 107–9, 112, 122–3, 127–8, 137
Constitution of Liberty, The, 33
constitution
  ancient *see* fundamental laws
  modern, 9, 34, 72–4, 76–7, 101–2, 109, 131–2, 143, 150, 191n1
control, 105, 119, 122–6, 133, 135–8, 140, 149–50, 161
Cornier, H., case of, 127–8, 130
corporations, 64, 69, 92, 120
cosmopolitanism, 149–50
counter-conducts, 156
critical theory, 151–2
Critique of Judgement, 186n150
Critique of Pure Reason, 186n150
Cromwell, T., 79

De Potestate Regia et Papali, 42
Defensor Pacis, 43
Deleuze, G., 15, 25, 27, 122–4, 162
democracy, 32–3, 49, 51, 53–7, 60, 66, 69–70, 83, 88–9, 119, 136, 142–5, 146–8, 192n6
  agonistic, 213n50
Democritus, 125
dialectical method, 63–4, 187n154
discipline, 4–11, 14–16, 17–21, 35, 38, 105, 113–16, 118–19, 122–3, 127–9, 131, 134–7, 144
Discipline and Punish, 19, 27, 31
dispositif see apparatus
dominium regale et politicum, 80
Dworkin, R., 156

empire, 43
Encyclopaedia, 66
England, 73, 75–80, 82–5, 87, 90, 92, 94–6, 102
English constitution, 80–4
English Revolution, 77–8, 82–3, 87–8
Enlightenment, 22, 146

equality, legal, 33–4, 41, 44, 48–50, 52, 54, 56, 60–70, 72–3, 83, 86–7, 90, 92, 96, 100–1, 107–11, 144, 155, 16, 189n171
estates, 77, 92–3, 120
État Providence, L', 13
etiamsi daremus hypothesis, 47–8
European Union, 145, 147
eventalisation, 27
Ewald, F., 14–15
expulsion thesis, 10–12, 14, 16–18, 21, 32, 35, 113, 116–17, 119

federalist papers, 88–90
feudalism, 38, 72, 92
Filmer, R., 79
Fitzpatrick, P., 16–19, 113
Forget Foucault!, 1
Fortescue, J., 80–1
Foucauldian studies, 18, 21, 24, 27, 116
Foucault and Law, 10
Foucault's 'toolbox', 21, 27
free will, 63
freedom
  concept of, 2, 8, 11–12, 21, 23–5
  individual, 33–4, 41, 44, 48–9, 53–4, 56, 58, 60–70
  legal, 72–3, 83, 86, 90, 92, 96, 100–1, 107, 109–10, 144, 155, 161
France, 42, 73, 75–7, 92–7, 102
French Revolution, 93–6, 112, 201n106
French Universal Declaration, 95–9, 98, 100–1, 110, 192n6, 201n105, 202n119, 202n121
  Preamble, 87, 98, 204n139
  Article One, 100, 110, 204n141
  Article Three, 99
  Article Four, 100, 204n142
  Article Six, 99–100, 204n142
fundamental laws, 78–85, 89–90, 94–5, 97–9
fundamental rights, 99, 132, 149, 153, 155

genealogy, 1, 3, 27–9, 34–6, 113, 153, 160–1
general will, 58–60, 63, 68, 97, 99
generality, of law, 33, 41, 44, 56, 62–3, 67, 70, 72–3, 83, 86, 90, 92, 100, 107–8, 138–9, 144, 155, 161, 172n157

INDEX

Gerard I de Cambrai, 201n97
globalisation, 141, 145–6, 150
Glorious Revolution, 73–4, 77–9, 84–6, 89
Golden Bull, 40, 175n13
Golder, B., 16–19, 113, 153, 156–9
governmentality, 5–8, 10–11, 14–21, 24, 35, 53, 91, 105, 113–16, 118–19, 127, 129, 131, 134–7, 155, 161, 164n26
Grotius, H., 46–9, 52, 55, 60
Guattari, F., 15
Guicciardini, F., 31

Habermas, J., 1, 9–10, 21, 57, 118, 141–3, 145–8, 150
Hale, M., 79, 82
Hamilton, A., 88
Hart, H. L. A., 33, 80, 139
Hayek, F., 33–4, 91, 106–7, 109
Hegel, G. W. F., 34, 56–7, 63–8, 70, 162
Held, D., 32, 142, 149–50
heterotopia, 151–2, 159, 212n49
hierocracy 42
Hobbes, T., 20, 31, 46, 50–5, 60, 162
Homo Economicus, 20
Homo Juridicus, 19–20
Hooker, R., 81
humanism, 43–4, 57
Hunt, A., 10–12

identity, 31–2, 110–11, 105, 117–18, 121–4, 129, 136, 144–8, 151, 153–4, 156, 186n150
inclusiveness, 131, 135–7, 148, 150, 191n183, 209n71
independence, personal, 54, 73, 106
individual, concept of the, 23–4
insurance societies, 13
internalisation of norms, 6–7, 23, 112, 130–1, 134; *see also* apparatus
intolerable acts, 86
investitures controversy, 40

Jasanoff, S., 116
Jean de Paris, 42–3
Jefferson, T., 88
judicial system, 17, 26, 81, 139
juridical, the, 13, 15, 21, 26, 152, 165n70, 166n73

juridico-political discourse, 4, 13, 19–20
'juris-diction', 26–7, 166n74

Kant, I., 56–57, 60–3, 66–8, 70, 142, 162
Kelsen, H., 33

Lacan, J., 153
law
  as apparatus, 25, 27–9, 32–5, 37, 44, 47, 49, 56, 62, 68–9, 71, 104, 113–14, 118, 134, 148, 160–2
  as command, 7, 10, 28, 33–5, 40, 44, 46–8, 52–3, 55–6, 59–60, 61, 66, 69, 76, 80, 87, 101, 106–10, 112, 192n3
  as norm, 13–14, 28, 34–5, 37–8, 47, 52–3, 57–8, 60, 62, 67–9, 74, 79–83, 87, 90, 99–107, 113, 119, 131, 165n70, 166n71, 167n79
  civil, 13, 93, 192n6
  criminal law, 10, 29, 39, 123, 127–8
  of law, 14, 28
  rule of, 33, 78, 84–6, 109, 148–9, 143, 151, 155, 174n192, 176n26
  social, 78, 81
legitimation, political, 37–8, 41–2, 44–7, 49, 51–2, 54–60, 67, 91, 101, 145
Leviathan, 50
Levinas, E., 153
Lévy, P., 124–5
lex aeterna, 40, 43
lex humana, 40
lex naturalis, 40
liberalism, 133, 135–7, 141, 144–5, 149–51
liberty *see* freedom
liquid modernity, 3, 35, 105, 119–21, 123, 125, 133–4, 148, 162
Locke, J., 20, 46, 53–5, 60, 70
Loizidou, E., 155

Machiavelli, N., 31
Madison, J., 88–9, 200n89
Madness and Civilisation, 38
Magna Carta, 83
Marsilius of Padua, 43
Massumi, B., 124
mixed government, 78–81
Montesquieu, 20, 38

Nagel, T., 156
Napoleonic Penal Code, 127
nation, 52, 93, 97, 99, 118, 135–6, 145–6, 149, 202n121, 209n71, 210n21
nationalism, 118, 147
natural law, 14, 40–1, 46–50, 52, 54–7, 95, 99
neo-liberalism, 19, 145
Neumann, F., 33
Nietzsche, F., 3, 22
norm
    concept of the, 7–8, 12–14, 28, 34–8, 44–7, 52–3, 57–8, 60, 62, 67, 69, 73–7, 80–4, 87, 89–90, 93–4, 101–2, 104–7, 111–13, 117–20, 122–4, 126–39, 165–7
    socio-scientific, 7, 12–17, 28, 35, 114–17, 131
normalisation *see* norm, apparatus
normalisation, *strictu sensu*, 35, 83, 89, 91, 101, 111
normation, 35, 83, 89, 91, 101, 111
Nozick, R., 156

'Of Other Spaces', 151
Order of Things, The, 38, 161
Otherness, 36, 105, 129–30, 132–3, 135–7, 139–40, 152–3

Paine, T., 200n92
parliamentary sovereignty, 79, 87, 200n93
parliaments, 76–88, 91, 94, 102, 194n13, 195n24
parody, 153, 155
patriotism, Constitutional, 145–6, 148, 150
Patterson, O., 41
Philosophy of Right, 63, 65–7, 188n166, 189n172
population, 5–7, 9, 19, 119
postmodernism, 141, 145
Poulantzas, N., 1
power
    concept of, 4–7, 21–4
    pastoral, 6, 19, 45
    political, 31–2, 38, 42, 45, 49–51, 54, 56–8, 62, 68–70, 78–9, 83–4, 87, 89, 92, 95–8, 101, 131

sovereign, 6, 9, 55–7, 60–2, 83, 101–2, 119, 154–5
power/knowledge, 3, 22–3, 25–7, 35, 46, 68, 114, 116, 126–8, 131, 148, 160
practices *see* subjectivation, practices of
problematisation, 2, 24, 27–8, 96, 125, 159–60

R v. Board of Visitors of HM Prison, The Maze ex parte Hone, 168n101
Rabinow, P., 29
Rawls, J., 59, 149, 156
Reason of State, 19, 45
Reflections on the Revolution in France, 77
Renaissance, 44, 177n46
rights, 1, 8–10, 12–13, 19–20, 49–51, 54, 56, 62–3, 65–6, 72, 74–5, 77–8, 85, 90, 92, 98–100, 107, 109–10, 119, 132, 142–4, 146, 149, 151, 153–60
Rose, N., 11, 24, 29
Rousseau, J.-J., 20, 56–61, 63, 66, 68, 70, 100
rule of judgement, 8, 13–14, 99

Scanlon, T., 156
scholasticism, 47
Science and Technology Studies, 116–17
secularisation, 14, 34, 37, 40–52, 57, 61, 69, 99, 134, 139, 142, 176
security, 9, 19, 77, 154–5
Security, Territory, Population, 19
self, the *see* identity
self-consciousness, 65, 188n160
self-government, 48, 75, 82, 85, 87, 198n67, 200n93
separation of powers, 88–91, 93, 102, 151
Sittlichkeit, 64, 188n156
Social Contract, 58
social contract theories, 20, 33
societies of control *see* control
Society Must Be Defended, 19
sovereign people, 32–3, 70
sovereignty societies, 6–7, 19, 37–9, 41–2, 44–6, 49, 52–4, 66, 69, 74–5, 84, 87, 91, 101–2, 110, 130, 161
state, 5–7, 31–2

subject
  non-normalisable, 3, 36
  of rights, 3, 20, 26
  universal, 112–17, 138, 155
subjectivation, 11, 25–7, 33, 49, 68–9, 104–5, 113, 119, 124, 131, 134–5, 144, 146, 148, 158
  practices of, 5–11, 17–18, 22, 24, 27–8, 50, 72, 113–16, 118, 123, 126–7, 130–1, 134–5, 137, 144, 152–4, 161
suicide, 156–7
syntax of law, 14, 29, 34–7, 50, 57, 62, 66, 68–9, 72–4, 76, 90–2, 94, 96, 98–9, 101–2, 104–7, 110–12, 117, 137–8, 141, 149–50, 155, 159–62, 172n157

Theory of Justice, A, 187n151
Thomson, J. J., 156
truth
  concept of, 2–3, 21–3, 25–7, 29, 116
  individual, 42, 44, 46–7, 49–50, 55–8, 62, 68–9

  social, 72–3, 75–6, 81–3, 87–9, 91, 96, 98–9, 101–2
Truth and juridical forms, 26
Two Treatises of Government, 54–5

universal, subject of law, 3, 105–6, 111–12, 115, 138, 155
USA, 76, 85–8, 90, 92, 94–6, 102, 192n6

Valverde, M., 11
veridiction, 26–7, 171n151
virtual, 35–6, 104–5, 119, 124–6, 132–4, 136, 138, 140–1, 148–9, 151, 153, 162
volonté générale, 63

Wahrsagen see veridiction
Washington v. Glucksberg, 156
Weber, M., 32–3
Whig history, 78
Wickham, G., 10–11
William the Conqueror, 81
Wrong-doing, Truth-telling, 26

Xenos, 136–7, 140, 151

EU representative:
Easy Access System Europe
Mustamäe tee 50, 10621 Tallinn, Estonia
Gpsr.requests@easproject.com

www.ingramcontent.com/pod-product-compliance
Lightning Source LLC
Chambersburg PA
CBHW051114230426
43667CB00014B/2578